ADVANCE

Path of the Novice Mystic is a penetrating suggestion of how you could live your life today, gracefully steering clear of the soul and spirit-wounding ways of modern culture. Paul Dunion writes from his experience and broad learning. He writes with style and vitality, with fresh takes on the main issues that cause us to stall and lose a sense of meaning. He writes as an inspired artist and an experienced therapist, driven by a vision that gets more honed and energized with every book he puts out. Paul is one of few writers I know who can reveal the creative fire that appears when you get soul and spirit together, when psychology and spirituality join, and when you reach a point where you see eternal truths in a simple story from everyday life. This is a beautiful book."

> —Thomas Moore, author of *Care of the Soul* and
> *A Religion of One's Own*

"Paul Dunion's *Path of the Novice Mystic* offers us a unique invitation to live intimately, deepening our devotion to know life and to be 'known by it.' The author shows us the power of self-examination, what it looks like to give voice to the truths we discover within ourselves. He calls us to remain beginners on the spiritual path—no matter how long we've been on it—so that we may always be stirred, moved, and touched by life's mystery."

> —Jennifer Read Hawthorne, co-author, *Chicken Soup for
> the Woman's Soul* and *The Soul of Success*

"Paul Dunion offers us an insightful travel guide for the journey of making peace with the uncertain world we find ourselves in today. He invites us back to what most of us knew in life, but then over time forgot: the joy and wonder that comes from accepting life's impenetrable mystery."

> —Thom Allena, professor of peace studies, University
> of New Mexico, and co-author of *Restorative Justice
> on the College Campus*

PATH *of the* NOVICE MYSTIC

Maintaining *a* Beginner's Heart *and* Mind

PAUL DUNION

RIVER GROVE
BOOKS

Published by River Grove Books, Austin, Texas, www.gbgpress.com

Distributed by River Grove Books. For ordering information or special discounts for bulk purchases, please contact Greenleaf Book Group LLC at PO Box 91869, Austin, TX 78709, 512.891.6100. Design and composition by Greenleaf Book Group LLC
Cover image: ©iStockphoto.com/piskunov. Used under license from Shutterstock.com

Publisher's Cataloging-In-Publication Data
(Prepared by The Donohue Group, Inc.)

Dunion, Paul.
  Path of the novice mystic : maintaining a beginner's heart and mind /
Paul Dunion. -- 1st ed.

  p. ; cm.

  Issued also as an ebook.
  ISBN: 978-1-938416-39-2

  1. Mysticism. 2. Attention. 3. Spiritual life. I. Title.

BL624 .D96 2013
204.4   2013939675

Part of the Tree Neutral® program, which offsets the number of trees consumed in the production and printing of this book by taking proactive steps, such as planting trees in direct proportion to the number of trees used: www. treeneutral.com

Printed in the United States of America

13 14 15 16 17 18   10 9 8 7 6 5 4 3 2 1

First Edition

TreeNeutral®

Dedicated to my children: Sarah, Jenny, and Jason.

Each has offered me the opportunity to remain

a novice of an essential aspect of Mystery:

Sarah—the mystery of simplicity,

Jenny—the mystery of a vital spirit,

and Jason—the mystery of living with immense heart.

As soon as we accept life's most terrifying dreadfulness,
at the risk of perishing from it . . . then an intuition
of blessedness will open up for us . . . Whoever does not,
somehow or other, give their full and joyous consent
to the dreadfulness of life can never take possession of the
unutterable abundance and power of our existence.

—RAINER MARIA RILKE

CONTENTS

GRATITUDE

I am especially grateful to the countless number of folks who have asked me to hear their stories and walk with them as they step closer to some forgotten part of their souls. Because of their courage, I have been able to remain a devoted student of the human condition, where I inevitably find some forgotten part of myself.

I am extremely thankful for those who took the time to read initial drafts of this book and offer me valuable feedback. Because of them, I continue to develop the craft of writing nonfiction. The readers include Peter Drake, whose vision of what it means to heal shame is unparalleled. Thanks to my friend Gary Blazer, whose feedback is inevitably laced with great heart and vision. Thanks to Michael Chell, who through the years has offered countless hours of caring listening to a variety of challenges I have faced. Thanks to Walter van Senbeck, whose offering of collegiality continues to ground me as a student of the human condition. Many thanks to Margaret Harris for her devotion to understanding and living a path with a heart, and to Jen Thompson for modeling what it means to maintain a beginner's heart and mind. Much gratitude for Amy Dunion, who relentlessly brings attention to my gifts and who consistently offers me some new way to view my thinking and my life. Also, thanks to Jennifer Hawthorne, whose blessing and critical feedback brought me closer to understanding the task of writing with more clarity. Many thanks to Thomas Moore for continuing to encourage the development of my writing. Unlimited thanks to Alaina King for relentlessly poking at my propensity for excessive abstraction, until the puncturing led to many of my ideas falling to the ground, gaining flesh and bones. Much appreciation to Elizabeth Chenette and Amber Hales for their editorial sensibility, to Kim Lance for her artistic acuity, and to Alan Grimes for keeping us focused and on schedule. I want to thank Rachael Tsokalas for tracking down numerous sources, allowing the poetry to land on the pages of the text.

I want to especially thank those who remain in conversation with me as we face our joys, fears, and losses while traveling a profoundly mysterious and insecure journey. Thanks to Joanne Reeves for a lifelong friendship that has held me in my efforts to know myself better and to learn to laugh at my buffoonery. Gratitude to Stuart Alpert for pointing me back toward the ground where my soul can once again be nourished. Much appreciation for Norbert Gauthier, Paul Gemme, Gary Blaser, Thom Allena, Jeffrey Duval, Michael Paprocki, and Clive West for sustaining a strong theme of brotherhood in my life. I remain deeply grateful to my wife, Connie Jones, for listening when I have lost my way. Her willingness to bring a heartful presence to my bewilderment continues to gently nudge me back to the light.

TO MY READER

My wish is that you will experience the words on these pages as a fervent invitation to live intimately. An ancient meaning of the word *intimate* is *to make known*. And so we live intimately by deepening our capacity to experience wonder and curiosity about life making itself known to us. The intimacy is not so much about knowing life, but rather living a devotion to know it and being known by it. We are known by life as we commit to live through self-examination, clarifying our values, beliefs, and emotions in an ongoing way. Then, by living with courage and discernment, we bring a voice to the truths we unearth within ourselves.

WHAT IS THE NATURE OF LIFE?

It can take awhile to grasp some simple truths about life. If we can endure disappointments, disillusionments, failings, and broken hearts, then we might loosen our attachment to idyllic, childhood visions of life. These early imaginings hold promise of love, fulfillment, success, and happiness. As these alleged assurances fall away, and if we are lucky enough not to be swallowed up by a groundswell of cynicism, we may begin to have some understanding of this journey we call life. And what we begin to grasp is that life is *mysterious, insecure,* and *unpredictable*. Once we are in possession of this understanding of the trip, we can decide who we are in some real way.

WHO ARE WE?

We are wayfarers on a deeply mysterious, insecure, and unpredictable journey. We can respond to such an odyssey and decide who we are by choosing from two different categories: 1) we can protest the trip or 2) we can accept the trip. If we insist upon protesting, then we define ourselves either as victims of life or conquerors of it. Both reactions place us in an adversarial relationship with life. We either see ourselves as being in a constant losing battle or are determined to be victorious over life's challenges. However, victory eludes us as we are unable to penetrate the immensity of life's mystery and power.

As protesters we fall prey to illusions of powerlessness (victims) or illusions of power (conquerors). In either case, we live in illusion, neither understanding the journey we are on nor understanding ourselves. We move out of our fight with life and liberate ourselves from illusion when we accept life as mysterious and insecure, as well as accepting ourselves as travelers on such a journey. This quality of acceptance is reflected in our willingness to remain mystics, novice mystics.

WHAT IS A NOVICE MYSTIC?

We can understand a mystic as someone willing to be devoted to accepting life's mystery, while remaining curious about life and curious about who we are. The reference to a novice mystic is simply a reminder that making peace with life's mystery calls for a devotion to remaining a beginner. When we remain a beginner, we allow life's mystery to stir, move, and touch our hearts. People with a beginner's heart start the day open to what's new; open to feeling excited, scared, joyous, sad, or loving—or to being loved. The beginner's heart knows that the feeling of today possesses a unique texture and tone, not to be compared to some past feeling experience.

We also remain beginners or novices as we lean into our experiences with a beginner's mind. This mind lives from curiosity rather than conclusions. Even when it settles into the comfort of some satisfactory answer, it may ask: What else is here? What's another way to look at this situation? Is there a larger way to look at this? What is this situation asking of me? This last question invites the novice to remain in a relationship with life. In this relatedness, the novice mystic is animated by life, a robustness fed by the energies of curiosity, awe, and wonder.

Being a novice does not denote naïveté. As novices, we can allow our curiosity to inform our discernment. Am I in the presence of a peacemaker or predator? Do I need to employ a boundary in this situation? What is being asked of me here? Is it possible for me to meet my needs here? These are examples of curiosities that can ground and guide discretion, bringing a sense of empowerment to the novice.

The twentieth-century Austrian poet Rainer Maria Rilke reminds us that the resolve of the novice or beginner may be our most significant hope for support from the Cosmos: "If the angel deigns to come, it will be because you have convinced her, not by tears, but by your humble resolve to be always beginning; to be a beginner."

THE DEVOTIONAL LIFE

"They forgot about the journey"
—HOMER (FROM THE ODYSSEY)

The waters of our culture wash over us again and again, shaping and reshaping our values and beliefs, smoothing our rough edges and unique contours, causing us to fit seamlessly into the surrounding landscape. The crash of the cultural waves reverberates a myriad of rumbles calling us away from authentic living and away from our own souls: Looking good is what matters, there's no need to suffer, death can be avoided, making material acquisitions is a sign of real power, fit in by adopting popular societal beliefs, aging is not acceptable, don't ask questions that disrupt your life.

Although I am intrigued by the question of how these petitions became central to American life, my passion pulls my curiosities in the direction of: How can we meaningfully and creatively find our way back to the authentic life? How can we remember the journey? So, we might begin our inquiry by asking: What is an authentic life? Or, What is the nature of the journey? We can respond by saying that the authentic life is not a thing but a journey. The word *authentic* can be traced to the early Greek and Latin, meaning *acting on one's own authority*. We can say that the authentic life has something to do with being willing to remain the author of our lives, defining ourselves by our heart's longing.

The first practice in reclaiming a beginner's heart is finding our way back to our hearts and living devotionally. I think of a devotional life as relational. On the one hand, we faithfully attend to creating our beliefs and values while deciding how we will live what we love. On the other hand, we respectfully honor the understanding that life is much larger than us by remaining close to the questions: What is life asking of me? What will it take to suitably respond to what is being asked of me?

MYSTERIUM TREMENDUM

Imagine you are a teenager and you are living communally with members of your own gender, actively learning from elders. You will remain separated from the general community for three to five years, until the completion of your initiation into adulthood.

It is about 2:00 AM, and you're asleep on a straw mattress with multicolored blankets, within the confines of a wooden hut. You and your dozen comrades are abruptly intruded upon, as the door of your shelter flies open and you are greeted by two dozen adults dressed in an array of costumes, with animal heads and an assortment of local demons displayed on masks. You and your peers are driven out of the sanctuary of your hovel into the cold and dark of the night.

These nocturnal visitors proceed to enact a drama (Ritual of the Mysterium Tremendum, or Great Mystery) aimed at teaching one vital lesson: *Life is much larger than you and this is the journey you are to remember. And in its largeness, you will be subjected to its mystery, its insecurity, and its unpredictability.* You sit huddled with your friends, shivering more from fear and terror than from the dampness of the night. You're being ritualistically introduced to the challenges of life: death, disease, suffering, and loss. These dramas will continue several nights a week for a number of years in the hope that preoccupation with your self-aggrandizement might be aborted in favor of a commitment to serve the community. These initiations have been popular for hundreds of years amongst most indigenous peoples.

The authentic life begins with a fervent devotion to the principle: *Life is much larger than me.* So large, that I will ultimately be unable to penetrate its mystery, protect myself from its insecurity, or accurately plan for my future. The authentic life, for so many of us, has been thwarted by the cultural suggestion that life is not larger than we are. That's what we have been told with certainty about our education, job, bank account, spouse and neighborhood; we will be spared life's unfavorable vicissitudes, leaving us as large if not larger than life! It's a life directive destined for disaster!

A warning about the distortion of certainty comes to us from the Indian mystic Tukaram (1608–1649):

Certainty

Certainty undermines one's power, and turns happiness
into a long shot. Certainty confines.
Dears, there is nothing in your life that will not
Change—especially all your ideas of God.
Look what the insanity of righteous knowledge can do:
crusade and maim thousands
in wanting to convert that which
is already gold into gold.
Certainty can become an illness
that creates hate and greed.
God once said to Tuka,
"Even I am ever changing—
I am ever beyond
Myself,
what I may have once put my seal upon,
may no longer be
the greatest
Truth.[1]

The cultural invitation to certainty is seductive and potentially extremely dangerous. Rather than living life on life's terms, we childishly demand to live it on our terms. And our terms are typically a series of strategies and answers crafted by our egos and intellects aimed at prioritizing our personal interests. Of course, what is naïvely missed is that ultimately our personal interests are inextricably connected to the whole. We become prone to acting adolescent, believing that we can simply attend to ourselves with no concern for others, as witnessed recently by Wall Street investors and the action taken by BP after the oil spill in the Gulf of Mexico.

The central theme of the devotional life is that life is much larger than our minds will ever grasp and that life asks us if we are willing to unite with the mystery, surrendering to uncertainty. This act of surrender is the essence of what it means to be a *secular mystic*. Typically, mysticism has been a devotional, spiritual path affiliated with a particular religion. Secular mysticism is also a devotional path committed to deepening our unity with the mystery of life, but not necessarily reflecting some specific religious orientation. However, a person could integrate the mysticism described on these pages with a preexisting religious practice.

As we've seen, indigenous peoples such as the aborigines of New Guinea, Bushmen of Central Africa, and many tribes of South America have been willing to accept life's rightful size. We might say that anyone willing to unite with the prodigious and mysterious nature of life is a mystic.

THE MYSTIC

When we are devoted to creating a relationship to the mystery of life, we are essentially mystics. The mystic is willing to craft a unique and personal relationship with life's uncertainty, no longer strongly depending upon societal influences telling us what kind of relationship we should have with life. It will mean being willing to remain curious about what actually lives in us versus what was poured in by our culture. Wonder and curiosity, not answers, keep us in relationship to life's mystery. Some questions that help guide us in personalizing our relationship with life include: What is my heart's desire? What are my defeats? What are these defeats asking of me? What losses are asking for my attention? How can I live my love more fully? What do I truly value? What is life asking of me?

I find myself intrigued by the awe and wonder expressed by my six- and three-year-old grandchildren. They appear to be having a spontaneous relationship with life marked by an endless curiosity, which seems to renew their connection to the flow of experience surrounding them. In Keats's words, "they don't appear to be irritably reaching for fact and reason." Rather, their behavior reflects a quote from Einstein, "The problem is not that we have wrong answers, it's that our questions aren't big enough." The size of my grandchildren's questions is certainly big enough, but what strikes me more is the delight radiating from their questions.

I find myself saddened by the thought of a day coming when, like me, they will feel ridiculed for their unknowing, ashamed of their doubt and curiosity, and finally "irritably reaching for fact and reason." At that point their delight will likely wither from the drought caused by fear of having an inadequate reserve of answers. My hope is that they can sustain a novice mind or what Zen Master Shunryu Suzuki called "Beginner's Mind." As Suzuki points out,

"In the Beginner's mind there are many possibilities; in the expert's mind there are few." And so it is with the novice mystic, there are many possibilities to delight in.

One origin of the word *delight* comes from the French meaning *to please greatly*, with some reference to light. My grandchildren will learn that their paths will not be paved with immediate acts of gratification. The idea that we are here to be immediately gratified will have to die. The mystic deepens a capacity to relate to life's mystery by allowing for such a death and moving away from the expectation that it is the job of life to greatly please us. If that belief dies well, then it will give birth to a higher mandate, which is *"How can I best serve life?"* Unless this death-birth cycle takes place, we run a high risk of maintaining an adolescent posture of protesting the challenges of life that lead us out of delight and away from the light.

Is there a more realistic way to return to delight? Yes, by stepping out of denial and by stopping the war with life by being willing to live on life's terms rather than those created by an ambitious ego. We move away from denial by beginning to accept life as much larger than ourselves and by stopping our attempts to win some adolescent battle with life. The task is to accurately identify what lies in our control and what does not, and then find the grace to surrender to what lies beyond our best efforts. The denial of life's rightful size and this battling are inextricably connected.

When we believe we are larger than life, we are caught in a struggle to prove our largeness by attempting to conquer life, penetrate its mysteries, remove insecurity, and comfortably predict what will come. All of which lead to an inauthentic life, stripping us of meaning, peace, and joy. The illusion of our size can be seen when we attempt to be responsible for the happiness of others, deny our mortality, convince ourselves that we can make someone love us, believe we can save others from acting self-destructively, prevent injury and illness, and escape the hazards involved with a broken heart.

Before a truce is declared with life, we will need to face the illusions that served as our weapons and, one by one, put them down; as we do so, we will feel the vulnerability of our nakedness. These weapons include money, social status, education, religion, our intellects, and even morality, as we convince ourselves that bad things don't happen to good people. As our armistice with life takes place, we gradually begin to accept the journey we have embarked upon since our emergence from the womb, one deeply mysterious and inse-cure, with death always having the final say.

Once we put down our swords and sign a peace treaty with life, we can begin to live authentically and fully. Two predominant attitudes begin to unfold: The inevitable separation from life begins to transform into an interest in unity with life and a wondering about how life can serve us turns to a curiosity about how we might serve it. These shifts in being allow us to wrap ourselves in what might be called *adult delight*. That is, we learn to become *greatly pleased* about the unity we create with life and how we serve life. What courage it takes to choose to unite with that which is mysterious and insecure!

Mystics are devoted to making peace with mystery through acts of unity—unity denoting a sense of deepening oneness. The mystic is not naïve to the perils of life, but remains willing to let go of protesting what life presents, accepting the nature of the journey, rather than longing for a more enchanting trip. So many of us are like disappointed children on Christmas morning, disgruntled by the gifts found under the tree, as we complain about life's offerings. The mystic responds to life's arduous undertakings by having typical, emotional responses, including hurt, anger, sadness, and fear, and remaining devoted to the work necessary to strengthen the roots of unity.

The devotion to unity is renewed by living questions that are aimed at diminishing separation: What is life asking of me? What needs to be awakened in me? Who in me is asking for forgiveness? Who can best serve as an ally as I face this challenge? What do I need to ask for from this ally? Is there a belief or value I carry, asking to be released? Is the current challenge asking me to remember something about where I come from? Is there some sacrifice being asked of me? These questions reflect the mystic's reluctance to experience life as simply unfortunate and divisive. It can be extremely helpful to write about these questions and talk about them with friends.

We see this devotion to unity in all of the mystical traditions:

- **Taoism:** Unity of the principles of the Masculine (Yang) with the Feminine (Yin).

- **Hinduism:** Unity of the individual soul (Atman) with the universal soul (Brahma).

- **Judaism:** Unity of humanity with God's vision of the sacred life.

- **Islam:** Unity of humanity with the presence of Allah in joy and in service to all beings.

- **Christianity:** Unity of humanity with the Christ manifested by love in action.

- **Indigenous Shamanism:** Unity of humanity with nature and our deep wounding in support of healing.
- **Buddhism:** Unity with our own souls leading to enlightenment and a life of compassion.

Cosmic Engagement

There is a quality of engagement that unity or oneness requires, which necessitates a deepening, a movement that can hold more than our intellectual capacities. An ancient Hebrew word for knowing suggests an emotional, sensual, and even sexual connection to whatever we seek to understand. This kind of knowing far exceeds any cognitive comprehension that comes to us through detached observation. Unlike most of us, Einstein and my six-year-old grandson do not experience curiosity as a cognitive reflex seeking satisfaction, but rather as a channel of relatedness, opening to ever-deepening expressions of inquiry.

I watch my grandson's eagerness in response to the waters of a brook we encounter on our walk. He asks: Where does it come from? Where is it going? What lives in it? He wants to touch it, drink it, splash it, throw a rock in it, and sit in it; the latter calling upon my best discretion as his caregiver. He appears to be wired for unity, seeking it, surrendering to it, and delighting in it. I actually feel duly instructed by my grandson as I notice the late afternoon light shimmering on the flowing water as if reflecting a treasure of diamonds resting just below the surface. As we get ready to leave, Corey offers the brook a verbal farewell and I shed a layer of pretense that had me believing I was the one who truly understood brooks.

FOUR CALLS TO ONENESS
Dismantling Unnecessary Boundaries

First, oneness calls for a *disruption of boundaries*, or those things aimed at separating. The ancient alchemists suggested that when two elements are completely separated from the compound they compose, then the bonding that occurs when they are reconnected is stronger than the original connection. Unlike children who have not created significant boundaries in support of their core values and beliefs, adults have borders that need to be disrupted to allow for oneness.

Oneness calls for a letting go of intellectual and emotional structures we have called home. Our beliefs tend to offer a sense of stability and security. Opening to unity means generating a willingness to notice that we have given up wondering and settled into a world view that helps subdue the tension accompanying ambiguity and confusion. We begin to allow ourselves to be provoked, moved, and touched by new and sundry energies and novel perspectives and considerations.

I recently participated in a physical training session called cross-training. The trainer got me to stand and lie on a number of obstacles guaranteeing instability. I immediately felt disoriented, no longer able to support my body in old, familiar ways. I stumbled and fumbled until I just burst out laughing at my clumsy gyrations. The trainer continued to point out the numerous benefits of exercising with instability. I was reminded of how much we can gain from many possibilities when we move away from the stability of old beliefs.

Willingness to Be Penetrated

The second call to oneness is a *willingness to be penetrated*, denoting the act of being pierced or infiltrated by something new, either from outside of ourselves or emerging from within. This can be especially difficult for heterosexual men to grasp, since the idea of penetration is typically associated with the sexuality of women and gay men. With a willingness to push beyond the confinement of cultural expressions of sexism and homophobia, men can begin to open to the power of penetration.

We see this power of penetration exhibited in a description of a vision written by the Christian mystic Teresa of Avila:

> I saw in his [an angel's] hand a long spear of gold, and at the
> iron's point there seemed to be a little fire. He appeared to
> me to be thrusting it at times into my heart, and to pierce my
> very entrails; when he drew it out, he seemed to draw them
> out also and to leave me all on fire with great love of God. The
> pain was so great that it made me moan; and yet so surpassing
> was the sweetness of this excessive pain that I could not wish
> to be rid of it.[2]

Allowing for penetration can mean feeling more, thinking more, and being more, as the penetrating energies add contour and shape to our interior landscapes. Ground that was barren becomes fertile, eager to become generative.

The disturbance of penetration can be disconcerting, as we are often unable to predict the likelihood of a favorable outcome. However, the real risk may not be the possibility of less than desirable results but rather how we treat ourselves amid life's calamities.

Years ago, while shopping at a grocery store with my three-year-old daughter Sarah, whose disability included a lack of control over gross and fine motor movements, I sat her in the back of the shopping cart in the hope that her flailing arms would neither intrude upon other shoppers nor bring canned goods tumbling to the store's floor. When we finally made it to the checkout counter, I felt like a marathon runner, exhausted by the distance covered and relieved by the sight of an approaching finish line.

In order to empty the basket, I had to maneuver myself toward the front of the cart, leaving Sarah unattended for just a few moments. I frantically moved groceries onto the conveyor with such authority that I noticed the checkout clerk jumping back in fear of catching a bunch of bananas in the chin. As the last carton of orange juice bounced in place for its pricing, I noticed that Sarah had placed a vice grip on the arm of a frail-looking elderly lady who was facing her at the back of our cart.

I lunged, attempting to dislodge Sarah's hold on this unsuspecting shopper. "Oh no, let her be! I haven't been touched in over twenty years," petitioned the old woman, apparently taking an unpredicted comfort in Sarah's contact.

I stood there motionless and dumbfounded, as I was deeply penetrated by a plea seemingly as misplaced as a pedestrian warding off warnings of oncoming traffic. We all stood still—the old woman, Sarah, the young woman at the register, and me, as if we had been taken hostage by that moment that prevented us from moving on to the next moment.

To this day, I'm not sure how long we all stood there. What I do know is that my daughter's intrusive behavior had been transformed into the temporary fulfillment of an old woman's longing. And I had been penetrated by the unexpected hunger of a stranger at the supermarket.

A Yearning to Belong

Thirdly, the experience of unity or oneness is the natural outcome of *a yearning to belong*. We must be willing to feel the discontent of isolation and separation before the thirst for belonging can be experienced. So many of us have become effective at protecting against feeling disappointment by allowing dreams of belonging to die. We know what it means to expect kindred spirits to welcome and honor our uniqueness, only to fall prey to unresolved conflicts and fractured connections due to hurt and resentment.

The other option is to give in to a fraudulent experience of belonging, where we adopt and acquiesce to the prevailing expectations and beliefs of others. We feel some temporary relief from a burdensome isolation as we witness others take satisfaction in our speaking and acting in accordance with their views. As our uniqueness is sacrificed, so is any opportunity of a genuine belonging. We are fitting in as we move into some psychic space that eliminates anything we might call ourselves.

Belonging becomes unattainable when we ascribe idyllic, womb-like features to the experience, where our every need is attended to, with endless accommodations of our narcissism. It is helpful to become more modest with our visions of belonging. Such a perspective leaves us wanting and also grateful for the sources of belonging coming to us as authentic gestures of welcome. However, even where we feel warmly received, there is a need to acquire certain skills in support of our belonging.

Feelings of hurt and anger and misunderstanding and conflict must be addressed if our experiences of belonging are to take on the texture of real life. The goal is to be able to hold both the unfulfilled longing and the satisfaction of belonging that we occasionally experience, accompanied by a willingness to do the work required in an evolving experience of belonging.

Recently, while attending a conference in Brattleboro, Vermont, I was wandering side streets looking for a quiet corner to sit for lunch. I came across a small café where I purchased a cup of black bean chili and proceeded to sit alone on a wall in front of the restaurant. Surprisingly, I found the gentleman who had waited on me standing before me as I took my second sip of the chili. With arms outstretched, palms facing up, and a small package wrapped in aluminum foil in his hands, he said with a soft, engaging voice, "You forgot your bread; this is your bread." His kindness pushed me beyond the estrangement of not knowing one another. His offering of bread created a small place outside of his café where for the time being, I was welcomed and I belonged.

Belonging also becomes more real when we prioritize belonging to ourselves. How odd that most of us are never taught to welcome ourselves, and yet, what a wonderful place to begin. We can welcome our beliefs, values, injuries, gifts, emotions, dreams, successes, and failures by refusing to limit the amount of kindness we offer ourselves. Learning to hold whatever we discover about ourselves with compassion becomes a fulfilling way to create home, the place deep within, where comfort and gentleness dwell.

The following by thirteenth-century Persian poet Rumi captures the experience of inner belonging:

The Guest House

This being human is a guest house.
Every morning a new arrival.

A joy, a depression, a meanness,
Some momentary awareness comes
as an unexpected visitor.

Welcome and entertain them all!
Even if they're a crowd of sorrows,
who violently sweep your house
empty of its furniture,
still, treat each guest honorably.
He may be clearing you out
for some new delight.

The dark thought, the shame, the malice,
meet them at the door laughing,
and invite them in.

Be grateful for whoever comes,
because each has been sent
as a guide from beyond.[3]

Heart Knowing

The fourth call to unity is the soulful experience of *heart knowing*, which happens when we sense that our understanding is not attached to being divisive, but rather inclusive, and likely created by at least some small act of courage. This form of apprehension will find little or no favor in a culture devoted to the worship of intellect. The church of reason mandates its priests (scientists and academicians) to penetrate the mystery and to take a fervent vow of celibacy, whereby they will do all that is possible to prevent being penetrated by mystery. The goal is to be satisfied with the accumulation of data and information. We take great pride in our piles of facts and then refer to ourselves as knowledgeable, all the while ignoring the gold of heart wisdom. After all, if it can't be measured statistically, why consider it to have any value at all?

We might begin to understand this heart knowing by looking at the values and beliefs that make up our personal philosophy. In the Greek, the word philosophy is composed of two words, *philia* (love) and *sophia* (wisdom). What is immediately apparent is that when we devotionally create a personal philosophy, we are in the realm of love. We are entering the region of heart. Sophia is the goddess of wisdom, and it may be that love of her sits in some hidden chamber in all of our hearts.

The following passage from *Sophia: Goddess of Wisdom, Bride of God* by Caitlin Matthews may help sensitize us to the presence of Sophia: "The way of Sophia is the way of personal experience. It takes us into areas that we may label 'heightened reality'—those creative realms to which ordinary mortals are called by right of their vocational and creative skills. However, the poetic, the magical, the creative inscapes of vision are often denied us by our culture."[4]

It is curious that the word wisdom has consistently been pursued, structured, and defined in terms of the rational, always committed to avoiding the poetic, the magical, and the creative. Western culture celebrates itself as a paragon of intellectual inquiry, relentlessly folding one abstract consideration into another. Anyone who has studied Western philosophy is immediately struck by the imperatives to wonder the theoretical and recondite, avoiding at all cost the instinctual, emotive, and imaginative. Does the demand that we avoid the personal once again suggest that we are tenaciously holding on to being the penetrator, making sure that we will not be penetrated?

From a highly rational perspective, it would be only too easy to trivialize the idea of personal experience being a legitimate source of knowing. The danger here is to employ an excessive amount of brainpower to explain the heart's knowing. It may be helpful to distinguish a superficial attitude toward personal experience from a devotional one.

In one of his letters, the Swiss psychiatrist C.G. Jung describes the following devotional attitude as religious: "Hence we need religion, which means a careful consideration of what happens [*religio* is derived from *religere* and not from *religare*] and less sophistry, i.e., overvaluation of the rational intellect."

Unlike Socrates, who had an endless list of questions and was described by the Delphic Oracle as the wisest, have we succumbed to sophistry with a pedantic attachment to answers?

This knowing of the heart reflects the freshness of wonder and awe, where the accumulation of information is sacrificed in favor of the particular countenance, timbre, and color of the moment. We are willing to be moved and touched, suspending immediate judgment and interpretation in favor of tracking what's getting our attention, receptive to being further informed.

Mind knowing eagerly moves experiences under the umbrella of some generalized category. The goal of such a move is to strip away the novel features and quirks, enabling us to comfort ourselves with the illusion that we have successfully eliminated ambiguity, surprise, shock, and upset. The devotional mystic maintains an allegiance to the originality of life experience, understanding and accepting the inevitable state of novicehood. From this position, awe, wonder, and curiosity can be invigorated.

Sophia and the knowing of the heart will be discussed further in Chapter 4. For now, let us understand this personal path of Sophia: How can I allow myself to be penetrated meaningfully by my experience, and what is the role of the novice in allowing such penetration to happen?

THE NOVICE

A number of years ago I was downhill skiing in central Vermont with my friend Marty. The apprehension I had regarding our differing skill levels soon waned as Marty graciously shared his expertise, allowing me to find some acceptance of my status as a beginner.

After several hours of skiing under Marty's tutelage, he suggested we take a chair lift to the summit, where we would find a beginner's trail that gently traversed the mountain. At the end of the chair lift ride, I vaulted my body out of the chair, eagerly making my way in the direction of the green trail marker. Marty called me back. "Hey, where you going? Come over here for a moment."

I skied to where Marty was standing. "What's up?" I asked, uncertain why we were not proceeding down the mountain on a trail I was sure I could successfully negotiate.

"It would be good to pause here for a moment. Take a look; you'll never witness again this view with the eyes you have right now," Marty instructed, pointing to the southeast with his right ski pole.

I lifted my goggles, allowing my gaze to drift into the distance, understanding that there was something special about my novice eyes. I also knew that these were eyes I never appreciated. I had been duly acculturated, giving credence only to descriptions such as advanced, proficient, masterful, and expert. Our culture tends to relegate the novice experience to something childlike, suggesting that the novice is naïve, unseasoned, and immature. It may reflect our culture's confusion about authentic adulthood.

Any new learning or experience typically left me a bit shameful, eagerly awaiting a more revered status. The mystic learns about the sacredness of being a novice and the immensity of the offerings coming to the novice. As novices, we can maintain awe and wonder in our life experiences. We are liberated from mental categories that can narrow our perspective. Once we say we know something, there is a tendency to limit what we know to a specific description of characteristics. As novices, we make what we see more spacious, holding more room for the organic nature of reality. Holding the attitude of the novice is a great invitation to the unknown. Also, it is a wonderful way to pull back on the reigns of ego, convinced that its current bank of knowledge is prolific.

BIRTH AND LEARNING HOW TO DIE

At the heart of mystery there is change. Hence, our relationship to life's essential mystery calls for a receptivity to change. I think of the word *change* as a euphemism for birth and death. With every change, something dies and something is born. It is only too easy to rigidly fix our focus on one aspect of a change, whereby we either only see what dies or what is being born. Although, it is probably more seductive to attend to what is being born.

The French obstetrician Fredrick Leboyer (1918–) reminded us that we are inclined to view a fetus emerging from its mother's body as only a birth. He suggested that the fetus is dying; it is separating from the safest, most protective environment it will ever know. Its *womb-world* is ending and in order to properly attend to this death, we should dim the lights in the delivery room, place the child in warm water and speak in hushed tones in order to simulate the environment this child has just left. We can say that his vision reflects Sophia wisdom, as he encouraged a full facilitation of the change experienced by mother and child.

Death calls for a willingness to have a relationship with loss and our own mortality. When we are experiencing loss, it is an important time to slow down.

Death is about stillness and a lack of movement. Loss is asking us to be still, often bringing our attention to the past and what was lost, making it difficult to be present in the moment.

We may want to be alone or in the company of others. We may be sad or angry or depressed. There is no proper way to have a relationship with loss. It serves us to step into our loss by telling the story of the loss, and doing so a number of times. Grieving is a great preparation for more life, as we let go of that which is dying.

The births and deaths of each change reflect an originality that places us in a unique life posture. What ends and what begins will give rise to a particular expression of feeling, thought, desire, and perception. We are forever stepping onto new ground, moving with a new rhythm and cadence, with a body possessing a different molecular makeup than it did in the last moment.

The varying faces of change demand that the mystic remain a novice, open to the novelty of the emerging moment. We could speak of a hierarchy of mystical development that is indicative of most mystical traditions. For now, let us entertain the perspective that the devotional mystic remains a novice, willing to affirm the largeness and mercurial nature of life, willing to devote him- or herself to maintaining a Beginner's Mind and a Beginner's Heart.

Honoring the value of novicehood is an immense countercultural move. Our culture is preoccupied with substantiating who is an expert. We take great solace in the thinking that whatever problem we face, there is an expert who will provide answers and solutions aimed at subduing the tension we feel when facing ambiguity and uncertainty.

We have wandered a long way from the understanding that a relationship with our lives' challenges and problems crafts and deepens character. We want answers and are disinterested in what the travails of life might be asking of us! In order to facilitate and create a dynamic relationship with change (death and birth) we might commit to becoming midwives of our souls, thus deepening our capacity to shamelessly remain novices.

MIDWIFE OF THE SOUL

The path of the novice mystic is surveyed, graded, leveled, and chartered by the skills of midwifery. The midwife knows how to honor and support the uniqueness and distinctive features of what is being birthed while offering attention to whatever is ending as part of the change. We can understand midwifery as embracing a particular skill set that helps create our unity with life:

- **A capacity to observe:** What's asking for new life? What support and skills are necessary for a successful birth? What emotions accompany this birth? Who will be most impacted by this birth?

- **Support for the birth process:** Offering encouragement. Exercising skills necessary to support the birth. Employing boundaries to protect the birth.

- **The evaluation:** How did it go? Would I do anything different in the future? What died as part of this birth? Is some form of grief being asked for?

It may be helpful to look at a concrete application of these skills. I am reminded of a family friend who is a shaman from the Central Amazon region. He readily speaks with great admiration of a shaman in Ecuador who seeks vision by hanging upside down in a cave. I sometimes feel envious of such unprecedented quests for awakening. There is something deeply seductive about glamorous paths to enlightenment. My epiphanies typically take place in grocery stores, kitchens, and automobile service departments, and as life would have it, I'm routinely standing upright and either feeling or looking foolish.

Having been told that the Volvo dealer sold a bike rack that was easy to assemble, I decided to make such a purchase. I got the rack home and proceeded to identify a time when I would install it. As that time approached, I felt the angst that commonly accompanies my tackling a mechanical task. I scheduled plenty of time to complete the job with all the proper tools, which to my great joy, was one wrench. Within minutes, the nemesis of the mechanical world appeared because no part of the rack fit smoothly onto my vehicle.

There was a call to my midwifery as I decided that two things were asking to be born: 1) a gentler attitude replacing a tendency to berate my lack of mechanical prowess and 2) a willingness to ask for help when I decided that I had exhausted the obvious strategies. I was feeling worried that I would fail and treat myself unkindly. After several valiant attempts, I decided I would call the dealer the following day and first confirm that they had actually given me the right rack, and if so, then ask for help.

I made the call to the dealer on Monday morning and heard the attendant at the parts department explain that the paperwork substantiated they had given me the proper rack. I got off the phone and encouraged myself to drive to the dealership, prepared to graciously accept their support. Moments later, the parts manager called apologizing that they had actually sold me the wrong rack.

I was now feeling somewhat of a reprieve from my blunderings and more ready to have a mechanic help attach the rack to my vehicle. When I arrived at the parts department, the clerk immediately handed me the appropriate merchandise as I put the wrong rack back into his hands.

"I want someone to help me put this on," I declared, aware that what was birthing was not only a willingness to get help, but to actually insist upon it.

"I'm sorry, we don't have anyone available to do that right now," responded the clerk, casting his eyes toward the floor.

"Well, I imagine that there is *someone*," I asserted, employing a boundary that indicated that I found his response unacceptable.

"I'm your man!" boomed a faceless voice from the back of the room.

Up stepped the parts manager, eagerly grabbing the box containing the new rack and inviting me to follow him to my vehicle. He proceeded to install the rack, instructing me as to the nuances of the process and graciously responding to my questions.

I left the dealership grateful for what had transpired. I was now off to pick up my bike at the bike shop. My next task was to attach the bike carrier to the new rack, which would be a first-time experience. I pulled into the parking lot of the shop, affording myself plenty of room from the comings and goings of other patrons. With the carrier in hand, I reminded myself that I had plenty of time and that mistakes were absolutely permissible. Sure enough, ten minutes later, the carrier was on backward, testing my commitment to support this new experience with a supportive attitude, which I did find. With the task completed, I entered the shop to be greeted by Rob, the owner, who was holding my bill and pointing out that he had eliminated a specific $30 charge.

I pulled out of the parking lot with my bike secured on the roof of my vehicle. Driving down the highway I looked back favorably upon the experience. I wondered if some synchronicity existed between my inner attitude and how I had been treated by the parts manager and the owner of the bike shop. What I saw dying was my resistance to ask for help in the mechanical world and my old demeaning attitude toward my lack of technological skill. I experienced more celebration than grief as I appreciated what was being birthed.

Sometimes effective midwifery falls a bit short amid a challenging birth.

Such an event occurred at my favorite little grocery store in Mystic, Connecticut, an appropriate place to explore mysticism.

I entered the store intent upon purchasing one particular item and open to exploring others. I took a number at the deli and waited patiently in the queue. When my number was called, I found myself staring at the item I desired, completely forgetting its name. I needed time. So I let my eyes wander about as if I did not hear my number being called.

"Number 23, is number 23 here?" asked the clerk, preparing to move on.

"I have number 23," I responded, continuing to scan the case from one end to the other, pretending to be in the middle of some serious decision making, as a ploy to buy more time. "What is the name of that yellow stuff that I've purchased hundreds of times?" I thought.

"Yes sir, what can I get for you?"

"What about filet mignon, do you have any?" I asked, not seeing any in the case, suggesting he would have to go in the back room to check, giving me a little more time for my delayed recall.

"Sorry, no filets today. Is there anything else I can get for you?"

"No, I think that will do it," I replied, attempting to conceal my embarrassment and wounded pride.

About one mile down the road, I started yelling, "Hummus, that yellow stuff is called hummus!"

Every first-time experience will either invite us to pay primary attention to what is asking to die or what is seeking to be born. It is safe to say that within this change, there was more death than birth. A brain reacting with immediate recall was dying and some excessive pride was asking to die. What needed to be birthed was enough humility to ask, "Hey, what's the name of that yellow stuff?"

The mystic is devoted to unity and guided by a willingness to disrupt one's own boundaries, a willingness to be penetrated, a longing to belong, and the courage to drop into the knowing of the heart. The authentic mystic remains a novice willing to learn how to engage in the deaths and births accompanying change. In order to maintain an engaged relationship with the mystery and insecurity of life, the mystic must be willing to learn how to fail.

LEARNING HOW TO FAIL

In spring 2010, a CBS reporter interviewed Rahm Emanuel, President Obama's chief of staff. The following reflects excerpts from that interview:

"What was your childhood like?" asked the interviewer.

"Well, the sign on the refrigerator door summed up my childhood, which read, *Failure is not an option*," replied Mr. Emanuel.

"What about the schedule of your typical work week?" continued the reporter.

"My motto on Fridays is: There's only two days left to the workweek!" explained Mr. Emanuel with a note of pride.

"And your family, I understand you have children. What's family time like?"

"My kids and I swim in a pool from 5:00 AM to 5:30 AM every Tuesday and Thursday."

These quotes are not printed here as an indictment of Mr. Emanuel, but rather as a metaphor for a popular distortion about an authentic and engaged relationship with life. The focus of these remarks has nothing to do with a union between self and life. These quotes describe a separation the speaker undergoes with himself and from life. Rather than our refrigerators sporting mandates about the unacceptable nature of failure, our kitchen appliances might display the reminder that perfection is not an option. Hence, we could actually be called back to a relationship with life characterized by grace and humility.

We can think of failure as stumbling that results in our falling short of some desired expectation. The idea that we can simply sanitize the human condition of stumblings may be a cheap way to deny the perilous nature of the journey. Hence, accepting failure as a probable experience causes us to authentically relate to life as insecure and unpredictable.

Recently, while working with a young man who was strongly risk avoidant, a simple opportunity arose to offer him a welcome into the human condition.

"Every time I think about taking a risk, I have the thought, *What if something bad happens?*" said Michael, explaining how he stops himself from exploring some risk.

"You don't want to ask that question. Turn the question into a statement: *Something bad will probably happen!*" I pointed out, welcoming him to the world of inevitable failure.

We can begin to make peace with failure by viewing it as simply what happens when we authentically unite with life. Failure is a likely result when embarking upon an uncertain journey, unable to accurately predict the consequences of our choices. Michael began to see that in attempting to avoid risks, he was avoiding life, deepening his *necro-philia*, his affiliation with death (as opposed to *bio-philia,* or love of life). He was struck by the intensity of his existential dilemma. He could take risks and eventually fail, or he could avoid risks and experience the failure of an unlived life.

It is helpful not to excessively personalize failure. Our egos quickly decide that failure denotes a diminishment of our personhood, a reflection of being an inferior person. Having an adversarial relationship with failure while on a mysterious journey is similar to being on a nautical voyage and not wanting to get wet. We will avoid uniting with life if we insist upon seeing failure as completely unacceptable. We end up either turning against ourselves or against life, slipping slowly into the depths of cynicism, where our ideals rest quietly in the graveyard of dreams.

Another approach to making peace with failure is asking the question "What is this failure asking of me?" The question nudges us away from seeing our stumblings as simply unfortunate. We can see this idea of failure calling us beyond the familiar in the following by John O'Donohue: "The light of failure has no mercy on the affections of the heart; it emerges from beyond the personal, a wiry, forthright light that likes to see crevices open in the shell of a controlled life."[5]

The Gifts of Failure

One day back in the early '90s I was meeting with my mentor Ray at our regularly scheduled time. I began to explain how a number of colleagues were making the transition from psychotherapeutic work to executive coaching. I pointed out that the change provided a more lucrative income and avoided the challenges of managed care. I made it clear that if I took on the change, I would want it to be a success.

Ray leaned forward, saying, "Shit, any goddamn fool can succeed. It takes a hell of a man to know how to fail!" This sent a vibration of curiosity throughout my entire body.

The years have affirmed the credibility of Ray's remark that day and the gifts that come from a willingness to learn how to fail. One such gift is that our need to always look good might diminish. It is only too easy to turn responsibility for our essential worth over to someone who might have a favorable reaction to our physical or intellectual plumage. We easily come to believe that the other person's acceptance of us somehow possesses more credibility, as if it can strip away any contaminating biases, offering a more objective account.

We cannot unite with others or ourselves if we are busy attempting to impress. The more we let go of a need to impress, the lighter we carry ourselves, taking ourselves less seriously and possibly remaining in control of our own worth. However, it may take a situation laced with pandemonium and farce to bring us back to ourselves.

In an attempt to secure my athletic prowess against an ever-aging body, I registered for a National Tennis Academy tournament. I arrived at the well-groomed tennis facility prepared to play well and look good doing it.

I entered the locker room aware that I had fifteen minutes to dress and get to my assigned court. I laced my sneaker on my left foot, and much to my surprise, my other tennis shoe was also for my left foot. I feverishly rummaged through my tennis bag in search of a much-needed right shoe. No such luck. I had failed to properly equip myself for this tournament.

I thought, no need to catastrophize, as I adorned myself with two left sneakers, convinced that I could adapt to this precarious predicament. I darted back and forth in the locker room, testing the feasibility of my plan. When another player entered, witnessing me dashing from the lockers to the toilet, I puffed up my chest and lifted my shoulders, in the hope of communicating that my locker room scrambling suggested a zealous eagerness to begin play. I was thankful that he appeared so overwhelmed with feelings about his recent defeat that he did not notice my feet.

When I finally reached the upstairs lounge area, I was convinced that my Charlie Chaplin look was probably going to interfere with my play. I was instantly struck by a sea of players outfitted with the proper apparel. I approached the woman at the organizing desk in the hope of discreetly describing my problem.

She quickly mobilized her body out from behind her desk, and leaning over my feet, she confirmed my dilemma. "Oh my, you do have a problem! What size sneaker do you take?"

"Ten and a half," I replied, momentarily comforted by the idea that I had an ally.

Before I knew it, she had grabbed the microphone on her desk. "We have a guy here in need of size ten and a half sneakers. Can anyone help?" she solic-ited, ending the discretionary aspect of our liaison.

I stood there shocked and embarrassed as a wave of white and proper turned in my direction. I immediately looked over my right shoulder as if joining the mass in search of the dim-witted man in need of sneakers.

To my relief, a young man approached me and handing me a pair of sneakers, explained that he had just been defeated and would gladly share his footwear. His generosity went a long way toward abating my humiliation. I have told this story numerous times, each time laughing more vigorously than the last and noticing some small part of my humanity rejoicing in a homecoming.

Learning how to make peace with failure enhances a capacity to forgive ourselves and others. The more we accept life as much larger than we are, the easier it becomes to extend a gentle attitude to our fumblings.

Living with an acceptance of the inevitability of failure diminishes a pull toward perfectionism. We can acknowledge that our best efforts at getting life right will fall short. Perfectionism only guarantees unnecessary failure. As perfectionism wanes, humility deepens as the dance we do with our limits reflects more grace. Another gift is that failure might suggest a skill asking for development. It is only too easy to assume we possess some competency that remains in need of fine-tuning.

Finally, if we're lucky, our failings might strengthen an ability to ask for help. The cultural worship of rigid self-reliance often leaves us vulnerable to blunders that may have been avoided with appropriate help. Learning to ask and receive help is a major contribution to the deepening of character.

Victims or Bullies

The two most common ways to respond to life's insecurity and unpredictability are either as a victim or as a bully. Each response suggests that life should be something other than hazardous. These reactions are in protest of reality, a refusal to accept life on life's terms. The voice of the victim says, "Life is too big for me," "Someone should save me from life's unfortunate demands," "Awful things always happen to me," "I'm overdue for a break." The voice of the bully might say, "I can do anything I put my mind to," "People need to stay out of my way," "I know what needs to be done," "No obstacle is too big to deal with."

In order to remain united with life, we need to avoid reducing our experience to simply unfavorable and unfortunate, confirming our identity as victims. Victims avoid unity with life because life is perceived as a perpetrator of villainous schemes aimed at hurting and overwhelming us. When we embrace victimization we are typically not exercising enough will, not appreciating what actually may be in our control.

Time and time again in my work with couples, I have heard spouses describe themselves as a victim of their partner. With some assistance, they can describe what they want or need from their spouses. When I ask, "Have you requested more conversation, more affection, more attention, etc.?" the typical response is "No." Sliding into victimization appears to be more acceptable than taking the risk and exercising what is in their control by asking for what they want.

We fall prey to bullying ourselves when we do not accept our own limits. We can think of bullying as the image of a bull pushing and cajoling us to places we allegedly can't or don't know how to go to. Typically, when we bully ourselves, we also succumb to attempting to bully life. When the choices of others and life events in general do not meet our expectations, we protest and curse our fate. Life is supposed to please us, not be obstructive to our fancy.

Several years after my divorce, I continued to bully myself with the failure of my marriage. On one particular day when my self-indictments were hot and heavy, I took a position on a yoga mat to do some stretching before working out at the local gym. An old friend dropped down on a nearby mat.

"I can't believe that I screwed up three marriages," said Barry, immediately getting my attention with his self-effacing remarks.

"Funny that you say that. I can't believe that I was obsessed with the mission of making someone who didn't want to be married, want to be married to me," I confessed, not trying to hide the disdain I held for myself.

"Oh, it makes sense to me. You could have attempted anything in those days," responded Barry, his remark carrying a load of assuredness.

We support uniting with life by shifting our focus from the awful things life did to us or the awful things we did or didn't do, to wondering about what internal shift life may be asking of us. As I left the gym, I was ready to ask, "What was the failure of my marriage asking of me?" My initial response was that it was asking me to accept my limits and find some budding compassion for myself as a devoted husband.

Welcoming the Fool

Another important way to make peace with life is to welcome the fool. There is no greater invitation to unity with our humanity than remaining receptive to the fool who dwells within all of us. Often, just when we think we've got a good handle on this uncertain adventure called life, the fool comes calling us back to reality. Several years ago, I received a very unexpected visit from the fool.

I had just arrived at a friend's home and parked my vehicle in his driveway, glad to be traveling with him to a local conference. As I made my way into the house, I greeted my friend with exhortations of my newly found confidence.

"I'm really glad to finally be attending these events with no anxiety and just feeling really grounded," I explained, anticipating Charles's confirmation of my exuberance.

"Yeah, I get how good you're feeling," responded Charles, looking beyond me as if preoccupied with something outside of his home.

"What the hell are you looking at?" I asked, wanting more of his attention.

"Well, I'm wondering about just how grounded you're feeling, since it appears that you may have forgotten to put your vehicle in park. Your car is now sitting in the swamp across the street," Charles pointed out, obviously in doubt about my alleged confidence.

We both laughed heartily as we cut the brush away from the car so I might gain entry. I welcomed the fool who was pointing me back to my humanity.

The novice mystic lives with a devotion to uniting with life. The essential supports for this union are accepting the mystery and uncertainty of life, expanding a capacity for maintaining a beginner's heart and mind, meeting each change as a death and a birth, and making peace with failure. We now turn to an *exploration of love* as the vital energy connecting us to ourselves and everything outside of us.

LIVING IN LARGER
LOVE STORIES

"Thus far I have spoken of love as the
overcoming of human separateness, as the
fulfillment of the longing for union."
—ERICH FROMM

Sid had recently returned from a four-month trip to Australia and New Zealand. He defined his junket as a vision quest in support of his fiftieth birthday and in the hope of renewing a vision of his life's purpose. He entered my office eager to relate the story of his journey and extremely enthusiastic about detailing the final days of his pilgrimage.

"I decided to stop in San Diego on my way back home in order to visit old friends. When I arrived there, I called my sister in Massachusetts, whom I was accustomed to updating throughout the trip. She reminded me that the Anderson family had moved to San Diego. The Andersons owned the adjacent farm to ours in New Hampshire, where our family spent summers. I thought it might be fun to reconnect with the Andersons. I found a listing for Harold Anderson and, upon calling, had a delightful conversation with him. He offered a plethora of information regarding the lives of each of his five children. I took particular notice when he mentioned his daughter Julie had also settled in San Diego," recounted Sid, leaning forward in a posture that seemed to summon my undivided attention.

Sid went on to explain how Julie had been a tomboy with whom he had spent numerous enjoyable preadolescent days. They hiked together, swam, built forts, played ball, and on especially hot afternoons, they sucked on fudgsicles and sat under a giant elm tree fantasizing about the eventual emancipation they would experience as teenagers. It was a friendship that had warmly made its way into Sid's heart.

"As the summer ended when I was thirteen, I was determined not to leave Julie in the hills of New Hampshire, so I took her picture home to Boston with me and kissed it every night before going to sleep. She was my secret love, at least until the summer when I was fifteen, when I finally dared to hold her hand and kiss her. My childhood buddy had become my first love," Sid said, his facial muscles softening, capturing the tenderness of the narrative.

Sid paused as a wave of old grief made its way to him, which was made obvious to me by his increasingly moistening eyes. He went on to share how Julie had acquired her driver's license shortly after her sixteenth birthday that winter. She had only been driving for two weeks when an automobile accident left her with a head injury accompanied by amnesia. Memories of her entire childhood had been wiped out. That June found Julie not only unable to recognize Sid, but having a "stranger reaction" whereby she experienced his friendliness as intrusive and unwelcome. Their budding love withered under the choking grip of Julie's amnesia, leaving Sid heartbroken.

"So there I was in San Diego, thirty-four years later, hearing Julie's father suggest that I call her before flying east. I phoned her that afternoon and drove over to her home shortly after the call. As I walked toward the front door, she emerged from the house, moving briskly in my direction. The closer she came, the more I felt bolts of energy moving in multiple directions throughout my body," Sid said, becoming animated with the description of the extraordinary dynamics of his experience.

"It felt like the most powerful event of my life. We stood there in an embrace that felt designed to be endless. We finally made our way into her home and spent the afternoon talking about the twists and turns our lives had taken through the years. Throughout the conversation I could feel some stirring of my heart laboring to enter the dialogue. It was all I could do to keep the exchange appropriate to her perception of me as a friend of the family.

"That evening we went out to dinner and by the end of the meal, Julie spoke of an endearing kinship she was feeling toward me that she didn't understand. I reciprocated the feeling and as I hugged her goodnight, I heard her say,

'I don't know you but my body seems to know you.' My two-day stay in San Diego turned into a month of romantic ecstasy.

"Each night she had questions about our childhood together, which as I detailed, she seemed to claim for her own. I offered as much information as I could about where we had played, what we had talked about, and how we had gotten into trouble. She delighted in every word. I felt immense joy in welcoming her back to our childhood," Sid said, now with happy tears.

We sat in an extended silence that was imbued with magic, enchantment, and healing. Sid had stepped into a larger love story. The expansiveness began with his choice to offer himself Agape (love) that we will explore later in this chapter. He had defined himself as deserving of a vocation that would feed his soul, so he left a lucrative position. He had also believed that his life merited two months of exploration and seeking, which brought him the loves of Eros, Philos, and eventually Agape.

Sid and Julie's relationship had just begun with a sizable injection of magic. The hope is that they could develop a connection that honors their individuality while deepening what they share. Hollywood would suggest that nothing but romantic bliss could possibly come from such a wondrous beginning. What is the grand seduction of romantic bliss? It likely holds the promise that we will finally feel truly loved. Who knows, maybe the magical lover will love us in a way that neither our parents nor ourselves have been able to offer.

However, it's a mystery. We don't know what Sid and Julie will create from their magical start and it may be that no other experience quite possesses the power to call us to something within that we would not ordinarily get close to. Their relationship will likely call them each to their *love wound,* and if they carry enough courage and enough mindfulness, they will open to what their love wounds are asking of them, and possibly create a genuine union. If this kind of connection is possible, each will be called to darker inquiries: What do I fear about being loved? How do I feel about my capacity to love? How do I obstruct my movement toward deepened emotional intimacy?

LOVE WOUNDS

The novice mystic accepts love as the single most powerful way to open to union. Once the overzealous ego surrenders and accepts the human condition as mandated to an approximation of truth, we can bow in acceptance of our cursory understanding of love. We can allow the light of our hearts to show the way. The mystery of love is a demanding road, calling us to the frontier of ourselves, asking that we travel without a proper map. It was C.S. Lewis who said, "There are as many loves as there are hearts." We will not know our way, leaving us either pretending we do or accepting ourselves as apprentices of love, novices to how love lives in us.

Mindfulness of our love wounds is the heart's way of finding its rightful size and moving beyond artificial limits. These constraints of the heart are typically primitive protective devices aimed at helping us defend against being hurt. They tend to constrict the heart. We either received too much attention, regard, and affection, or not enough.

Parents who are desperately lonely or too frightened to see the uniqueness of their own children often call their children in too close, ignoring the child's needs, encouraging their offspring to be an extension of themselves. These children grow up convinced that love kills and maims individuality and freedom, never believing that their preferences and ideas possess any legitimacy.

Some did not receive enough care and attention. They believe that love leads to estrangement and abandonment. Love wounds leave us believing that we will either lose ourselves or lose those we love, with the underlying theme being that the risk to love is too great. Love wounds also tend to focus our attention on the quality of love coming to us and not on the value of the love we are offering. If we do happen to gain an interest in our capacity to love, the wounding easily moves us to discredit the merit of our loving. We believe that our love will leave the beloved wanting, unable to fulfill his or her need to be deeply witnessed and cherished.

Under another title, *Dare to Grow Up: Learn to Become Who You Are Meant to Be*, I have described the medicine needed by the wound as an embellishment of our love stories. We introduce healing by making the narratives of our loving larger and more beautiful.

The first step is to being willing to move out of our constricted personal love stories into the larger narrative of humanity. We can do this by acknowledging that love guarantees loss. Love will be withheld, someone will leave, or someone will die. When the inevitable loss comes, we might identify ourselves as courageous enough to risk loving, rather than being a victim of the circumstances. When we define ourselves as someone's victim, it prohibits union. We can only reinforce separation as we cling to strategies of survival and protection.

Here are some questions to help embellish love stories: Did I come from too much or not enough love? If I come from too much love, then what is my heart asking for? What is my heart asking for if I come from a deprivation of love? What stories of being personally victimized by love am I living in? How can I best support my individuality while building something meaningful with others? How can I best care for myself when feeling abandoned by another? What will it take to accept the worth of my loving? What is my fear of loving asking of me? What do I reject about myself that makes it difficult to strengthen my ability to love and be loved? We reclaim our souls when we remain devoted students of love. I encourage you to write and talk about these questions on a regular basis.

In order to remain loyal to love, we may need to unite with aloneness, as seen in a portion of David Whyte's poem "What I Must Tell Myself":

> ... *When you are alone*
> *you must do anything*
> *to believe*
> *and when you are*
> *abandoned*
> *you must speak*
> *with everything*
> *you know*
> *and everything you are*
> *in order*
> *to belong.*
>
> *If I have no one to turn to*
> *I must claim my aloneness.*
> *If I cannot speak*
> *I must reclaim the prison*
> *of my body.*
> *If I have only darkness*
> *I must claim the night.* [6]

Sometimes the most elemental expression of love is the unity we step into as we hold ourselves in our aloneness. The devotion of the novice mystic is poignantly lived when we choose to unite with the one lost and alone within us. You may be seeking love or grieving lost love; the love story is about listening to the request of your aloneness.

Is the aloneness asking to be felt? Is it asking for nurturance? Is it asking for companionship? Is it asking to be remembered? Is it asking for quiet? Is it asking for prayer? Is it asking to be witnessed? Is it asking me to move closer to nature? Is it asking me to remember another who is alone?

These are some examples of what aloneness could be asking for. Our love wounds are asking us to hold them as honorable life's work, rather than something to mend during a weekend workshop. We remain novices of love, willing to observe how giving and receiving work in our lives. We can identify what we want to learn about love and ultimately learn to live with more heart and more unity. Looking at the different faces of love may support a devotion to learning. We can begin with Eros, or the romantic love that is reflected in the story of Sid and Julie.

EROS

Let's define Eros as a romantic attachment, typically unconditional, energized by desire. To say that it's romantic is simply to suggest that it is accompanied by feelings of being charmed, delighted, and enchanted. It is commonly a reaction of feeling enthralled and pulled toward, rather than the result of a considered choice. The experience can involve another person, an animal, a place, or some passionate pursuit such as writing a book. We feel pulled, drawn, and out of control, properly expressed by the phrase "falling in love."

When Eros is under-developed, there is a loss of passion and desire. The energy of Eros lives in our bodies. If we take up residence in our minds, contenting ourselves with abstract concepts begetting more abstraction, Eros quickly withers. Our language becomes more polite, reflecting convention, removed from the fire of Eros. Because Eros is a creative energy, its absence sinks our lives into mediocrity, and we become spiritless. Large piles of earth replace the flames.

When Eros is reduced to the erotic, it remains underdeveloped. The reduction likely reflects our preoccupation with pleasure and excitement. As desire morphs into lust, we avoid the challenges of living love, in favor of simply feeling it and acting it out in a feverish burst. Unfortunately, our culture defines male sexuality as driven by lust and heartlessness. This understanding of men is so skewed that I frequently find myself reassuring men that there's nothing wrong with them because they bring heart to their sexual passion. How dangerous it is to suggest to men that their tenderness, gentleness, and sweetness are somehow antithetical to their sexuality!

Depression and shame go a long way toward keeping Eros in an underdeveloped stage of maturation. Eros' fire is the same combustion, giving rise to anger. When anger is internalized and depressed down into the body, Eros is reduced to a small flickering flame. Eros is often shamed by families, churches, and schools. The socially threatening fire of desire moves us away from the expectations and demands of others, anchoring us in the depths of our own longing.

The common shaming accusation hurled in our direction when we express desire is "My, aren't you selfish," which can be deeply injurious to the life of Eros. Of course, the person leveling the accusation likely wants consideration and attention for his or her desires, raising the question of who is really exemplifying excessive self-focus.

Honoring Wildness

The spirit of Eros is naturally wild and therefore illusive and unpredictable. It typically does not feel chosen but rather experienced as a gust of wind knocking us off our feet. We can experience it in the beauty of a sunset, the majestic prominence of a mountain, or the elegance of a woman when we feel the transience of the sublime. We are often not in control of our rendezvous with Eros. If we protest its wildness, we likely fall prey to attachment, depression, and possession. We can either be aroused away from the center of ourselves, or dispirited with little or no inner flame.

Eros undergoes an aberration when we either attach to what is desired, attempting to possess the object of our love, or allow fear to smother the fire. In the following passage from the book *How to Expand Love*, written by H.H. the Dalai Lama, we can see the malady that attachment can have upon Eros:

> Attachment increases desire, without productivity and satisfaction. There are two types of desire, unreasonable and reasonable. The first is an affliction founded on ignorance, but the second is not. To live, you need resources; therefore desire for sufficient material things is appropriate. Such feelings as "This is good; I want this; This is useful," are not afflictions. It is also desirable to achieve altruism, wisdom and liberation. This kind of desire is suitable; indeed, all human development comes out of desire and these aspirations do not have to be an affliction . . . when

you have attachment to material things, it is best to desist from those very activities that promote more attachment.[7]

Like attachment, a desire for possession, especially pertaining to people, is founded upon an illusionary sense of power and false security, often aimed at attempting to prevent abandonment. It is true that love only guarantees loss; someone will either walk away or die. It is what makes loving such a bold act. We believe that whoever we love will make us better, bigger, more lovable, or younger, if possessed. Sometimes we see our beloved as having the power to bestow value on us, a value we do not extend to ourselves, or we believe that somehow the journey will be made more secure if we possess what we love.

Attachment and possession are founded upon a belief in false security. We find ourselves needing to acquire more and more once we infuse our acquisitions with the power to make us okay or allegedly more safe. The flames of Eros are reduced to flickering embers as we attempt to escape from mystery through attachment and possession. The mystic is asked to welcome Eros, while remaining mindful of a possible tug toward attachment and possession. If we remain unconscious about those two possibilities, we actually weaken Eros's creative potential.

Yvonne came to me complaining about her relationship with Carol, whom she had met in massage therapy school. Both women were in their mid-forties with teenage children, and they had gradually created a deep friendship. Yvonne began to notice that Carol would pull away from her when she paid attention to another woman. Carol's possessiveness of Yvonne grew and she finally broke into verbal attacks of her. Carol's love had become compensatory as she attached responsibility to Yvonne to make her feel important by excluding others. Carol apparently was demanding that Yvonne make up for the depth of childhood abandonment she had experienced. The Eros of Carol's love grew into a debilitating possessiveness that Yvonne gradually could not tolerate.

Eros can be dangerous, capable of incinerating our compliance to who we were *told* to be and creating an opening to who we were *meant* to be. It can be difficult to maintain control over those who step into the flames of Eros. They may be driven by romantic enchantment, a deep desire to live their values and beliefs, or a desire to passionately follow a personal vision. In any case, it can be a formidable task to attempt to rein them in, in compliance with some acceptable social decorum.

Walking away from the fire of Eros is often fueled by a deep knowing that Eros always holds the potential of being disruptive. If we are caught in the primitive understanding that being lovable means being obedient, we run a high risk of Eros being reduced to a flicker. The power to be involved evaporates, as we await the fire of another person to direct our lives, allegedly allowing our acquiescence to demonstrate how lovable we are.

We see the blaze of Eros in Plato's *Apology*, where Socrates is accused of corrupting the youth:

> If you say to me, Socrates, this time we will not mind Anytus,
> and you shall be let off, but upon one condition, that you are
> not to inquire and speculate in this way any more, and that
> if you are caught doing so again you shall die;—if this was
> the condition on which you let me go, I should reply: Men of
> Athens, I honour and love you; but I shall obey God rather
> than you, and while I love life and strength I shall never cease
> from the practice and teaching of philosophy . . .[8]

Socrates would prefer to be put to death rather than violate his heart's desire. The fire of Eros burns in his devotion to his teaching and his self-proclaimed role as *midwife* of the soul.

The television journalist Bill Moyers once interviewed the mythologist Joseph Campbell, who coined the phrase "Follow your bliss." Moyers asked Campbell, "Joe, what's the big deal about the bliss?" Campbell responded, "No big deal, just no other place to begin."

Joseph Campbell was identifying our bliss, or Eros, as the authentic starting point for the hero's journey. With our desire as the beginning place, our journey is genuine; it belongs to us and us to it. The unity with the journey is deepened when we ask: What is the journey asking of me?

We may be in need of developing a stronger relationship with Eros. When it is suppressed, it becomes challenging to summon the will to engage life passionately and creatively. We become mere reflections of conventional beliefs and values, never truly knowing who we are, likely living someone else's life. We are either living in our own story or someone else's story. We can begin to awaken Eros by dancing, singing, playing, competing, going on adventures, creating, gardening, and being sexual. If all else fails, take a walk! Wherever there is an arousal of the senses or an experience of beauty, there is likely a call to Eros.

A Slow Burn

Eros is given ground and becomes more creative and less destructive when it burns slowly. We can think of grounded Eros or a strong, slow burn, as opposed to flames leaping out of control and threatening to torch the surroundings, when we move slowly. The fire of Eros ignites a strong emotion and if we do not move slowly with it, we run the risk of acting impetuously, lacking a mindful guidance to our fires. We also run the risk of becoming obsessed, addicted, unnecessarily vulnerable, seductive, hysterical, and compulsive.

We move slowly when we consciously bring our breath to the heat of our emotion. We can then allow our breath to bring our attention to being connected to the ground, feeling the connection of our feet to the floor or earth.

Next, we can bring discernment to the expression of Eros, guided by questions like: Does it serve me and/or others to speak the truth of this fire or act on it in some way? If so, what can be said that would be helpful to the purpose and values that guide the relationship? Would silence be more compatible with a desired discretion? What action might be most congruent with the purpose of the relationship? What is this fire asking of me? And what is my best understanding about the nature of such a request? Where there is significant doubt and confusion about what to say or do, silence and inactivity are probably preferable. The key is to keep Eros at a slow burn.

Freud suggested that Thanatos, god of death, and Eros remain in an important dialectical relationship. It may be that before we can open our hearts to Eros, we may need to grieve. Uniting with grief is not popular. However, denied grief is inevitably a heart-closing endeavor. Denied grief is a cold water, keeping us unconsciously in relationship with our losses. Rather than the energy of sorrow and loss being wailed and sobbed, the waters of grief stagnate and collapse upon the heart. We can step closer to our grief by asking: What loss is asking for my attention? Will it be helpful for me to write a poem or a letter in honor of this loss? Is there a way I might ritualize this loss? Do I feel called to build an altar in honor of this loss?

I recall once declaring to a mentor of mine that I wasn't sure what I wanted from life. He responded with great passion, "There is no greater insult to the gods than confusion about what you desire."

A willingness to long is a powerful way to step into uniting with life. It takes courage to want, since we don't know how life (fate) will respond to our wanting. Our desiring takes on an honorable sensibility, as we not only long for our private satisfaction but also hold a willingness to open to a larger consideration of stewardship for some small aspect of our experience. We take seriously what we can give, as we long to offer our skills and talents a place to develop and grow in the world.

There are a number of questions to be faced, especially when we encounter a response from fate that is less than fortuitous. Is this a time to remain faithful to my desire or a time to let go? Is my desire in accord with my values? What do I need to do in order to avoid victimization when fate responds unfavorably to my desires? Am I willing to unite with my experience when fate obstructs my desire? Am I willing to unite with gratitude even when circumstances are less than fortuitous? Am I willing to be receptive to a larger call from life than my desire? Am I willing to rejoice and celebrate when fate accommodates and supports my longing?

I found myself in such a quandary when my writing was initially greeted with countless rejections. Is it time to press on or let go? Maybe swap my computer for a good oven and open a pizzeria? When fate is not terribly accommodating of our heart's desire, it is easy to slip into bad faith and want to quit. It can simply be a time to slow down and allow fate's lack of cooperation to be an opportunity to choose ourselves on a deeper level. Consequently, I write this rather than check the oven.

Eros has the power to keep us awake, to keep us from succumbing to lethargy. "What is my heart's desire?" is a great call to Eros. We now turn to another face of love, Philia, or friendship.

PHILIA

For Aristotle, Philia was the most virtuous of the loves: "For without friends no one would choose to live, though he had all other goods; even rich men and those in possession of office and of dominating power are thought to need friends most of all; for what is the use of such prosperity without the opportunity of beneficence, which I exercised chiefly and in its most laudable form towards friends?"[9]

Philia is a conditional love; it is not offered arbitrarily. We choose our friends because they have earned our trust and because they possess characteristics we respect and admire. There is delight in anticipating being with a friend. Before taking a closer look at the heart-opening of Philia, it may be helpful to explore underdeveloped expressions of friendship.

One unseasoned expression of Philia is companionship that Aristotle described as a relationship driven by pleasure and/or usefulness. Companionship is typically what our culture allows men to share. They can get pleasure out of some shared activity like fishing or a ballgame or find utility in their connection by fixing or building something. Relationships based upon pleasure and/or usefulness are fine and they do not engender the meaning and depth of mature friendship.

Enmeshment is another expression of an underdeveloped friendship. In an enmeshed relationship at least one person's uniqueness is sacrificed, usually in the name of minimizing conflict and maximizing harmony. The assenting member of the relationship gives way to the will of the other, forgetting who they are or who they were meant to be. The self-sacrificing member typically forgets about what they want and value, taking their cues from the other's expectations. One person mimics the other. Enmeshed relationships depend upon a diminished opening of the heart. The thinking is that we can avoid risks of discontent, upset, and conflict if we are working with only one set of desires and needs.

Isolation is another form of underdeveloped friendship. It takes place as two people practice physical and/or emotional avoidance. Isolation is a relationship committed to supporting the independence of the participants, with a willingness to sacrifice a meaningful rapport. It is another form of avoidance as the members hope to escape from the common entanglements of intimate relationships.

In a maturing friendship there is a desire to know the other and be known by them. The relationship is characterized by shared values, mutual respect, gratitude, generosity, and offerings of truth and compassion. When our hearts open to the love of Philia, we are choosing a particular person to explore who we are and who they are. The relationship becomes a container for creating ourselves, infused by the energies of self-examination, curiosity, and receptivity to the perceptions of others.

In *The Four Loves*, C.S. Lewis described Philia "as that attachment where we ask the same questions while offering different answers." Lewis's remark captures the element of shared values while accommodating differing beliefs and views. Common values allow two people to share a common vision. The relationship becomes a reference point where they can explore the implications of implementing their values. Consequently, it might be difficult for a Christian mystic to experience the love of Philia for a neo-Nazi. Other expressions of love might exist between them, but not likely Philia.

Mutual respect is another characteristic of Philia. We can think of the word *respect* from the old Latin, meaning *to look back at*. When respect is present between two friends, they deserve one another's attention on a deep level. There's comfort in disclosure about what is loved, lost, longed for, feared, and what they may be willing to fight for. Each finds him- or herself in a new way because of the offering of mutual attention. There's something about how the other chooses to live that summons heed. That is, respect reflects the belief that our friendship truly benefits us. What is gained is an opportunity to tell our stories and remember who we are.

I met Thom twenty-five years ago at a conference. Since that time, our mutual respect, our devotion *to look back at one another* has gradually deepened. The looking back can be seen as a gesture of invitation, which says, "I want to know what you see, how you feel, and how you're thinking, especially as it relates to your experience of me." Our relationship became a place to remember who we are.

We often come to one another with a story of some temptation that challenged us or called us away from ourselves. Sometimes it is a story about an event that invited us to think poorly of ourselves or a remark that was cutting, which left us wondering if it was deserved. However, my deepest appreciation is Thom's ability to hear and hold my defeats with deep compassion. He hears my remorse and regret while reminding me of the courage that allowed me to risk stepping onto some unfamiliar terrain. His respect for me has forged a resolve in me to continue to dare to be myself.

Recently, I mentioned to him that when acts of kindness and love are presented to me, I drop my mindfulness just enough not to fully take in the offering, and that I wanted to work on becoming a better receiver of these offerings. He responded, "Then, I'll have to tell you I love you more, so you can practice." I shyly smiled in gratitude.

Gratitude and generosity are features of a maturing Philia. We are grateful for the friend being in our lives and the offerings of shared adventures, good conversation, support, and care. Likewise, there is a desire to offer time, energy, and money that we believe might be helpful to our friends or that simply allows us to step into a larger story of generosity.

Our hearts open to the depth of Philia when we are willing to engage in personal truth-telling accompanied by compassion: compassion for our struggle to represent the truth clearly and compassion for the listener. This kind of compassion calls for an endearing sensibility for our use of language and the present emotional status of the listener. This level of friendship calls for consciousness (union) with our own desires and values, and a willingness to disclose them to our friends. Philia also lives as we open ourselves to the values and desires of our friends that are different from ours.

Philia suggests Eros as we express what we want from our friends. We may want to be heard, encouraged, loved, guided, or joined in collaborative efforts, as well as play and work together. It is quite common for spouses and friends to experience their relationships growing numb and embittered in the absence of clarity about what they what from one another. It calls for a level of inner resources that allow us to move from hearing the other's want as a demand to hearing we have been chosen as a valued source of fulfillment. Our responsibility is to respond to a request honestly by saying, "No," "Yes," or "I want to negotiate."

The second expression of truth-telling is holding ourselves or friends accountable. Here, we can either offer a blameless account of our own behavior when we violate our own values or hold friends accountable when they violate some agreement they have with us. An example of the former might be helpful.

I employ two specific protocols in my counseling practice. The first is that clients are held financially responsible for a missed session unless they make a twenty-four-hour notification of the cancellation. The second guideline is that if I overlook an appointment, the client receives a session at no charge.

On one particular Tuesday evening, I stepped into the hall outside my office to find two couples waiting for the next appointment. After one couple graciously deferred to the other, it became obvious that I had double-booked.

When the deferring couple appeared the following week for their session, I explained my protocol regarding no fee for the session due to my error. The husband insisted that my gesture was unnecessary. I went on to explain that my offering of a free session was not mostly for them. Rather, it was my way of remaining accountable for my choices and my values. I suggested that I wasn't opposed to them benefiting, but the decision was mostly made to serve me. After some time, we went on with the counseling session, with the husband willing to carry his confusion about my decision forward.

When we hold others accountable, we offer a blameless account of their behavior when their behavior has left us feeling hurt or angry, or when some agreement has been violated. It might sound like "When you agree to pick me up at 6:00 PM and you arrive at 6:30, I feel frustrated and angry. I wanted to hear the opening remarks at the meeting." And not "You were supposed to pick me up at 6:00 PM and I can't believe how insensitive you are and how you only think of yourself."

Experiencing hurt and angry feelings are usually reflective of a deepening connection between people. Both sweet and bitter feelings indicate a stronger level of involvement in one another's lives, something that goes beyond a perfunctory exchange.

Not knowing what to do with feelings of hurt and anger is the most typical place where Philia breaks down. We often either attack our friends, leaving the relationship permanently ruptured, or we withdraw, pulling back warmth and attention.

Our bruised feelings take place under two very different situations. In the first circumstance we are solely responsible for our injured feelings. For example, we may not have told a friend what we wanted, which led to our dissatisfaction. Or we may have created a story that a friend was not interested in pursuing us when we experienced a lack of contact, which left us feeling hurt and/or angry. In this latter case, it may be helpful to tell a friend about the story we created, in order to gain a better understanding of the reality of the friend's absence.

In the situations described here, our feelings are due to our own choices, and if we want something, it would be from ourselves. That is, we may want to be clearer about what we want from our friends and clearer about the stories we create in order to explain their behavior.

In the second circumstance, we either have been clear with a friend about what we want, or we believe there is an agreement in place regarding some specific need of ours. In either case, what we're looking for has not taken place.

In order to deepen Philia, an account of a friend's behavior must be blameless, that is, not diminishing of the other's character. The hope is that we can communicate with some level of compassion, and if that's not possible, then our language can at least not attack the friend's character. Some examples might be helpful. "When you say you'll pick me up at 6:00 PM and arrive at 6:30, I feel angry." "When you say you're willing to cook for our communal meal and you arrive with a bag of potato chips, I feel angry." "When you forgot to acknowledge my birthday, I felt hurt."

The opening of the heart, characterized as Philia, will inevitably have us stumbling into fear, hurt, and anger. I often refer to this heart-opening as "getting bumped." The key is to learn how to feel these feelings, identify them, and communicate them clearly to our friends. Blame is corrosive to Philia and learning to eliminate blame from our friendships is a worthy lifelong endeavor.

We now turn to Storge, another face of love.

STORGE

I had just finished my course work for my doctoral degree and was preparing to begin my dissertation. During a meeting with my adviser, Al, he suggested I put some ideas together for the first three chapters of my dissertation and that we meet again in a month.

I returned a month later to Al's kitchen, where we usually met. He had prepared cups of tea for each of us, and we took our places around the kitchen table.

"Well, I'm anxious to hear what you've been thinking about. I think you can do a lot with the topic of trust," explained Al, eager to hear about the direction of my research.

"I've been pretty focused. I hope that I've put this together okay," I responded, ready to hear Al's feedback, as I dropped one hundred pages of material on the table.

Al sat there speechless, looking stunned, with a tear slowly moving down his cheek. "It would have been a grand collaboration. One I would have thoroughly enjoyed," said Al, obviously more saddened than pleased.

It took quite awhile that morning for me to grasp what Al was experiencing. I was not accustomed to being the recipient of Storge love, a love in this instance that a mentor offers his protégé. The elders to whom I had been exposed expected my self-reliance and independence. I had learned not to burden them and to demonstrate that I could be self-sufficient, even if it had been in my best interest to access their support and guidance. Al was introducing me to the love of a mentor who delights in helping with the development of gifts and holding a vision of their manifestation.

Storge love is an attachment to nature, youth, and ancestors, as we remain mindful of the sacredness of these three expressions of life. We suffer greatly in regard to Storge love as we forget about ancestors, lose interest in mentoring youth, and remain determined to conquer nature. It supports the mystic's interest in union by exploring how we can begin opening our hearts more fully in these three aspects of life.

We can get curious about where we come from by gathering old photos and asking relatives about family members who have passed on. We can identify legacies that strengthen and honor our ties to ancestors. We can appreciate the struggles they faced and hold a vision of them devoted to our enrichment. Similar to a common Alcoholics Anonymous protocol of "Hi, I'm Jim, a grateful alcoholic," we can also learn to be grateful for the victories and the defeats experienced by our ancestors. We unite with our own past by accepting what it was rather than longing for a more glamorous path.

There was a time when I viewed my male relatives as simply unfortunate, caught in a destructive relationship with alcohol and feeling victimized by life. Over time, I began to realize that their stories were larger. Woven through the family was a fervent capacity to dream, a wit that subdued the tide of cynicism and humbled exhortations of arrogance, and most of all, an abiding devotion to gather together, honoring their common bond and the uniqueness of each man's story.

We have walked a long way from our union with nature. The beginning of the distancing likely took place when we moved from an agrarian society to an industrial one. The former required an intimate connection to the earth, as did hunting and gathering. The factory insulated us from nature, as does the thirty-second floor of an office building. Physical separation from anything tends to inhibit emotional and spiritual union with that thing.

We can reduce our relationship to nature to a variety of recreational activities. Or, we can move beyond recreating and learn to honor nature as being much bigger than us and deeply mysterious. The mystic remains committed to shedding the identity of conquerer, remaining mindful that the human body and the earth are composed of the same material. Gratitude for the gifts of nature contributes greatly toward honoring them. The following poem, *Sleeping in the Forest* by Mary Oliver, expresses the depth of Storge honoring of nature:

Sleeping in the Forest

I thought the earth remembered me, she
took me back so tenderly, arranging
her dark skirts, her pockets
full of lichens and seeds. I slept
as never before, a stone
on the riverbed, nothing
between me and the white fire of the stars
but my thoughts, and they floated
light as moths among the branches
of the perfect trees. All night
I heard the small kingdoms breathing
around me, the insects, and the birds

who do their work in the darkness. All night
I rose and fell, as if in water, grappling
with a luminous doom. By morning
I had vanished at least a dozen times
into something better. [10]

There is a deep relatedness with nature for Oliver as she says, "the earth remembered me" and "took me back tenderly." She sleeps as never before, as a child would in that place providing deep comfort. We see the unconditional love of Storge in the phrase "perfect trees." She has the experience of rising and falling throughout the night, believing such movement to be dangerous. However, she says she "vanished at least a dozen times into something better," suggesting that her relationship to nature moves her into a quality of being that previously lay dormant.

Storge can be an unconditional love we offer to youth. The nuclear family may be an aberration of the human condition, because children for thousands of years were raised by the clan or tribe. In 1992, I was promoting a mentoring project by addressing groups of social service providers. A year earlier, our town experienced its first drive-by shooting, which killed a teenage boy named Corey Benton. At the start of each of the presentations I would ask the audience to close their eyes and raise their right hands if they were responsible for the death of Corey Benton.

Typically, less than one third of the room raised their hands as my question challenged them toward a new paradigm of responsibility. The old paradigm said, "If I don't know you or don't live in your neighborhood, and I didn't pull the trigger, then I'm not responsible." Whereas the new paradigm declared, "If I contribute to creating the values in this community, if I am an elder in this community, then I am responsible for what happens in this community."

I would end my talks by encouraging the gathering not to see young people as simply misguided, but rather to view gang participation and violent actions as heralding the death of authentic community. Heart-opening often calls for a larger story than accounting for the behavior of others as simply degenerate, which takes us to unconditional love, Agape.

AGAPE

Agape love is expressed through offerings of kindness and compassion, with no conditions other than a willingness to give. We can see this love as a heart-opening to our common humanity.

In the late '70s, my wife and I decided to implement a neurological reha-bilitation program called Patterning for our disabled daughter, Sarah. In order to properly administer the recommended techniques, we would need one hundred volunteers. I was overwhelmed by the prospect of that many people making offerings of time and energy to our family. After running ads in several locations, one hundred people stepped forward in the next two weeks offering their support for Sarah.

It can be as challenging to receive Agape love as it is to give it. My ego was struck by the urgency to be loved in this way, as well as by the compassionate offering from so many. Was I not strong enough to take care of myself and my family? Was the offering a testimony to my neediness? Would I be viewed as somehow less than?

Gradually, I grew to accept myself as needing help and was grateful for the many kindnesses extended to my family. Some of my compulsive self-reliance eroded away along with a limited vision of my common humanity. Years later, I asked Sarah if the exercises in the program helped her. She replied, "I don't know if it was the exercises or that so many people came to love me, but some-thing was helpful."

Agape is greatly about acceptance and humility. It can be a profound way to step into the mystery of the other's journey. In the small town where I grew up, there was a Roman Catholic priest, a Father Henry. Every Tuesday, like clockwork, he would disappear after early morning mass for the rest of the day. Unable to bear the mystery of Father Henry's Tuesdays, my friends and I decided he was having a romantic rendezvous in the neighboring town.

As the years passed, the stories of his coital adventures were greatly embel-lished. Until one day shortly after Father Henry's death, the topic of his Tues-day escapades came up among a group of us who had been childhood friends. Norm quickly interrupted the conversation, pointing out that Father Henry had worked at a shelter for homeless men every Tuesday. When we questioned the new version of the Father Henry story, Norm explained how his father accompanied Father Henry whenever some carpentry work was needed at the shelter. We all paused as we listened to Norm's description of Father Henry's work with the homeless, with our silent apology hanging in the air.

The ego ardently wishes to penetrate mystery rather than be penetrated by it. Agape creates union through acceptance without having to define what it accepts. This level of acceptance often calls for a suspension of the categories of "right" and "wrong." We can see such an attitude in a verse from a poem by the Islamic mystic Rumi:

Out beyond ideas of wrongdoing and rightdoing,
there is a field. I'll meet you there.
When the soul lies down in that grass, the world is too full
to talk about. Ideas, language, even the phrase "each other"
doesn't make any sense.[11]

Agape stretches beyond individuality and personality to embrace the human condition. Agape wants to create a story of our common plight and our common connection as sojourners. We might hold the awareness that like us, others fear rejection, want to be loved, fear pain, and hold some uncertainty regarding the mystery of death. Agape energy invites us to relax into the embrace of our common humanity.

Although Aristotle believed Philia was the most virtuous of the loves, it may be that the most virtuous is a willingness to attend to what our open hearts are asking for and to be willing to live devotionally in support of that heart-opening. Or it may be that all heart-openings are dependent in some way upon our willingness to extend Agape love to ourselves.

Agape for the Self

The most challenging and arduous love story is the offering of Agape love to the self. Kabir, the fifteenth-century Indian religious reformer, captures the importance of self-love as we strive toward deepening our capacity for unity:

I don't know what sort of a God we have been
    talking about.

The caller calls in a loud voice to the Holy One at dusk.
Why? Surely the Holy One is not deaf.
He hears the delicate anklets that ring on the feet of
    an insect as it walks.

Go over and over your beads, paint weird designs on
    your forehead,
wear your hair matted, long, and ostentatious,
but when deep inside you there is a loaded gun, how
    can you have God?[12]

Just about everyone appearing at my office door for the first time arrives exhausted by carrying "deep inside" them a "loaded gun." The loaded gun can be deep self-loathing, shame, self-ridicule, or many forms of self-abuse. Unfortunately, there is almost no cultural accommodation for learning how to extend unconditional compassion to ourselves. After all, as long as we're carrying a loaded gun deep inside, there will be something to sell us in order to temporarily alleviate our burden. We are encouraged to believe that there is some product we can acquire that will mitigate our distress rather than point us in the direction of learning to hold ourselves with compassion.

It is a curious dilemma; we very much want to feel good about ourselves, and yet we spend our days in self-contempt. Like the characters in Beckett's play *Waiting for Godot,* many of us are shrouded in self-hatred, waiting for that special someone who will come, choose us, and bestow the love we so much resist offering ourselves. The novice mystic is willing to give up the wait and take back the responsibility for offering Agape love to oneself.

At my Love Workshops, I often ask the participants to imagine two representatives of humanity, Amy and Adam. I ask folks to identify common positive and negative characteristics of Amy and Adam. The positive list typically includes sensitive, giving, receptive, generous, thoughtful, caring, cooperative, patient, resilient, and productive. The negative list is composed of traits such as selfish, cynical, insensitive, petty, unavailable, self-righteous, bitter, arrogant, and unreliable.

Of course, our fictitious characters Amy and Adam are projective screens. Consequently, when I ask the audience who else the list of positive and negative characteristics might represent, they often respond by saying, "All of us."

I confirm that each of us in the room likely possesses all of these traits, and after some discussion, it becomes obvious that we are also talking about humanity in general, which places the conversation in a much larger story. At that point, a meaningful exchange can ensue about self-loathing and Agape love for the self. I go on to ask the group why Adam or Amy is highly focused on his or her negative traits. It begins to be obvious that our fictitious characters have both sets of qualities and that self-contempt is getting fixated on the negative only.

We often stay preoccupied with our shortcomings because if we dare claim our positive attributes, we run the risk of betraying our parents. This is especially true if all we heard from them were demeaning remarks regarding our character. Betrayal of a parent who was abusive or cruel can be very difficult, especially if as children we saw our survival as being dependent upon maintaining at least an illusion of rapport with the abusive parent. The work is to grow an interior parent who takes the place of our biological parent, enabling us to depend upon ourselves for our safety and love. (I have treated this idea of growing an interior parent in more detail under the title, *Dare to Grow Up: Learn to Become Who You Are Meant to Be.*)

Maybe Adam and Amy are engrossed with their flaws because they are willing to settle for what I call *negative self-esteem*, where they are willing to offer themselves endless amounts of negative attention. The ego will either be positively special or negatively special, by exaggerating either what's good or what falls short. It abhors being ordinary. A not too distant cousin to negative self-esteem is an attachment to a sanitized personality, one crowned with perfectionism.

A more popular purpose for staying focused on what's negative is the desire to remain *risk avoidant*. This undertaking can commonly be heard as "I'm not deserving of that!" or "I'm not good enough to pull that off." The risk avoidant individual employs self-loathing to evade living life on life's terms, not wanting to unite with life. The hope is that they can avoid failure, not because failure is such a taboo, but because of the cruel way they will likely treat themselves when they do fail. Of course, not living fully may be itself the greatest failure.

A preoccupation with our invalidating traits may reflect a resistance to leave childhood by taking responsibility for defining ourselves as lovable. We descend into the depths of being victimized by our self-contempt with the ego often waiting for a possible reprieve. We either pause in the hope of some benevolent other coming to affirm that we are good people or manipulatively strategize toward procuring such a response.

We can prepare for union with the self by getting honest about our excessive vigilance with our shortcomings. We can acknowledge that we are much larger than our negative attributes and we focus on them for very specific reasons, as outlined in this section. Even in its most precarious moments, the psyche remains resourceful in its attempt at achieving some special status, even if the price paid is extremely high.

I recently made a commitment to be more conscious of my own attachment to attaining some distinguished status. I decided that paying attention to my need to be impressive would be a valued beginning place. I soon found myself in a discussion with someone, and I was pleased to note a mounting pressure in my chest to saying something impressive. I had enough trust in my listener to give a voice to my need to make an impressive remark. The person looked at me and said, "Aren't I impressed enough?"

I chuckled and went ahead asserting my alleged inspired idea, as if the declaration had a will of its own, with no hope of my interruption. The staggering size of my attachment to impress could no longer be veiled.

What about the small story of staying focused only on what's positive about us? Of course, that venture is also purposeful. The primary objective is to desperately attempt to secure some semblance of self-love by denying the negative. However, what we know about denial is that the stronger it gets, the more denied negative traits are actually lived out.

Preoccupation with positive traits is also an attempt to substitute pride for authentic self-love, since we are falling way short of accepting who we truly are. We inflate what helps us to present well, condemning ourselves to a contingent personality. We become prisoners of whatever situations we find ourselves in, unable to accept what we deem as unimpressive. It is likely that we will fall prey to an excessive vigilance, as we monitor what we look like, how we talk, how we're dressed, the vehicle we drive, and the neighborhoods we live in.

Union with the self begins to be possible as we accept what is both positive and negative about ourselves, creating union with our humanity. Such acceptance is no trivial matter. It opens us to the possibility of making offerings of unconditional love if we are willing to let go of an obsession with one set of traits or the other. The initial step is commonly holding that our unworthiness has no truth, it is simply a story aimed at supporting one of the purposes previously mentioned. Then the work is to let go of whatever our self-contempt story is in the service of and to create a new and more compassionate narrative about ourselves. And these stories often best begin with some willingness to offer ourselves forgiveness.

Forgiveness for the Self

The prefix *for* comes from the German meaning *away*. We can understand the word *forgive* as meaning *to give away our sin*. When we are not forgiving ourselves for some behavior we deem unacceptable or sinful, we are cursing ourselves, blotting out our essential goodness. How do we come to sustain years of self-cursing? Do we believe that the intensity and frequency of cursing ourselves will help prevent future enactment of unacceptable behavior?

Self-forgiveness is discussed in the following passage from John O'Donohue's book *Eternal Echoes*:

> It is such a great moment of liberation when you learn to forgive yourself, let the burden go, and walk out into a new path of promise and possibility. Self-compassion is a wonderful gift to give yourself. You should never reduce the mystery and expanse to a haunted fixation with something you did or did

not do. To learn the art of integrating your faults is to begin a journey of healing on which you will regain your poise and find new creativity. Your soul is more immense than any one moment or event in your past.[13]

With these words from O'Donohue in mind, we can ask "Who in me is asking for forgiveness?" This can be a powerful question, initiating some meaningful attention to forgiveness. The hope is that it will lead us to a large story of union with the self guided by love, which inevitably opens us to greater union with others, nature, and God. Much more will be said in the last chapter about forgiving others; for now, let's look at what it means to forgive ourselves.

Marybeth, a fifty-two-year-old high school teacher, came to see me complaining of unfulfilled relationships with men.

"I really don't expect to be treated well by men," she explained, looking puzzled.

"Tell me more about your story with men," I encouraged.

"Well, they either don't listen to me, don't respect my opinion, or they leave me," she said, succinctly describing her journey with men with a hint of disdain.

"It certainly sounds like you've had a challenging time with men. I'm wondering about your relationship with yourself," I suggested.

"What do you mean?" she asked.

"Do you listen to yourself and respect your own opinions, and do you stay with yourself?"

Marybeth's face dropped, her breathing became shallow as she gently wept.

"No, I don't listen to myself and probably don't respect my own opinions," she said, her voice deepening with resignation.

"Listen, I don't want to get men off the hook for how they have treated you. However, it seems to me that it might be empowering for you to examine your relationship with yourself first. You've been treating yourself poorly. Is there some reason for that?"

She sat motionless in an extended pause in the conversation and then said, "Yes, I had two abortions in my early twenties. I haven't felt right since, and I don't know what to do about it."

Marybeth had been carrying the curse of her abortions for an extended period, for reasons common to many of us. First of all, she was experiencing a level of ignorance about the curse she was perpetuating. She believed that her response to her abortions was simply a natural way to go through life after having violated one of her values. I introduced the idea that it might be her responsibility to explore how she might forgive herself.

Her distrust of herself also contributed to her protracted cursing. She was convinced that in maintaining the curse, she would not likely commit another act as despicable as the abortions. Over time and with commitment to her therapy, she began to see that her attachment to the curse would not prevent her from violating her values in the future. She understood that indulging in the curse had nothing to do with the development of a mature conscience.

Marybeth also figured out that the cursing gave her an illusionary sense of control. If anyone ever found out about her abortions and rebuked her for such choices, she could take some solace in having already admonished her behavior. She could take the sting out of someone's ridicule of her by having already inoculated herself with her own curse.

She increasingly accepted responsibility for her own forgiveness. She created a ritual involving close friends aimed at addressing the two lost fetuses, to whom she wrote a letter of amends, expressing her remorse. She read some poetry, handed out flowers, and for the first time, told a compassionate story about a young woman who had decided to have an abortion. She was willing to give away her sin and accept her goodness. Her attitude toward men shifted from one of undeservedness to a receptivity to being seen and chosen. She became increasingly curious about welcoming good love into her life.

GOOD LOVE

An old mentor of mine would regularly speak of "good love." I came to understand that by good love he mostly meant the kind of love that is devoted to championing the uniqueness of the beloved. Good love encourages the beloved to remain mindful of his or her innate gifts and talents. It also heartens the beloved to live close to what they love and rejoice in living their love.

Good love is welcomed when we are willing to remain curious about how love is living in our relationships. We typically like knowing about our financial status, how stocked the cabinets are, what clothes might need to be purchased for the start of school, or how to beautify our lawns and gardens. We seemingly prefer these focuses rather than taking on the task of examining how love lives in our lives.

There are a number of good love questions aimed at raising our consciousness about how our love with other people is being lived. We can regularly ask: Is my love supporting your freedom? Do you feel good about yourself in my presence? Do you feel accepted by me for who you are? Do you feel chosen by me? Do you feel known and understood by me? Do you experience my love supporting your empowerment? Do you feel appreciated by me? Does being loved by me bring joy to you? Do you experience my love as welcoming what is growthful in you? We can ask the same questions regarding how we experience the love offered to us.

Good love honors the bond between love and authentic power. Love without power is a sentiment spinning its wheels, unable to create life. Power without love becomes an array of heartless expressions of energy. Real power unites. Sometimes a level of separation is called for, such as in the example of needing to separate from someone in order to unite with ourselves.

We can see the essential relationship between love and power in the following excerpt from Martin Luther King Jr.'s 1967 speech "Where Do We Go from Here?":

> Now, power properly understood is nothing but the ability to
> achieve purpose . . . And one of the great problems of history
> is that the concepts of love and power have usually been con-
> trasted as opposites, polar opposites, so that love is identified
> with a resignation of power, and power with a denial of love
> . . . Now, we got to get this thing right. What is needed is a
> realization that power without love is reckless and abusive,
> and that love without power is sentimental and anemic. Power
> at its best . . . is love implementing the demands of justice,
> and justice at its best is love correcting everything that stands
> against love . . . It is precisely this collision of immoral power
> with powerless morality which constitutes the major crisis of
> our times.[14]

We have seen that in order to live in larger love stories, we need to be willing to take on the tasks of love. Remaining an apprentice of love is probably the most honorable of life's undertakings. Love will remain a deep mystery and the mystic is willing to remain curious about one's own loving and the quality of love being received. Love is not a place to get perfectionistic, but rather a place to be humble and curious enough to remain a student.

We will at times need to forgive ourselves for the failures of our loving, which happens when we do not live with the level of heart-opening we expect. Our humanity has us falling prey to blaming, shaming, gossiping, ridiculing, losing empathy for others, becoming excessively self-focused, and living with a diminished sensitivity to the impact we have on others. Bringing mindfulness to what we are giving and what we are receiving, and the amount of grace and compassion accompanying what we say to others keep us united with the mystery of love. They are small portholes into the immensity of love.

Once we are willing to accept and maintain responsibility for our own goodness, we can expand our story as seekers of unity by devotion to a *soul practice.*

A SOUL PRACTICE

*"You would not find the limits of the soul
although you traveled every road:
it has so deep a mystery."*
— HERACLITUS

David, a fifty-two-year-old architect, entered my office for the first time, moving with the elegance of a high priest, every gesture suggesting command of purpose. As he positioned himself in the seat eight feet in front of me, his facial muscles softened while the rest of his body stiffened. I wondered if he would allow our engagement to impact him, nudging him somewhere he did not expect to go.

After he meticulously filled out some intake material, I asked, "What brings you here?"

"There's a lot about my life that I like. I mean, in many ways life has been good to me," he explained, outlining the joys and fulfillment of both his professional and family life.

I nodded, allowing for an ensuing silence aimed at inviting the rest of his story.

"Well, there's emptiness and I don't understand it. There's no reason for such hollowness; my life is rich," he insisted.

"Tell me about the richness of your life," I encouraged, believing he wanted to think that his life was not simply falling apart.

"As I said, I love my work, and my wife and I have a great relationship. I'm close to my teenage daughter and recently inherited enough money to provide for me and my family for the rest of my life," he explained, with a hint of anger.

"Are you telling me that you're angry because these life circumstances are not appropriately delivering as planned?"

"Yes, I think so. Besides, I really pay attention to my spiritual life. I pray regularly and meditate ninety minutes twice per day," he remarked, with the sound of disillusionment deepening.

I went on to explain to David that he obviously had invested time and energy in support of his spiritual life, but at the possible expense of soul. After agreeing to back his meditation practice off to an hour twice per day, I was encouraged to hear his curiosity about what it might mean for him to live with more soul and develop a soul practice.

SOUL AND SPIRIT

Thanks to the work of Thomas Moore and others, we can begin to explore the distinguishing features of soul and spirit and deepen our understanding of their interdependence. In his book *Care of the Soul*, Moore states, "Soul is not a thing, but a quality or a dimension of experiencing life and ourselves. It has to do with depth, value, relatedness, heart and personal substance."

Soul	Spirit
Engagement	Detachment
Slow moving	Propensity for swiftness
Attached to being emotionally and sexually intimate	Attached to being analytical and reflective
Willing to be lost	Attached to clarity
Welcoming darkness	Prefers the light
Movement toward a descent	Movement toward an ascent
Attached to beauty and love	Attached to understanding and meaning
Receptive to chaos	Prefers order
Water and earth	Fire and air
Incubation	Penetration
Immanence	Transcendence

SPIRITUAL PRACTICES

Before exploring a variety of soul practices, it may be helpful to acknowledge the spiritual practices available to the novice mystic: meditation, prayer, reading, reflection, contemplation, yoga, martial arts, chanting, ecstatic dance, singing, drumming, meditative walking, ritual, and ritual art. I encourage the reader to explore these practices and decide if one offers spiritual support or an ability to help generate greater meaning and vision.

SOUL PRACTICES

Engagement

We engage as we move beyond the borders of ourselves and meet another person's body, emotions, and beliefs. However, the engagement of beliefs can easily move into an exercise of spirit, with ideas flowing back and forth.

Recently, while having an engagement of beliefs with a friend, I asked that he not disagree with my ideas. He was quickly incensed, imagining that I was suggesting he should simply acquiesce to anything I said. I explained that I didn't want him to agree, which puzzled him thoroughly. I then asked if he would consider responding to my convictions by telling me that he either liked or disliked what I was saying. I suggested he then share the story of his emotional reaction, which keeps us more emotionally engaged.

As we engage we take ourselves to the other rather than remain behind the fixed contours of our personalities. Engagement suggests *involvement*, which in the Old Latin means *to entangle or roll into*. Our soul lives as we roll into life and allow ourselves to be touched and moved by people and nature. The word *engagement* in the Old French means *to be under pledge*. We might understand this as a kind of promise to be vulnerable enough and permeable enough to be contacted, so that we slide into involvement.

We can be called into engagement by art and music, as depicted by the following quote from the film *Zorba the Greek*: "It was the dancing when my little boy Dimitri died . . . and everybody was crying . . . Me, I danced, I got up and I danced. They said, 'Zorba is mad,' But it was the dancing, only the dancing, that stopped the pain."

Zorba describes the music calling him through the pain as his entire body expresses his loss. He allows the music in and he becomes the dance, he becomes the music.

Engagement calls for our willingness to loosen a grip on how we might define the next moment and enter into the realm of the other, risking confusion and possible pain. An engaged self welcomes the moment as pregnant with possibility, yielding to the creative forces surrounding it. It calls for a willingness to embrace unknowing and to allow for the deepening of rapport.

I once received a call from the mother of a ten-year-old girl. I explained to the parent that I did not work with girls. The mother insisted that her doctor had recommended that her daughter see me. I again let her know that ten-year-old girls simply were not part of the population that I treat. She implored me to see her daughter Sally at least one time. For some reason, possibly the respect I held for her physician, I dropped the boundary and agreed to see Sally.

As Sally entered my office and took a seat, I was convinced that I had made a foolish decision.

"So, Sally, why you are here?" I asked, expecting an elongated silence accompanied by much confusion.

"I'm here because I just know that my tears want to tell me something and I'm having a hard time listening to them," she explained, demanding my attention.

"What makes it difficult for you to listen to them?"

"I think my tears make my mommy sad and I don't want that to happen."

"Okay, if your mommy were comfortable with your tears, would it be easier for you to listen to them?"

"Yes, I think it would be easier for me," Sally explained with a palpable certainty.

I encouraged the mother to allow Sally to have her tears and not to get so worried about something awful happening. Sally came in the following week and told me that her tears told her that she was sad about her friend Lisa moving and going to a different school. Sally became a great listener to her tears and I became more engaged with a ten-year-old girl who told the story of her tears. She challenged my belief that a healing engagement was not possible between me and a young girl.

Engagement reflects the presence of Eros with a desire to be with what is presented. It is inevitably the place where we are invited to be body, allowing ourselves to become visible, releasing ties to anonymity. Something deeper has the opportunity to be created as we temporarily relinquish a hold on the sovereignty of separate individuality.

The novice mystic supports stepping into engagement with the spiritual practice of detachment. We can bring more grace to our engagement as we develop an inner observer, a watchful eye, offering discernment to our choices and allowing us to be moved by the quality of a more mature engagement. We can lessen our propensity to act impetuously, which often results in hurt and confusion.

When we are not able to step back, we move into situations where our presence may not be life evoking. It becomes only too easy to offer advice and counsel where it was not requested or to take action toward some goal that is out of our control. Such decisions diminish our unity with life because we are unable to be open-minded enough to hold what we are hearing and witnessing.

When engagement is guided by an inner observer, we can mature our ability to witness rather than react. The job of the observer is to decide where our engagement or involvement is most beneficial, most generative of life. The development of an inner observer will likely happen as a result of trial and error and be determined by what we desire and value. With engagement being guided by an inner observer, we grow a deeper authenticity when we say "yes" and "no." We must also attend to a delicate balance. We either remain engaged with little or no observation and act without discretion, or we are heavily into observation, placing ourselves in some marginalized position with diminished involvement.

I recall my youngest daughter, Jenny, coming home from school one afternoon announcing that she believed it was her fifteen-year-old prerogative to shave her head. Her mother and I stood there shocked, mostly resulting from our attachment to her thick, shoulder-length, chestnut hair. When I finally shook off the staggering impact of her declaration, I asked if she would give me twenty-four hours to respond. She agreed.

I made numerous phone calls to friends and colleagues, hoping to gain some insight about how to prevent this travesty. It became gradually clear that the status of her hair did not fall under the domain of my influence or control. Her mother and I agreed to share a simple statement about our appreciation of her hair and tell her that we believed that ultimately she was responsible for her own hair.

The following day, at the time designated, Jenny heard our prepared statement as I appropriately suppressed my preference to say, "You shave your damn head and you're grounded for a year." Two hours later our daughter returned resembling a refugee recently released from a prison camp.

Detachment guides our individuation, allowing us to give back to family and culture what does not belong to us. We let go of opinions and ideas that are not truly ours. Through separation we create an invitation to our unique preferences, beliefs, and values. Detachment allows us to respond to the call of who we were meant to be while holding on to the uniqueness of the other.

There are questions that may help guide how we live engagement facilitated by detachment: Is the present story of my life asking for more engagement? Where in my story does more engagement seem appropriate? What do I risk by seeking more engagement? Am I willing to take the risk? Is there something I want to say to a particular person? Where in the present story of my life is detachment being asked for? What fears result in me becoming overly attached? Where am I inclined to attempt to control what is out of my control?

Slow Moving

Our culture appears to be obsessed with speed. We want our computers, our cars, our careers, and the development of our children to all go faster. I am increasingly asking people to speak more slowly so that I might understand what they are saying. It seems there is some attraction to the illusion that moving faster equals more life, when the exact opposite is typically true. Moving our bodies through space at some accelerated rate dulls our senses, pumps adrenalin that makes it more difficult to feel our emotions, blurs clear thinking as we typically move into an anticipatory mode of thought that is aimed at preparation for some future event. This happens when we interrupt our ability to listen by quietly preparing our next statement.

It appears that we have attached several illusions to living the fast life. Some of us survived childhood by becoming a moving target rather than a stationary one. We learned that staying busy and on the move might prevent us from being an easy mark for abuse. A great survival skill in childhood leads to hyperactivity as an adult, accompanied by excessive fatigue, anxiety, and an endless flight from the moment with an itinerary pointing us toward the next event.

Many of us have ascribed our worth to being busy, living by the misconception that we must be good people because of all we do. The problem is that there is no time to settle into the comfort of a moment of self-appreciation, and any true valuing of ourselves remains ever so illusive.

Also, our fear of death is pulling us into overdrive, and we are guided by the distortion that as long as we're moving quickly, we are definitely not corpses. How true it is—a cadaver does not move! However, our acceleration is no indication of being fully alive. We see less, hear less, and ultimately live less under the seduction that our increased velocity actually has something to do with living, rather than simply rushing toward death.

We likely have discovered that life mostly takes place in the moment, and if we dare allow ourselves to settle into it, we become vulnerable to the inherent predicaments of life that take place in the present. Of course, settle into it or not, life will have its way with us. Moving quickly is likely characteristic of the ego demanding that its intentions govern life rather than fate playing a larger role in our development. With speed naturally comes a growing anxiety announcing that we are not living where we belong. We are living too far from ourselves, unconscious of what we feel, what we want, what we believe and cherish.

We can understand slowness as passivity, which in the Old Latin means *capable of feeling and suffering*. Are we rushing away from feeling? Has suffering been defined as failure? It would appear that in the alleged game of life, our suffering denotes that life wins and we lose! However, allowing ourselves to suffer reveals that we have some understanding of how to live, how to endure loss, how to take risks, which moves us beyond a shielded existence. We can also see slowness as what we need to do in order to get ourselves in place for meaningful engagement rather than maintaining the evasiveness of speed.

Slowness and passivity are essential conditions for healing as we allow restorative energies to maximize their impact upon us. In the common language of "I need a vacation," we can hear a need for less thinking and less doing, a call to slow down. We can actually fall prey to the belief that when we are not highly active, nothing is occurring. It may be useful to remind ourselves that our lungs are exchanging carbon dioxide for oxygen and our hearts are pumping blood and nutrients to every organ and cell without our direct involvement.

Soulful stillness—a softening into allowing life to live us—acknowledges the immensity of life. The ego recoils, yelling out, "I will live life!" And so we are invited to subdue the ego and not run from life as a child avoiding contact in a game of tag. The soul longs for a stillness, whispering to life, "I'm here; I'm waiting; touch me and teach me. I'm here."

We can see the value of stillness and hereness in the following blessing by John O'Donohue:

For Presence

Awaken to the mystery of being here.
And enter the quiet immensity of your own presence.
Have joy and peace in the temple of your sense.
Receive encouragement when new frontiers beckon.
Respond to the call of your gift and the courage to
Follow its path.
Let the flame of anger free you of all falsity.
May warmth of heart keep your presence aflame.
May anxiety never linger about you.
May your outer dignity mirror an inner dignity of soul.
Take time to celebrate the quiet miracles that seek no attention.
Be consoled in the secret symmetry of your soul.
May you experience each day as a sacred gift woven
around the heart of wonder. [15]

The spirit energy of swiftness certainly has its place, especially as a call to action. However, speed has greatly gleaned cultural approval, leaving many confused about the value of slowness. When we fall captive to lethargy, mediocrity, apathy, and fear, we may be called to become more decisive, speeding up our process in order to evoke more life. Becoming maudlin as we slip easily into the past may be a cue that speed is being asked for in order to let go of where we have been.

Attached to Being Emotionally and Sexually Intimate

Soul is about intimacy. We can be emotionally intimate with God, people, places, and animals. However, soul is also at home when we are emotionally intimate with ourselves. Common growthful inclinations point us toward who we wish to be, how we want to better ourselves. Soul invites us as novice mystics to move closer to who we are rather than who we might become. This invitation is guided by a devotion to knowing who we are, or as Socrates described, "living the examined life." It must be a knowing guided by care and compassion.

Imagine getting to know someone but remaining critical and shaming so that the relationship quickly deteriorates into avoidance and estrangement. Soul asks that we remain devoted to knowing ourselves with acceptance and kindness, or likewise we succumb to self-alienation and avoiding ourselves.

Soul is enriched by participating in an emotionally intimate event where people are committed to being honest, supportive, and encouraging. Soul flourishes in an emotionally intimate relationship where the task of intimacy calls for more depth and meaning.

Soul loves living in personal stories of intimacy. An ancient meaning of the word *depth* is *limitless* and as such, soul places no limits on the strength of emotional experiences of connectedness. Soul thrives on feeling seen, heard, considered, loved, and welcomed and is open to feeling rejection, hurt, and vulnerability. That is not to say that a soul practice involves getting off on feeling unappreciated. Rather, there is a willingness to experience intense emotion that indicates an openness to endure the risks involved in genuinely joining another.

Soulful meaning happens not so much due to the intensity of feeling but more because of the range of feeling. Meaning expands as we welcome the other into playing, planning, solving problems, fighting, dreaming, creating, exploring, and making love.

Soul is enlivened through sexual intimacy, especially when it is accompanied by depth and meaning. When the inner well or Eros spills from genitals to hearts, and back again, soul is awakened. Being sexually intimate means being chosen and choosing the other in a full way that is not meant to be limiting.

We can see the relevance of the French euphemism for orgasm—*la petite mort* or small death—because some limitation between two people may pass away during orgasm and something new, a new feeling of unity, may be born. In soulful sex there is a hunger for more, more feeling and more desire. As this desire builds, there is an increasing likelihood that there will be some loss of ourselves as we get lost in the rapture of connection.

Maturing intimacy can be supported and guided by the spirit energies of analysis and reflection. The heart and mind inform one another. I suggest avoiding pathologizing (by the use of labels such as codependency) the experience of getting lost in the other. Our intimacy stories can be richer by allowing spirit to expand the vision of ourselves as lost, inviting and welcoming new understandings of the one who is lost.

Intimacy may be a story about getting lost and finding our way back to ourselves. We don't need to catastrophize our situations because we seem to be more interested in what our partners desire than in our own needs and desires. Emotional intimacy involves both the courage to feel so deeply that we become lost in the other and the courage to find our way back. The soul practice begins by allowing for enough vulnerability and permeability so that we *do* get lost.

There are some questions that can help build the story of loving, getting lost, and finding our way back home. Have I ever been lost in love? How do I feel about myself as someone who got lost in love? Do I need to forgive myself for choices I made while I was lost? Have I allowed myself to get lost again? If I have never been lost in love, what do I need to do in order to allow it to happen? What's at risk if I do let myself get lost? What's at risk if I don't let myself get lost? What might need to be sacrificed in order to find my way back to myself? Who might be a valuable ally in support of my trip back to myself?

As we gain more of ourselves, celebrating the uniqueness of what we cherish and long for, the soul's hope is that we are courageous and foolish enough to live deeply passionate lives. Any story infused with Eros will include a daring that will call us away from the comfort of the familiar.

Willing to Be Lost

Truly one of our greatest cultural taboos is getting lost—lost not simply in love, but lost in life. Consequently, most of us embrace the familiar, condemn ourselves when we are lost, or do our best to pretend we are above such an inane ordeal. In order to gain some appreciation for the soulful practice of getting lost, we'll need to stretch ourselves beyond our cultural indoctrination. As illustrated here in Gonzales's five stages of getting lost, the first four are mostly about denial, depicting the ego's mad tenacity to see itself as knowing, or at least pretending to know, regardless of whether it leads to one's own peril.

In his book *Deep Survival*, Laurence Gonzales outlines five stages of getting lost in the wilderness that are also extremely applicable to getting emotionally lost in our own living rooms:

> The research suggests five general stages in the process a person
> goes through when lost. In the first, you deny that you're
> disoriented and press on with growing urgency, attempting to
> make your mental map fit what you see. In the next stage, as
> you realize that you're genuinely lost, the urgency blossoms
> into a full-scale survival emergency. Clear thought becomes
> impossible and action becomes frantic, unproductive, even
> dangerous. In the third stage (usually following injury or
> exhaustion), you expend the chemicals of emotion and form a

strategy for finding some place that matches the mental map. (It is a misguided strategy, for there is no such place now: You are lost.) In the fourth stage, you deteriorate both rationally and emotionally, as the strategy fails to resolve the conflict. In the final stage, as you run out of options and energy, you must become resigned to your plight. Like it or not, you must make a new mental map of where you are.[16]

Why would soul possess an affinity with getting lost? Well, one reason is that soul desires to be intimate with life, and as we have seen, life is a mysterious, insecure, and unpredictable journey. Such an odyssey guarantees getting lost. One measure of a well-lived life will be the degree to which we allowed ourselves to get lost.

Do you know the one in you willing to be lost in order to stumble across a deeper truth within yourself? We can also understand getting lost as the movement away from the familiar: the old ends, heralding something new. Such an ending may be accompanied by grief, fear, and the loss of faith that something greater will take the place of what was so recognizable.

A time that cast me into the wilderness of the journey happened when I decided to leave my marriage of twenty-five years. I was truly lost, no longer knowing what to believe in or what to trust. Luckily, I had a mentor who consistently reminded me that I was lost, so the first of Gonzales's stages quickly lost it potency. However, I did quickly lose my capacity for clear thinking. My cerebral musing went from moving to the West Indies, to buying a sports car, to joining a monastery.

In the third stage I was attempting to "find a place that matched my mental map." I met a beautiful ballerina, imagined developing a wonderful monogamous relationship and living happily ever after. The map was perfect for a week, until she discovered I was fifteen years older than her. True to Gonzales's fourth stage, I became more depressed, more desperate, more confused, and more frightened as my identity crumbled before my eyes.

My mentor knew I needed a new map describing where I was and recommended a Vision Quest in the Adirondack Mountains with two dozen men. His suggestion sounded like a great way to make matters worse. I acquiesced not out of some confidence in his suggestion, but rather by surrendering to the hopelessness of my situation.

I had no idea then that the deep forest was analogous to where my soul was. Nor did I understand that the Vision Quest was a ritual or a funeral for a dying husband. At one point, I collapsed into the arms of men, screaming and sobbing tears of deep devotion that herald a broken heart and the death of a dream.

The familiar cradles us in the hope that we might be immune from the torrid vicissitudes of life, that we will not be torn away from our temporary comforts. And it is so challenging to believe something greater awaits us with open arms. As the sanctuary of the familiar is cracked open and we fall to the ground, lost, we have an opportunity to step away from the supremacy of our egos. If we are willing to learn to bear the tension of the unknown, we will be carried to a deeper experience of ourselves and of life.

After my funeral in the mountains and by continuing to remain lost for a number of years, I learned how much my soul hungered to be lived by life, calling me to the unknown that was pregnant with evolving possibility. The ultimate purpose of getting lost is to be found by life in a new way, under the guidance of a new clarity. The familiar shelters me from change and growth, allegedly protecting me from the dynamic and turbulent forces of life that cajole and push me to the unknown.

There are some questions that might be helpful to the soul practice of getting lost. Am I willing to stop pretending I'm not lost when I am? Am I willing to hold some compassion for myself while and after I'm lost? Am I willing to find a place to tell the story of being lost, not allowing the listener to attempt to rescue or shame me? Am I willing to experience the feelings and tension that accompanies being lost? Am I willing to feel the grief associated with letting go of the familiar? Am I willing to be curious about where I belong?

Clarity is the spirit characteristic we may benefit from when we are willing to bear the tension of being lost. Often the gift of such a resiliency is new eyes that find their gestation in wonder and curiosity. With a little luck, this unfolding clarity may deepen our knowing and our capacity to unite with life.

Welcoming Darkness

Soul hungers for the opportunity to be intimate with life and intimate with God, the Transcendent Other or the Creator. There's so much to let go of—distortions aimed at stitching a torn and overworn ego, which minimize the vastness and impervious mystery of life.

In Dante's *Divine Comedy* we are offered images of the transformative offerings of darkness, as depicted in the dark wood: "Instead I found myself a middle-aged man with a torn tunic, swollen ankle, and hemorrhaging pride in the bottom of a gulley. The lofty sentiments of my intellect were useless. My philosophy and poems were futile to explain this abhorrent situation."[17] What once provided illumination falls away; our old beliefs and ideals no longer provide an adequate beacon. We are lost and desperate, moving closer to an opening of the heart ushered in by darkness.

"But after I had reached a mountain's foot, at that point where the valley terminated, which had with consternation pierced my heart."[18] It would appear that a heart piercing is the gift of darkness. The piercing is necessary as we attempt to avoid feelings of vulnerability and fragility by garrisoning our hearts with hubris, narcissism, and an inordinate amount of self-reliance. Without sufficient darkness our hearts remain shielded and removed from any longing to unite with life, convinced that every task can be addressed by a fine-tuned ego.

"How many times had I been seduced by the likes of the leopard, mesmerized by form, beauty and grace devoid of character and depth? How many times had I met this leopard in the arms of a lover, poetic or real? I had bartered beauty and lust for truth and lost my way."[19] When the walk into the dark wood is not accompanied by enough desperation, the ego will insist upon defining such a trial as simply unfortunate, characterizing darkness as an evil perpetrator who victimizes but teaches nothing. We then fail to ask: What did I barter for truth? In my case, I once learned I had bartered a denial of my limits and an obsessive self-reliance on truth.

My middle child, Sarah, was born with a neurological condition that left her susceptible to seizures when running a fever, especially if she fell asleep. We were caught in a no-win situation, where her healing required rest, while preventing a seizure meant keeping her and me awake. I would lie near her, talking and gently rocking her in an attempt to avert sleep. Inevitably, I would fall asleep, awakening to Sarah's quivering, seizing body and feeling ashamed of my negligence.

There were no simple answers in those trying times, when my own exaggerated pride and confidence were being tested and broken. My heart was pierced by desperation, helplessness, and love for Sarah. "I needed something I rarely sought. I needed not to lead, even to lead myself, but to be led. I was ready to put my trust in another for my self-recovery. I resolved to follow if ever a teacher would come."[20]

Following Sarah's sixteenth birthday, my heart piercing opened me to receiving help. A group of friends and relatives began to meet twice per month with the purpose of supporting our family. I learned that when the heart is pierced by darkness, vision can happen with a new luminosity. A new light shown and I accepted my limits and accepted the strength of a communal effort to support my disabled child. I saw myself capable of carrying and expressing deeper levels of gratitude. There was a new welcome offered to my humanity, which had previously been thwarted by my heroic inclinations.

I was a bit more open "to follow if ever a teacher would come." One of the great gifts of darkness can be a new openness to being informed by sources outside of ourselves. Darkness encourages us to remain students, to remain novice mystics, ready to unite with a source of light greater than ourselves.

Movement toward a Descent

In Greek mythology the *katabasis* was typically a hero's descent into the underworld, or hell. Such descents can teach us about death and how to die. An example of such a downward journey is Odysseus's descent into Hades, the land of the dead, as he makes his way home from the Trojan War.

While in Hades he learns of his fate, as Tiresias explains how he has incurred the wrath of Poseidon by killing his son, the Cyclops. Odysseus's mother explains to him how she died, modeling what it means to learn about dying. His cleverness is no match for Poseidon's determination to launch a series of calamities in Odysseus's path. In order to reach his destination, he will need to be humble enough to allow his experiences to teach him.

A descent may be about the death of some limitation or whatever obstructs a larger vision or blocks us from living in a larger story. The descent is typically an opportunity to bring understanding and peace to our fate. It is a chance to give up some way in which we unnecessarily struggle against life and against ourselves.

Christ's descent into the tomb symbolizes the death of his humanity and the ensuing birth and ascent into his divinity. Typically, a descent is heralded by being lost and being pierced by the darkness of deep self-doubt, as reflected in Christ's sweating blood in the Garden of Gethsemane, where he asked to be relieved of his destiny. Coming to a point at which we simply want to quit is one of the essential challenges of a descent.

One of my initial descents took place when I was twenty-two years old. I worked in retailing as an assistant buyer of women's plus-size dresses. Newly married with my spouse newly pregnant and a full-time student, I experienced the burden of being a provider who was quickly slipping downward.

I was drinking heavily, smoking a pack of cigarettes per day, and tipping the scale with an extra forty pounds.

I dragged myself to work in the hope of a miracle that would transport me anywhere but the boring world of large dresses and the haughty airs of corporate life. I was scheduled to visit showrooms in the garment district every afternoon, allegedly educating myself regarding the new and hot styles. Instead, I took my leisure in the back office with a salesman or an administrator of the manufacturer, indulging in good whisky and conversation.

Much was dying for me. My idyllic vision of collegiate life and skewed beliefs about the work world being creative and fulfilling were rapidly decomposing. Life seemed empty, cruel, and meaningless. My impending addictions and obesity quickly took a backseat as a new nemesis demanded my attention. The divisional manager was about to impose his expectations on me.

The divisional manager called me and the other five assistant buyers into his office. He explained that the time had come to measure what we had learned about buying and selling our respective merchandise. He described how the company was cutting each of us sizable checks, whereby we were to make purchases from our manufacturers that were to be distributed among sixty retail stores. He pointed out that we would meet again after he received sales reports from the stores regarding the merchandise we sent to them. He wished us all well and I remained in my seat, stunned.

"Any questions, Paul?" he asked, probably thinking that my pause likely indicated some relevant inquiry regarding the task.

"Oh no, sir. I'm just going over a few things in my mind," I responded, hoping to conceal the gripping terror that had resulted in my temporary paralysis.

"Great! I like a young man who wants to get a jump on things!"

"Thank you, sir," I said, now quickly taking leave, thinking more about the possibility of jumping out the window.

I returned to my desk convinced that my incompetence would be exposed, surely leading to my dismissal. How could I have failed at my first job? How would we pay the rent? How would my wife finish school? My thoughts quickly moved to catastrophic dimensions.

As I sat at my desk heaped in worry and staring out at the street where delivery boys pushed racks of clothes, the phone rang, interrupting my tragic musings. The voice on the other end was Steve, vice president of a dress manufacturer. He and I had shared numerous backroom raps ranging from philosophy to baseball. He immediately heard my fading energy and asked if anything was wrong. From a combination of desperation and a trust in our rapport, I decided to tell him about my predicament.

Rather than chastise my ignorance about dresses, he responded with enthusiasm and hope, instructing me to come to his showroom with the check. He outlined a strategy of tracking styles sent to other stores that were fast sellers. Once he identified the movers, what was selling, he would send those styles to my stores. I left his showroom relieved to have an ally and forlorn about the hypocrisy to which my business ignorance had led me. I justified my decision by acknowledging that I was in survival mode and by increasing my alcohol intake.

Three weeks later the divisional manager called for the follow-up meeting of the assistant buyers in order to evaluate our progress. I moved slowly from my desk to his office, flooded by embarrassment about a suit that seemed two sizes too small and the portrayal of a business savvy several sizes too big.

The divisional manager grabbed piles of reports off his desk revealing the successes and failures of the six of us. As I sat there, I felt more like an uninvited guest than an employee. I was prepared to hear the bad news.

"Well, I only wish that the five of you would have come close to Paul's monthly results!" he said, proclaiming a success that shocked me.

Several of my peers cast suspicious glares in my direction, as they knew full well my commitment and competency were a long way from stellar. I did my best to appear pleasantly surprised, determined to conceal any amazement that might expose the depth of my self-doubt. The manager was granting us another opportunity to illustrate our skills as buyers by cutting us more checks. I left the office and immediately called Steve, gratefully sharing the result of our collaboration and hoping we could reproduce the success of our initial venture. Steve assured me of the imminent realization of our goals.

The next meeting with the divisional manager went similar to the first. Only this time the manager detailed numerous purchases I had allegedly made and the copious sales reported by each store. He applauded my business prowess, as I reminded myself to appear neither overly confident nor unduly modest. I thanked him for his support and eagerly left his office, catching the eyes of my colleagues that had shifted from suspicion to disdain.

I called Steve to offer my gratitude, and he reminded me that we all won: him, my company, and me. I wondered why I was so critical of a business plan that involved utilizing my good rapport with Steve—a man who knew much more about dresses than I did.

The following week I was called to the company president's office. He introduced himself and promptly offered me a promotion. I graciously declined, explaining that I felt called to explore teaching. He said he understood and that there would always be a position waiting for me in his organization. Two months later I left the world of dresses and took a position at a small New England prep school teaching philosophy and American history.

I learned to die in the garment district. I went to New York believing that money was the best reason to work—that belief died. My attachment to looking good began to die. I had been in the first male beauty pageant at my university. Although I lost the contest, the attention I received elevated my vanity, making me value how I looked rather than who I was. My descent into the world of buying dresses ushered in the death of valuing how much I earned and how I looked. I learned a little about dying and living at a considerable distance from myself.

My ascent had a lot to do with the value of authentic rapport and how it saved me. I left New York a bit less naïve, trusting in the creation of mutual respect and its power to support any task. The idea of descent is discussed further when we address the experience of resurrection in the last chapter.

Attached to Beauty and Love

As we saw in the last chapter, love is a profound call to unity. Our souls long to find a path through the briars and thicket of our existential separateness and aloneness, where the heart welcomes. Soul wants to offer love and receive love. There is no soul life outside of love.

Soul celebrates its journey in the world as love moves and disturbs, calling us to unlock small hidden chambers of the heart where old hurt dwells. A heart-opening to love allows soul a pulse and a deep knowing about its presence on the earth plane. Those emotional aches collected along the way are an inevitable event in a life lived from love. The hurt is not damaging to soul, but the heart contractions aimed at protection impair soulfulness. Soul asks us to learn how to be hurt, how to bring a suppleness and resiliency to blows to the heart.

Learning to be heartfully hurt first means being mindful of how we presently deal with hurt. Do we attempt to pretend that the hurt never happened? Do we demean the perpetrator or diminish our own characters? At times, such attacks seem necessary. The key is not to dwell in attack mode too long.

One example is when we get hurt and launch an attack on the heart, deciding the hurt happened because we're unlovable. Or we decide we love wrong, lacking the necessary skill in order to master love. However, there is no mastery of love! Love is simply too immense and vast to imagine becoming a love expert. At best, we remain devoted students of love. When we can call off the narcissism that focuses our attention on our love ineptness, we hold ourselves open to love again.

When we lock ourselves into the fires of anger and revenge, we prevent the healing waters of hurt to wash over the wound. We define ourselves as the unfortunate victims of perpetrators who mishandled our tender hearts. We can pretend we are safer when we go on the attack.

Learning to be hurt entails several simple focuses that we will explore in detail in Chapter 8 as related to strengthening our capacity to forgive. For now, I suggest the following:

1. Remain close to the truth of being hurt instead of being distracted by anger, revenge, or a heart attack.

2. Allow yourself to feel the hurt, such as through crying.

3. Tell the hurt story to supportive allies, increasingly moving toward clarity about what's to be learned about love and living with heart.

This third step involves the spirit energy of understanding and meaning. The soul is dependent upon spirit in order to remain devoted to a life of love, which helps us learn how to be hurt and how to live in a large love story.

I recently stepped into a larger love story while leading a workshop. During the day I told Sid and Julie's story as an example of a larger love story. When I got to the part of the story where Sid helps Julie reconstruct their childhood together, I wept uncontrollably, frequently needing to pause, in honor of the deep feeling finding its way to the surface.

I left the workshop more willing to allow for confusion regarding how deeply touched I was. I did not understand the intensity of my feeling. The soul celebrates the opportunity to bathe in deep emotion before being elucidated by the probing energy of spirit and liberated into a larger story because of spirit's luminosity.

I initially attributed being so touched to the urging of some unresolved romantic sentiment. That explanation simply did not hold the power emanating from my heart. Several days later, I was struck by the awareness of having helped to reconstruct hundreds of childhoods in my work, which always called for as much truth and compassion as I could muster. I sat gazing at the last leaves holding to their lofty postures in high branches on the trees outside the window. A wave of gratitude swept over me, as I held the immensity of such an opportunity, to help build a past that allows folks to make peace with their fate and more fully participate in the creation of their destinies.

In his book *Beauty: The Invisible Embrace*, John O'Donohue writes, "When we experience the Beautiful, there is a sense of homecoming." Similar to the soul's attachment to love, it also holds a deep knowing that it belongs to beauty. The question of whether beauty lies inherently in the thing observed or in the eyes of the observer is irrelevant to soul. Soul longs for the embrace of beauty. In order for the soul to unite with the sublime, there must be an honoring of simplicity.

Sometimes it is only through a lens developed over time that we can see the beauty that always surrounded us. When I was five years old, my grandmother allowed me to leave the sanctuary of women gathered in the kitchen and sit with the men in the living room. The day she delivered me to this male lodge, she cautioned them about the use of obscenity in the presence of my virgin ears. Within minutes of occupying my new station, the verbal banter weighed heavy with profanity.

These men—my grandfather, his five sons, and his three sons-in-law—gathered every Sunday afternoon to tell stories whose imaginary borders flowed seamlessly into reality. They spoke loudly, drank hard, and celebrated themselves as Irish rogues resembling Celtic warriors following a decisive victory. Every Sunday they were determined to give themselves the deep warmth of their passion and their company. Their stories lifted them out of the mediocrity and emptiness of their lives, offering temporary refuge from a life they knew they did not know how to live.

Every Sunday I took my place near my grandfather, whose gentle hand on my shoulder reassured me that I belonged among this male assembly, my clan. It was many years later that I saw the beauty that embraced these men. There was rapture in the tenacity and devotion they possessed as they addressed the hallowed with a relentless irreverence. They soothed the sting of their deep sense of inadequacy by dismantling every sacred cow that presented itself for their proper evaluation.

They possessed a wit that rattled through their bodies, filling the air with a laughter that exonerated them from feeling victimized by life. The tears of their hilarity washed away the dust of cynicism and despair from their cheeks. Their eyes brightened with a new light as the robust nature of their humor confirmed their vitality and potency. These men truly knew how to gain comfort from one another's company.

I recall one Sunday when my father briefly detailed his challenges at work, attempting to conceal the thrashing his pride endured daily. As my parents and I walked to our car, my father's brother, my Uncle Ace, threw open the front door of my grandmother's house. With his chin raised and his right fist thrashing into air of the night, he yelled, "Kick their ass, Billy!" My father smiled in gratitude and opened the car door for my mother.

The image of my uncle standing on that porch cheering and refusing to leave the side of his brother, who would again and again step into sure defeat, remains for me a silhouette of great beauty. When my Uncle Ace died, I wrote to his wife, explaining that no man brought greater joy to a brother than her husband did for my father.

There was another man in my childhood who introduced me to beauty. Father Ray, a priest who came into my life when I was eleven, also taught me that beauty surrounded me and was eager to embrace me. This was a lesson I would not acquire for many years.

We enjoyed taking rides in his car, a vehicle fast enough and sleek enough, and more fitting to a young man seeking adventure than to a member of the clergy. This particular Sunday we were driving down a four-lane highway hours before my graduation from grade school. Father Ray abruptly pulled over into the break-down lane and exited the vehicle as if to put out a brush fire. I sat there stunned by his bizarre behavior. My religious mentor was dancing on the nearby hill, both arms flailing in the air, yelling, "Look at this! It's everywhere!"

I yelled back, "What are you looking at?" I was somewhat relieved by his exuberance, which suggested that he hadn't encountered something dead.

"The Mountain Laurel, it's incredibly beautiful; it's everywhere! Can you believe it?" he exclaimed with the enthusiasm of a boy on Christmas morning. It was beyond me at the time how anyone could get excited about anything other than girls and sports.

This past autumn, some fifty years later, I pulled my vehicle to side of the road, struck with awe as I saw a tree with new eyes. The leaves were in their transformative state, not their original green nor their emerging yellow. I was being presented with at least a hundred different shades of green! I never realized there were so many greens. I wanted to bow in the presence of nature's sublime offering. I finally understood Father Ray's encounter with the Mountain Laurel.

Spirit can offer curiosities that help strengthen soul's relationship to beauty if we can focus our attention. What beauty is attempting to get my attention? Which of my senses is most receptive to beauty? What expressions of beauty have recently touched me? Am I able to see the external or internal beauty of the people in my life? What might I need to let go of in order to be more available to the embrace of beauty? How do I resist being touched by my own beauty? What's at risk to let go of this resistance?

Receptive to Chaos

Several ancient meanings of the word *chaos* include *unformed* and *chasm*. We can image the soul's affinity with chaos to reflect that in-between place where the old is dying and the new is yet to breathe life or be formed. Soul appears to thrive on inviting possibility, eluding definition that may be limiting or diminishing. This in-between place typically involves a great deal of tension. It is the space before the grab that takes place between two trapeze artists. There's so much we no longer are and so much we have yet to become! The experience of chaos can be a large declaration that we are opening to mystery rather than attempting to sooth ourselves with the familiar.

Peter, a forty-eight-year-old nautical engineer, came to my office overwhelmed by chaos. He explained how a week earlier he had attended a weekend retreat sponsored by his church. Upon his return home, he found his wife's closets empty and a note on the kitchen table describing how she was taking leave of their marriage of twenty-six years. His attempts to reach her were met with defiance and repulsion.

Peter spent a number of sessions with me in shock, moving from feeling completely victimized to lamenting a lost marriage and a dream to grow old with a woman he dearly loved. Chaos was gushing down on him, with his old life crumbling before him and nothing new yet having formed. Gradually, he learned to make peace with the tension of life in the chasm, and he became curious about what the chaos was asking of him.

He began to see how he had swallowed the American dream whole. He had totally accepted our culture's mandate for success. He went to the right college, married the captain of the cheerleaders, got an appropriate job, and moved into a very appropriate neighborhood, where he raised the appropriate number of children while maintaining his membership in the appropriate country club.

His wife's departure had hurled him into a whirlwind of self-doubt and chaos, which called him to mend the rupture of his life from having married the right cheerleader. Peter slowly surrendered to the chaos as an opportunity to allow his borrowed self to die. He grew to tolerate the tension of his turmoil and even appreciate it as a large invitation to prepare for a more authentic life, one more friendly to his soul.

Spirit takes great satisfaction in providing our lives with order. An ancient meaning of the word order is *arrangement*. We take great solace in arranging our beliefs, values, and commitments so they might comfort us from the vicissitudes of life, but we're never quite sure if the arrangement actually reflects who we are. It is a precarious journey as we eagerly arrange ourselves, only to be subjected to the next tempest of chaos. However, this process of moving from chaos to order and back again may reflect the soul's passion to create itself.

Water and Earth

The elements of water and earth feed soul. Water can easily reflect the soul's comfort with deep emotion and grief. Since water is a conductor of light, we can say that at times of great grief, the waters of the soul are receptive to the luminosity of the spirit's fire. This light moving through water can offer an epiphany, clarifying what is dying in our lives, the beliefs and choices that crafted the old life, and possibly a hint of what is asking to be born.

Water can also represent the soul's need for flow, always moving to a lower level, bringing us to new depths with an enduring flexibility. Water's relationship to earth allows us to stay in the flow, being escorted and directed toward our destinies. Like earth that makes up the banks of a river, the concreteness of our senses and our actions offer guidance to the waters of our feelings, keeping the flow while avoiding flooding and stagnant pools.

Earth not only supplies a container for soulful waters but also the support deeply desired by soul. Soul longs to be nurtured by deep earth energy, such as arms holding us in the embrace of a safe harbor or the warmth of a gaze offering an invitation that washes over us. When we experience continuity in terms of home, friendships, and where we belong, soul rests in the arms of the earth.

Spirit can provide air, strong winds that clear away dead limbs and brush, symbolic of old ways that no longer work. It also offers fire that can clear away convictions that have outlived their relevance. Air is symbolic of a willingness to bring new meaning and clarity to the soul's experience, while fire can be symbolic of an infusion of passion, a rekindling of Eros.

Once again there are questions that can help focus our attention on the soul's need for these varied elements. What emotions are asking to be expressed?

Where is my life asking for more flexibility? What losses are calling for my grief? Where is my home and where do I belong? Is there a position I need to take? What beliefs appear to no longer work for me? Am I living my passion?

Incubation

Soul prefers to linger. An ancient meaning of the word *incubation* means *to lie in or upon*. We can say that soul has a propensity to lie on or in its experience. We are offered this deeply sensual image of soul lying upon its experience, merging with it, receptive to the unexplored nuances of the encounter, as soul deepens itself.

There is a sense of a creative passivity where soul is touched, moved, and aroused toward something new and different. Soul appears convinced that in its passivity it will be impregnated with new and vital energies. This level of receptivity calls for a suspension of the tyranny of ego that is determined to give governance to the moment.

In this soulful incubation there is patience, grace, and faith that much is happening for us in the absence of our intentions. Soul opens to what is hidden, much like nature in winter as the indiscernible life of plants lies quietly beneath the snows and frost, waiting to emerge with new vigor.

During incubation the soul rests easily with the curiosity "What else is here?" I had an important awakening about incubation while visiting my friend Thom in New Mexico. We had just left a video shop. Lingering longer than my blood sugar and hunger could tolerate, I was more than ready to get back home for dinner.

We were driving slowly through a large parking lot when Thom yelled, "Hey, there's old Pete!"

I saw an elderly man shabbily dressed, with all the stereotypical signs of being homeless. Thom slowed the vehicle as we approached the vagabondish figure, and I hoped it would be a cursory greeting with us being on our way. But, oh no, my friend decided to pull over and engage this fellow in conversation that I immediately judged as excessive and unnecessary.

As we finally pulled away, my silence announcing a protest of my friend's indiscriminate actions, Thom said, "Did I ever tell you about old Pete?"

"No, you haven't," I responded, having no need to conceal my annoyance.

"Yeah, old Pete is known as the oldest living Lakota medicine man. He was the principal consultant to Spielberg's television epic *Into the West*," explained Thom, as my indignation quickly evaporated.

Soul lies comfortably with "There's much more here than I know." Sometimes when I am eager to display my knowing, I can support the soul's wondering about what else lies before me. However, there are still those times when I'm convinced I know exactly what is in front of me, deciding that the moment is undeserving of my pause, certainly not warranting my time and energy.

An immense soul practice is the devotion to track and interrupt an attachment to being right. The ego demands its supremacy as it asserts the rightness of its claims, gaining some temporary reprieve from whatever self-loathing dwells within. As we undo our embrace of being right, we welcome the opportunity to incubate, which allows us to learn more about ourselves and about life.

Incubation is a holding. The following is a blessing of incubation as a holding.

HOLDING

Is it possible that the time of unholding could be a violent time?
That time when you frantically tear at the structure of beliefs
which hold up the one who stands before you, struggling to make
himself known to you?

Have you asked your listener to help confirm some idea destined
to fall way short of undeniable certainty? And when the uniqueness
of his vision pushes against your desperate need for agreement, have
you responded in violence?

In that moment, you can't allow the timbre of his words to shake
you into a cascade of fear, desperately fleeing from the possibility
of being wrong. So, you offer the other an invitation to abandon
himself, hoping he will surrender to your strivings to convert him.

Can you remember the sacredness of moving slow? And in that
restraint, loosen your grip on the shackles of right and wrong?
Can you hold the other in the invitation of your curiosity?
And can you hold him through the veil of your fear, allowing
the tension to subside, replaced by an abiding calm?

Then, you can hold the both of you in the faith that the pause
will allow the two of you to lie together, relinquishing the struggle

to demonstrate and prove. And from such a joining comes a sacred germination yielding new life, life that has been waiting for such a holding.

You will learn to hold yourself and hold the other. And in the warmth of this embrace, violence comes to an end as the desperate need to be right is sacrificed. And in its place, you come to understand this holding, this offering of sustenance, as stillness replaces impetuosity, respect replaces irreverence, gentleness replaces force, welcome replaces domination, and peace replaces violence.

. . . .

Spirit enjoys its capacity to penetrate the moment. When we penetrate, our physical, emotional, or intellectual energies are breaking into the moment. We can penetrate in order to make a genuine offering. This happens when we believe our energies will make a welcomed contribution. When that happens, penetration is not something done to the moment or done to someone, but rather it's a cocreative act.

Because our culture prizes penetration, it is often done indiscriminately, lacking a refined sensibility. I am regularly struck by a penetrator offering advice and opinions in the name of demonstrating intellectual prowess, which ignores either the needs or the receptivity of those penetrated. When penetration is used as the ego's need to authenticate itself, we often lose sight of the possibility of creating a deeper rapport, harvesting the creative energies of union.

During social interaction, penetration typically occurs verbally. We can bring more maturity and depth to our penetration by asking: Do I feel urgent about penetrating this moment with my ideas? If so, what's my urgency about? Is my need to penetrate simply self-serving? Will it serve me in this moment to incubate a bit, by asking, "What else is here?"

Immanence

We can understand immanence as the sacred or the divine being here now, in our midst, right before us. The novice mystic is asked to seek the sacred, that which is deserving of one's devotion. It is through devotion that we consecrate our experience, creating the sacred. The soul personalizes the task of bringing the sacred to life. The novice mystic welcomes the chance to deepen a kinship with life through devotion. What deserves our devotion? How do we know we are living devotionally?

A BLESSING FOR DEVOTION

What calls to your faithfulness?
It may all begin with a despondency and a loss of faith. In this place,
there is only a vision of a large chasm
separating you from life.
Can you hold a longing for the other side,
a fervor for life's welcome? A tiny
flame is ignited, slowly burning away
small stories about life not wanting to live you.

A surrender to your own body is repaid
by informing you of what deserves your
devotion, your loyalty. You lose breath,
gain breath, a warmth cradles your cheeks
like tender hands and your heart aches with
a new fullness.

Whatever deserves your devotion calls you
to more feeling, more thinking, and more
dreaming in the embrace of an ever-enlarging
story. You know where you want to live and
be lived.

Now, the life of devotion is pregnant with a
wish for generations to come. You know what
you want for those waiting to follow you and you
know you'll forget what serves so many beyond
your immediate gratification. And you pray for
the reminder. Then and only then, can life be
truly lived devotionally.

The consecration of life, here and now, takes place as we honor our experience through gratitude and an eagerness to give back. We can let go of ruminating on all the ways we've been deprived of attention, love, and success. We turn toward the endless bounty of life's offerings, recalling kindnesses received, moments of joy, the company of good friends, and the myriad ways to be embraced by life's sweetness. Even the breath given to us in this moment deserves gratitude and allows us in the simplest way to consecrate our lives.

The soul longs to be the recipient of its own consecration as we live the blessed life. This happens as we love ourselves for who we are rather than what we do or accomplish. Mystics unite with the mystery of self as we hold ourselves deeply deserving of forgiveness, honoring our limits, seeing ourselves as deserving of love, and accepting our place in the family of humanity. We can remain eager to make an offering to life with a presence that remains deeply welcoming. The sacred then abounds, without and within.

Spirit contributes its attachment to transcendence where the sacred dwells beyond this time and this place. The experience of the beyond points us deeply into the heart of mystery, reminding us of the immensity of the sacred, asking us to stretch further, asking more of our experience and our imagination.

The transcendent calls to our sense of wonder and awe, allowing our egos to dim their auspicious brilliance. We move closer to a genuine expression of our humanity, with hopefully less need to impress and claim victory. The transcendent sacred can teach us to bow, not in humiliation but in thanks for the opportunity to hold reverence and recognize the enormity of what is.

It serves the novice mystic to open to a soul practice that can deepen and expand the experience of unity. There's so much about soul calling to the divine energy of Sophia, where unity truly lives. Now, we turn to the mystic's welcome of Sophia.

The heart of a twenty-two-day-old fetus generating brain cells. Source: *A Child Is Born*, Lennart Nilsson and Lars Hamberger, Tidningarnas Telegrambyrå, National Wire Service, 105 12, Stockholm, Sweden. Reprinted with permission.

WELCOMING SOPHIA

*"I will tell you what wisdom is and how she came to be,
and I will hide no secrets from you, but I will trace
her course from the beginning of creation and make
knowledge of her clear, and I will not pass by the truth."*
—BOOK OF WISDOM, 6:22

I don't know when I first met her. I remember hearing the crunch of snow under my feet and the sun rising directly in front of me, as if leading me forward to something ancient, something my body knew as home. I was eleven years old and making my way to the parish chapel in order to serve 7:00 AM Mass. I knew I belonged in that chapel the same way I knew about belonging on a baseball diamond. Each was a house permeated with welcome.

That year, I found Sheila Bonforti, a dark-eyed Italian girl in the fifth grade, who brought my bodily sensibilities to a dimension I was convinced had never been experienced by other males. My longing to touch her, smell her, and maybe even kiss her escalated until fears of my fumbling were replaced by an unflinching determination to make contact. And make contact is what I did. The hand-holding, kissing, and petting vaulted me to celestial realms. I now understood what the *Baltimore Catechism* meant by its descriptions of heaven.

When I was sixteen, I fell in love, and the call to Sophia possessed more depth and more meaning. My teenaged self-centeredness began to dissipate as heartful forces constellated in my chest, extending my abilities for empathy, sensitivity, and consideration for another. Commitment took on new meaning as I felt an abiding respect and protection for Annie. A heightened curiosity stirred, launching waves of intrigue about this teenage girl's mind, heart, and body. I wanted to know all of her! I was beginning to learn Sophia's demand that we open to experience, letting it touch and move us, rather than begin reflecting and analyzing.

My love for Annie was driven by curiosity and wonder. The more I wanted to know her, the more I wished to know myself. I had never before experienced such love, desire, and passion. To be near Annie meant there was a vast increase in my life energy. There was more of everything in me and around me. I have come to discover that the presence of Sophia amplifies life forces exponentially, which seems better communicated by poets than theologians and social scientists. In fact, I have noticed that religious thinkers and social scientists tend to squeeze the life out of her, apparently attached to disembodying Sophia.

ALLOWING EXPERIENCE TO SHAPE US

Because Sophia is about experience, she is about body and about our connection to the earth. Old meanings for the word *experience* are *feel*, *suffer*, and *undergo*. These meanings suggest a fullness of life, and a willingness to approach life rather than retreat away from life. We need stories that present her and introduce her, not abstract analysis that attempts to control her. These stories can be seen as a move away from seeing ourselves as informing and a move toward allowing ourselves to be informed. The control associated with being the one who does the informing, the knowing, peels away, giving way to a deepened receptivity. Sophia calls us to larger love stories, to narratives infused with deep soul, feeling, suffering, and undergoing various conundrums, pressing us closer and closer to Sophia's touch.

I believe I was twenty-nine when Sophia thrust herself upon me with great vigor and heartiness. At the time I had been teaching philosophy at a small college for some five years and although I loved philosophy and loved teaching, my teaching felt empty and terribly unfulfilling. I had adopted the teaching methods of my own professors: standing in front of forty students, pontificating on the varied treatises of major philosophical thinkers. I finally became overwhelmed by the vacuous stares on the students' faces and a palpable mediocrity that engulfed my classroom.

The presence of Sophia is often summoned by some dispassionate experience leaving us feeling flat in the grips of a relentless monotony. Welcoming Sophia often involves finding the courage to admit that our lives aren't working for us and confronting feelings of inadequacy and hunger. She often comes to us by way of a deep hunger. I was tempted to criticize my students' lack of interest in philosophy rather than stay close and curious about my hunger. What was I truly hungry for?

Fortuitously, my mentor was willing to listen to the voice of my hunger and name it for me. He suggested I visit an educational institute in Amherst, Massachusetts, where teachers could learn to teach holistically and build learning communities in the classroom. I discovered I was hungry for authentic engagement in my classes, driven by my curiosity and the courage to have a voice. I hungered for the ability to be the muse inspiring a creative energy and bringing students closer to themselves and one another. Before the end of the semester in 1977, I was learning how to invoke more self-responsibility, imagination, and commitment from my students.

Before I began to introduce any philosophy, students learned how to communicate more effectively, build trust, and take responsibility for their learning. I recall one incident where I had just returned to the college after a week of the flu, and a colleague stopped me in the hall and asked, "Weren't you sick last week?"

"Yes," I responded, explaining how I was feeling much better.

"I'm glad to hear it. I noticed all your classes were meeting," he added, looking quite puzzled.

I pointed out that the students were clear about their task and could proceed without me, receiving the necessary guidance from one another. He walked away looking more confused than he had before our conversation.

I was a thirty-year-old professor learning what it meant to bring more heart to intellectual inquiry. I increasingly witnessed students taking their learning personally, invested in understanding how varied philosophical perspectives could bring more value and consideration to crafting a meaningful life. My job lost its bareness and was replaced by a richness of soul and spirit, which I had thought impossible in an academic environment. Sophia's kiss came like a wild wind sweeping away old beliefs and practices, expanding and deepening a young man's vision of learning and creating.

SHE IS THE LOVE OF WISDOM

I didn't become acutely aware of Sophia and her past visits until spring 2010. My awareness came with a fierce anger that inoculated me with a series of vexations of which I have yet to purge myself. I had been a devoted student of philosophy since was seventeen, when I would sit in the stacks at the university library reading the works of Miguel de Unamuno, a Spanish existentialist. Any serious student of philosophy knows that the word *philosophy* in the original Greek means *love of wisdom*. My contentment with the translation came to a screeching halt as I discovered the word *philosophy* more accurately means *love of Sophia*. Once I got somewhat beyond feeling duped and misled, I began to wonder, Who the hell is Sophia and where does she come from?

Where Does She Come From?

In Western culture, reference to a divine feminine energy first appears in the Apocryphal Book of Wisdom in the Old Testament and later in Gnosticism. The first citation was likely a member of the Hebrew community in Alexandria, Egypt. Probably written around 100 BC, the author speaks in the person of Solomon, lending more credibility to his remarks. "Wisdom is radiant and unfading, and she is easily discerned by those who love her, and is found by those who seek her" (Wisdom 6:12).

This passage suggests that it is in loving her and seeking her that her wisdom becomes available to us. Loving her can be seen as the courage to live with enough heart to risk feeling deeply, suffering and undergoing the trials of living intimately. We live intimately when we allow our hunger to call to the mystery of life in the hope that some small vision will be granted. We seek her from our love and hunger for her.

"Found by those who seek her" suggests we must become seekers in order to access her. What does it mean to become a seeker? The seeker is willing to live a life of curiosity; to dream, become disillusioned, and dream again; to be willing to get lost and wonder beyond convention.

Pythagoras's Love of Sophia

I found myself becoming more interested in the historical origins of Sophia. In the sixth century BC some Greek teachers were referring to themselves as *sophos—a wise one.* However, it appears to be Pythagoras (570–490 BC) who first refers to Sophia as something other than a testimony to his own wisdom.

At age eighteen, Pythagoras is advised by his teacher, the Greek astronomer Thales of Miletus, to travel to Egypt in order to further his studies. He remained in Egypt for twenty-two years studying with Egyptian priests. In 525 BC the Persian army of Cambyses invaded Egypt. Pythagoras was captured by the Persians, and their admiration for his knowledge of mathematics landed him in Babylon where he created collegiality with Zorastrian Magi priests and, likely, Hebrew scholars.

After years of study in Babylon, he returned to his homeland, the Greek island of Samos, referring to himself as *Lover of Sophia.* He became disillusioned with the political leadership of Samos and traveled to the town of Croton in southern Italy, where he established a mystery school. In identifying himself as Lover of Sophia (*philo-sophia*), he located wisdom somewhere external to his own ego, with love being the connective energy.

His teachings went far beyond mathematics, as he created a cult of the *mathematikoi* (learners) who vowed years of silence before being able to actively learn with Pythagoras. They believed in reincarnation, were devoted vegetarians, and owned no personal possessions. They practiced a monastic lifestyle composed of spiritual teachings, common meals, exercise, music, poetry, and philosophical study. Women participated as equals with men.

If we consider Pythagoras to be the first philosopher (Lover of Sophia), then we are offered a holistic model of what it means to be a philosopher. More than a course of study, it is a way of life devoted to the heartful pursuit of wisdom. We see this attitude exemplified by Pythagoras as he emerges from his initiation into an Egyptian mystery school: "Before this training I could only understand through the intellect, through the head. Now I can feel. Now truth is not a concept for me, but a life."

Socrates and Plato

Socrates is often referred to as a mystic. He would enter ecstatic trances, becoming receptive to an inner voice he referred to as the *daemon* or source of inspiration. He postulates the "examined life" as the highest pursuit of philosophy, with authentic knowledge manifesting itself in virtuous living. He is described as somewhat of an ascetic, roaming the streets of Athens attending to what he described as his vocation, a midwife of the soul.

Plato, like Pythagoras, was likely initiated into the mystery schools and an adherent of a theory of reincarnation where the soul's aim was to live the just life. Philosophy for Plato was the pursuit of *noumenon,* or ultimate reality, that transcended the material world. Similar to Socrates and Pythagoras, the purpose of rational inquiry is to discern right living.

Unlike Pythagoras and Plato, Aristotle was not initiated into the secrets of a mystery school; consequently, he relied much more on rational thought as a way to uncover layers of reality. Hegel would later describe Aristotle as attempting to elevate Sophia to the rank of science, which might suggest that Hegel himself may have reduced Sophia to a minor form of rational inquiry. With Aristotle, philosophy begins to lose its devotion to exploring how to live, inclusive of matters of the heart, and is relegated to a mental activity characterized as inductive reasoning. Detachment replaces unity. Sophia is replaced by Logos. According to Robert Powell in his book *The Sophia Teachings,* "Plato's philosophy is Sophinaic and Aristotle's philosophy is more related to the Logos." [21]

Lovers of Logos

The original Greek translation for *logos* was *word,* and it was later broadened to include *speech, mind, thought, reason,* and *logic.* I refer to those individuals who are heavily attached to thought for thought's sake as *philogrophers,* lovers of Logos. Their love remains in the ethereal realm of spirit, where rational inquiry is highly regarded but where there's little or no curiosity about what it means to live with more heart. Their tendency is to ignore what an act of courage life may be asking of them, such as, "Why did this transition take place? One reason is that the overemphasis upon the Logos, the masculine side of existence, had to take place in order for Western humanity to develop its philosophical, theological, and scientific faculties." [22]

In *Walden,* Thoreau references the distinction between philosophers (lovers of Sophia) and what I have termed philogrophers (lovers of Logos):

> There are nowadays professors of philosophy, but not philosophers . . . To be a philosopher is not merely to have subtle thoughts, nor even to found a school, but so to love wisdom as to live according to its dictates, a life of simplicity, independence, magnanimity, and trust. It is to solve some of the problems of life, not only theoretically, but practically. [23]

We can understand the devotion of Pythagoras, Socrates, and Plato in the above passage by Thoreau. It is easy to identify the three as lovers of Sophia, and being her consort, demanded that Logos (thinking) be in support of living with more soul, more heart, and more courage. Although there have been many individuals committed to the marriage of Logos and Sophia, such as Immanuel Kant, Martin Buber, Thomas Hobbes, Soren Kierkegaard, and C.G. Jung, so many have and continue to turn away from Sophia. Why denounce Sophia? Is there anything to fear about her? Why does it appear so difficult in academic settings to wed Sophia to Logos? Are we naïve enough to think that science and intellect would suffer in the wake of a welcome extended to Sophia? At what cost do we walk away from her? In order to better understand these reactions to her, we might need to deepen our acquaintance with her.

WHO IS SHE?

Since becoming more acquainted with Sophia last spring, I have felt disoriented, blissful, angry, aroused, defeated, charmed, intrigued, and lost. So, it seems appropriate to say, she's one hell of a lady! She has been referred to as a divine feminine entity, consort of God, a psychoid entity (both spirit and matter), and the deep expression of personal wisdom. What I have noticed about her is that she demands love and creativity, or we can say she compels us to make love. Hence, we will move toward her without a heavy overlay of theology. Rather, our interest will focus on what it means to be touched by Sophia's spiritual energy, the one that touches our hearts and asks to be lived through our bodies.

Her love is lived as an opening of the heart, an appreciation of beauty, and a desire to give and receive. Her creativity may manifest as we take old ideas and considerations and make them our own by impacting them with our passion and our values. Jakob Boehme describes her as firm and persuasive, and when it comes to bringing more heart to where there is either apathy or a diminished heart, she may be less than gentle.

I appreciate the story of Saint Paul on his way to Damascus to persecute Christians as an example of Sophia acting less than gently. At that time Saint Paul is actually Saul of Tarsus, a zealous Pharisee and tent maker. The story has him blinded by a bright light and thrown to the ground from his horse. We can say that often Sophia's intervention in our lives involves being dismounted abruptly from our *high horse*.

High horse can be a metaphor for being arrogant, haughty, pompous, or simply excessively prideful. Have you experienced such a dismount from your high horse? How did you deal with it? Were you able to identify what learning or heart-opening was being asked of you?

In our endeavor to know her, we will follow the Hebrew description of Sophia (*the plan for creation*) asking what role heart has in whatever plan we have to create. We will also allow the Gnostic perspective (*at the heart of matter*) to lead us. We could also imagine adding the article *the* before the word *matter*, shifting the meaning to *at the heart of the matter*. We can understand this phrase as a deepening curiosity about what is heartful and deserving of our attention regarding any situation. It would be naïve not to notice that the words *creation* and *matter* do refer us to what is physical, that is, our own bodies and our relationship to other natural and human bodies.

As we ask what role heart plays in anything we plan to create, and the place of heart in any situation, our hope is that we will be deepening our personal wisdom. In may be appropriate for the wisdom of Logos to ask: What is wisdom? However, in regard to Sophia or personal wisdom, the more relevant question is: How is wisdom? Her wisdom is personal because it calls for an intimacy with life and with our own souls. Such an inquiry will itself call for heart; hence we take our lead from Pythagoras and dare to define ourselves as philosophers (lovers of Sophia). Coming to know her will happen as an act of love. It will be an intimate knowing, leading us to the union desired by the mystic.

KNOWING INTIMATELY

How do we come to want to know intimately with open hearts? Are we born with Sophia energy or does our life experience infuse us with it? Powell (in *The Sophia Teachings*) mentions that a transition must take place:

> Just as three thousand years ago there was a transition from ancient clairvoyance to the rational thinking of Greek philosophy, so now there needs to take place a transition from mechanical thinking to a new kind of clairvoyance, a new seeing, a new thinking that is able to "see" in pictures. This is the transition that is to take place now. We can call this the thinking of the heart, and it is characterized by a new radiant faculty of thought that is made possible through opening up the heart to the inspiration of Divine Sophia.[24]

How do we open our hearts and avail ourselves of knowing intimately? Kabir reminds us that this business of knowing intimately with open hearts must be desired:

> Friend, if you've never really met the Secret One,
> what is the source of your self-confidence?
> Stop all this flirtation using words.
> Love does not happen with words.
> Don't lie to yourself about the holy books and what
> they say.
> The love I talk of is not in the books.
> Who has wanted it has it.[25]

We may emerge from the womb holding Sophia's hand. However, I am more confident that my desire to know has come from an enduring reliance upon ego and intellect, which was doomed to failure. This reliance upon ego to know seeks comfort from the angst of not knowing.

Dethroning Ego

The ego celebrates its supremacy, convinced that it holds jurisdiction over much that is way out of its control. One of its favorite illusions of control is the belief that it can penetrate the mystery of life with intellect. The declaration of "I know" offers a temporary respite from the tension that accompanies ambiguity and mystery. I have declared some alleged knowing many times under the pretense that I had mastered some understanding. It may be the deconstruction of the sovereignty of ego that begins to stimulate a desire to know intimately.

I recently had a dream where I bought a bottle of vodka. Before I opened it, I reminded myself that I had been professing a strong commitment to sobriety, and yet, I had been drinking. I refused to drink the vodka, as I was overcome with the hypocrisy of my ways. One response I had to the dream was that ingesting the vodka symbolized my tendency to go unconscious about how assertive I can be with clients as a way of demonstrating my intellectual prowess rather than remaining a student of the human condition.

I see that in order to deepen my desire to know intimately I need to continue to deconstruct an embellished ego. The moment when the glory and exuberance flow through us may be an invitation to ask the beginner's question, What else is here? The challenge may be to learn how to hold entitlement to draw conclusions, while remaining curious.

Ego desires separation as a testimony to how special it is. It easily slips from its uniqueness to claiming its special nature. Ego disconnection especially happens as we weave our social stories with themes of comparing and contrasting ourselves to others. This typically leaves us either feeling inadequate or temporarily strutting over some alleged triumph. As ego finds a more modest way to affirm its identity, it begins to let go of sizing itself by distancing from others.

I highly recommend the poem *Call Me by My True Names* by Thich Nhat Hanh. The poem captures the simple truth that what I welcome within myself, such as an impoverished child, a weapons dealer, a girl who commits suicide after being raped, or a dying man in a labor camp, I come to hold as part of a large vision of who I am. With ego reduction, it becomes easier to live by the notion that what is within is without and what is without is within.

This mantra becomes a plan for how we create ourselves and our vision of others. We begin to grasp that what we see outside of ourselves is in us, and what is in us is likely also in humanity generally. When I hear of a predator who preyed upon a woman walking home alone or a young boy after serving mass, I can end the folly of my moral immunity by recalling the times I preyed upon someone's individuality by either trying to talk them out of what they believed or simply dominating them in the name of winning an argument. It can be extremely liberating to notice that some of the fear we carry is simply indicative of the human condition; it strips us of being an aberration and asking for acceptance.

As we welcome Sophia, our perceptions begin to move beyond the apparent differences between the impoverished child in Uganda and the Wall Street investor who absconds with the retirement funds of thousands of folks. The very thought of these two having something in common can leave us dumbfounded and bewildered.

What separates the two images are the despairing feelings we carry. For the investor, we likely feel disgust, indignation, and repulsion, and for the child, pity and sympathy. Yet, at the heart of the matter, or how they live in their bodies, they both hunger for food, attention, warmth, safety, affection, support, and a chance to live. Of course, they also both live within us—the frailty, vulnerability, and longing of the orphan and the greed and callousness of the financier. As we learn to accept the orphan and investor within, our knowing becomes intimate, cloaked with the energy of Sophia, in our relatedness.

The dethroning of ego does not have to be quite so dramatic. I recall being a teenager gifted with athletic ability, which resulted in my either being the first chosen as teams were being formed or being the one doing the choosing.

Occasionally, a kid would show up at the playground with a new ball and sneakers, possessing little ability but being eager to play. I would notice him standing to the side, hoping to gain entry into the fraternity of hoopsters. I knew he would not be offered admittance. I felt some sympathy for him, knowing full well that my desire to win would prevent me from offering him a welcome. I remember taking some solace in reminding myself that he and I were quite different. I didn't know that I was destined to meet him again in a very personal way.

Some forty years later, accompanied by my spouse and an old friend, I entered a popular, private bookstore carrying a plastic bag that was filled with a dozen copies of a book I had recently self-published. Once the proprietor knew my book was self-published, she emphatically declared there would be no opportunity for a book-signing event at her establishment.

I turned, humiliated and defeated, remembering the kid I had not chosen at the basketball court. I now knew him intimately, and although there remained stirrings of repulsion and even contempt for my books, I knew I was being asked to find a welcome for the both of us. It would be some time before I would find enough courage to extend a hand to he who shuffled out of that bookstore with a plastic grocery bag filled with his books. Sometimes, ego finds its proper place not because of a new level of humility but because our hearts have blown open.

Heart Blown Open

Quite often, coming to want Sophia to be present and to know intimately happens as it did with my bag of books. She comes to us on the winds of fate, blowing our hearts open. A man once said to me, "I'm not sad, but I'm feeling something very deeply." I suggested he was allowing himself to be touched. Being touched became a whole new lens for him to understand his emotional life. When we are touched in a big way, our hearts will likely be blown open. It may happen in a simple encounter with nature, as depicted in this poem by Seamus Heaney:

Postscript

And some time make the time to drive out west
Into County Clare, along the Flaggy Shore,

In September or October, when the wind
And the light are working off each other
So that the ocean on one side is wild
With foam and glitter, and inland among stones
The surface of a slate-grey lake is lit
By the earthed lightning of a flock of swans,
Their feathers roughed and ruffling, white on white,
Their fully grown headstrong-looking heads
Tucked or cresting or busy underwater.
Useless to think you'll park and capture it
More thoroughly. You are neither here nor there,
A hurry through which known and strange things pass
As big soft buffetings come at the car sideways
And catch the heart off guard and blow it open.[26]

Getting our hearts blown open can feel frightening, overwhelming, exhilarating, and deeply fulfilling. As Heaney describes in the poem, the experience can feel "neither here nor there" where "known and strange things pass." When we are at the neither here nor there place, we are at the precipice, the edge of two worlds where we are called to experience something out of the ordinary. We can think of this as Sophia's plan for creating us, and the plan is happening to us, not because of us.

It is only too easy to grab something known at the precipice, to offer ourselves temporary sanctuary from strange things. The ego typically protests feeling out of control and may even launch a torrent of shame aimed at driving us away from the experience, leaning us into denial and secrecy. It can be helpful to tell the story to a helpful listener, someone who can acknowledge the emotional impact of the event, with some familiarity with such heart-opening. A compassionate reception can help to alleviate the sting of shame and strengthen our ability to accept the depth of humanity our blown-open heart has brought us to. Again, the beginner's question may be appropriate, What else is here? This kind of curiosity tends to invite Sophia to bring her stirrings and awakenings.

When my daughter Sarah was sixteen, I had my heart blown open accompanied by Sophia's stirrings. Shortly after Sarah was born, she was diagnosed with cerebral palsy, which left her with an estimated IQ of 40. Although there were myriad challenges, we decided to keep Sarah at home with us, resisting the idea of institutionalizing her. As she aged, she was offered the typical educational services geared for special students.

Around her sixteenth birthday, we received a call from the high school principal, who suggested an immediate Pupil Planning Team (PPT) meeting. My wife and I were not clear about the urgency of the meeting, but we were seasoned veterans when it came to attending meetings aimed at clarifying services.

At the meeting, we were met by two dozen professionals rather than the customary five or six who usually designed Sarah's program. The principal, who was typically not in attendance, greeted us, and our curiosity and suspicion quickly mounted. Our trust in the willingness of school systems to allocate appropriate funds for services had dwindled over the years.

The principal explained how a speech therapist had made a breakthrough with Sarah, a profound breakthrough. He went on to say that Sarah had typed out a sign the previous day that read, "I'm Sarah Dunion and I deserve your respect," and that she had proceeded to hang it in the cafeteria.

We were now being told that the daughter whose IQ had been estimated to be similar to that of our border collie was more likely above average. Since intelligence is commonly measured by the use of language, Sarah's nonverbal status had proved to be a major obstacle in ascertaining who she actually was. Each professional took his or her turn confirming Sarah's new intellectual status. They encouraged a supportive and gentle transition for our daughter who had been locked away in her body for sixteen years, unable to let us know she was there.

Our hearts had been blown open. We were being called to accept the tentative and ambiguous nature of reality, the reality of our own family. Pat and George, two people who had dedicated their lives to the support of folks with disability, stepped forward, and a supportive group was formed to advocate for Sarah's development as well as her family's.

The power of Sophia's energy brought me to a new level of intimate knowing. I saw how attached I had been to a compelling self-reliance that only left me in the depths of helplessness and hopelessness. Sophia prodded me in the direction of learning about receiving. I had taken great pride in my capacity to give whatever helped me to avoid the loss of control that often accompanies receiving and the possible shame of feeling needy.

I witnessed friends and relatives take joy in creating a container dedicated to the sustainability of our family. *At the heart of the matter* of Sarah's disability was an evolving community. These folks were willing to take on an assumingly impossible task, pool their resources, and remain accountable for the needs of our family. What continued to touch me the most was their willingness to witness the physical, financial, and emotional nuances of a family coping with severe disability. These people would be called to accept something fragile and unconventional in themselves in order to embrace the struggles and contentions of our family's life. They joined us, refusing to take the high ground of being able-bodied and culturally appropriate.

I continue to be amazed about Sarah's ability to call me back to myself. Just when I have grown content to attach myself to either my achievements or my popularity, Sarah beckons me back to what is ordinary and sacred about my humanity. I have come to think of Sarah as Sophia's handmaiden. Sarah is about to turn thirty-six, she owns her own home, hires her own staff, and writes and lectures on behalf of folks with disability and their families. And like her father, Sarah continues to live the tension of remaining a unique character in search of that place where she might deepen her experience of belonging.

A heart blown open by splendor and beauty is one thing. A heart smashed open is another. It can be extremely difficult to understand that we may be called to a larger vision while enduring a broken heart. Typically, the fracture of loyalty, trust, and love can throw us into the depths of anger, cynicism, and feelings of victimization.

Linda and her husband Adam came to see me following Linda's discovery that Adam, who worked as a physician at a local hospital, had engaged in several sexual affairs with staff. Initially, Linda was inconsolable while Adam was drowning in shame, unable to offer his wife an explanation of his acting out. After several sessions, they both became clear about their commitment to heal their marriage. They began to understand that they each had a broken heart. Linda's shattered heart was due to Adam's betrayal of her, and Adam's heart splinter was the result of betraying his own values and hurting his best friend.

"I want to know if there is any way in which I might have colluded in this situation," explained Linda, willing to take a large step closer to the heart of the matter.

"Well, tell me the story of this marriage leading up to the betrayal," I suggested.

"I know that I have felt responsible for the emotional life of the marriage. Adam gets easily confused about his emotions."

"How has it felt for you to do that and what message have you been sending to your husband?"

"Well, I'm going to be honest; the responsibility of it has been a considerable burden. And I guess I've been letting him off the hook when it comes to emotionally growing up," Linda offered, stepping closer to her collusion in the betrayal.

"Not only has she been responsible for the emotional life of the marriage, but she's also controlling! She won't let me make any decisions about our sons!" piped in, Adam.

"So, what have you been doing with your parental responsibility?"

"She's really passionate about her ideas when it comes to the kids, and she discredits my suggestions," said Adam, with his voice trailing off.

"You've been deferring to Linda regarding parenting and, I believe, became damn resentful along the way," I confronted.

"It's true. I have felt resentful and I guess I allowed her to make all the decisions," reflected Adam, loosening his grip upon being Linda's victim.

"You seem to be getting it that Linda didn't dominate you as much as you allowed her the authority to make decisions regarding the children. I'm wondering if the resentment, on some level, didn't lead you to find a way to punish her."

"Makes sense, I've been pretty angry," admitted Adam.

"Let's be clear here. When you, Linda, decided to not have expectations of Adam regarding his emotional maturity, you placed yourself in the role of his mother. And when you, Adam, decided to define her as responsible for the emotional life of the marriage, you made yourself her son. And once you had a mom, you would likely be interested in a girlfriend," I said, watching them take in for the first time the environment they had created that would likely be the prelude to betrayal.

"Linda, tell me, did you ever see any of Adam's behavior that might suggest his boundaries with women might be somewhat shabby?"

"Yes, I have. He would either move closer to a woman than what I would consider common social distance or make physical contact with someone he hardly knew."

"How did you deal with what you saw?" I asked.

"I didn't. I mean, I didn't say much. I complained every now and then," responded Linda, dropping her gaze.

"My take is that you are a fairly assertive woman. You didn't tell him to get clear about his boundaries. How did you lose your voice?"

"I didn't want him to see me as a bitch. Whenever I confront him, he makes some reference to his mother, who reigned over him," explained Linda.

"You lost your voice in the name of attempting to control Adam's emotional response to you."

"Yes, I guess that's colluding with his bad boundaries," admitted Linda, sounding less attached to being Adam's victim.

Adam and Linda continued to work on becoming less and less a victim of one another. They were willing to focus on how they betrayed themselves in their marriage. Each was learning to live with more heart. Due to their resilience and devotion, their broken hearts were leading them to identify how they wanted to remain loyal to themselves and one another.

Besides getting our hearts either blown open or broken open, we can allow our hearts to be touched and moved. Every Wednesday and Thursday evening, I descend a set of stairs, headed to facilitate two separate men's groups. Regularly, I hear men's voices raucously telling stories, greeting one another with warmth and laughter.

At those times, I am often reminded of childhood friends who would call me out to play. Their bidding was a foreshadowing of games to be played, adventures to be quested, and the anticipation of endless discoveries. I am touched by the men gathered in the basement who are bold enough to live the examined life, who invite and challenge each other to shed cultural maxims of manhood aimed at distancing them from themselves and those they love.

SHE IS PERSONAL WISDOM

Above all else, Sophia is personal wisdom. I often wonder about impersonal wisdom, which I imagine to be exhortations of platitudes, clichés, and typical pontifications aimed at reducing life to a formula. None of which strikes me as having anything to do with authentic wisdom. Actually, wisdom may be a great deal like love; it must be personal, and when it belongs to Sophia, it is otherworldly in its attempt to find its way to us. She comes to us when we are devoted to living intimately, which is the call to union experienced by the mystic.

In keeping with the Socratic bidding to live the examined life, we can deepen our investment in being intimate with ourselves. This quality of intimacy is reflected by a devotion to what is true about us and accompanied by compassion. Like a lover who continues to arouse our curiosities, we can remain interested in who we are, willing to offer compassion (an open heart) to the person we discover within.

We can employ the four elements of earth, fire, water, and air to guide the deepening of an intimate relationship with ourselves. From the viewpoint of earth, we can make use of the following: How would I describe the relationship I have with my body? What brings stability to my life? How do I attain balance and rootedness in my life? What is the status of my personal boundaries? Am I experiencing a desire for mobility and movement in my life?

Fire enables us to consider: Do I live my passion? Does my anger receive a proper voice? Am I regularly expressive about what I want? Does joy have a place to live fully in my life? Do I create?

Water invites: Do I live my love? What sorrow is asking to be expressed? Where is my life asking for more compassion? What loss is asking for my attention? Do I allow myself to be emotionally touched?

Air beckons us to: What ideas do I carry about my wounding and my healing? What understanding do I have about my gifts and what they intend to offer? What values guide my more important life choices? Am I willing to return to my breath as a way to focus inwardly? Do I dream?

I have said a great deal about living the intimate life with others under other titles (i.e., *Shadow Marriage* and *Dare to Grow Up*). For now, I offer a simple reminder that deepening a connection to others is about being with ourselves in their presence. We cannot leave ourselves and hope to be with the other. We typically leave ourselves by attempting to impress or becoming highly adaptive. We must be present before another can join us or we can join them. Our sense of presence is a reflection of our breathing as we focus on how we feel and what we want. So, we take several deep breaths and allow our bodies to inform us about whether we feel sad, lonely, scared, angry, or glad. Then, we need to allow for the possibility that we might want something, maybe some form of comfort or an opportunity of some kind.

Once that internal connection is made with breathing, I can represent my truth with as much clarity and compassion as I can muster. I express what I feel and what I want. A third focus is to create room for the other's truth, what he or she feels and wants, without attempting to influence them or talk them out of their truth. In doing so, I allow the other's truth, in the true form of Sophia, to inform me regarding what we might create together. Fourth, learn to hold the tension when our truths are significantly diverse. Sometimes what we want and what others want are quite different, and from Sophia's energy, we consciously avoid holding the difference as if someone must win and someone must lose. Rather, we can use the opportunity to examine our own beliefs with more scrutiny, become a source of support for the other, deepen our capacity for acceptance, or learn from one another.

These steps guarantee nothing. They simply represent an attitude of living the intimate life. However, such an emotional posturing does have the tendency to be visited by Sophia's wisdom.

Recently, while participating in a seminar on Jungian psychology, a colleague reported, "I worry that if I allow my emotions to impact my thinking, I will get excessively sentimental." The statement reflects a concern that almost anyone who values serious reflection experiences at one time or another. It is noteworthy to see how common it is to worry about our thinking being contaminated by too much heart. The challenge is to allow the moment of great sentiment to open us to self-examination. We can do this by stepping away from our beliefs and attending to the feeling directly.

It will call for patience, curiosity, and courage. When we cannot attribute some meaning to strong feeling, we typically feel out of control. If we attempt to quickly subdue the angst, we run the risk of prematurely naming what our strong feelings are about. These urgently driven conclusions are typically rigid, poorly conceived, and narrow. Our very worry that strong sentiment will contaminate our thinking becomes a self-fulfilling prophecy as we press for some explanation of our strong feelings.

Hasty thinking often shows up as strong moralizing, advising, accusing, excessive analyzing, justifying, commanding, threatening, stereotyping, and criticizing. Strong sentiment does not lead to unsound thinking, but the lack of patience, curiosity, and courage do. If we can remain patient and curious about how our strong sentiment might want to inform us without interrupting the emotional experience, then we may allow for some deeper truth to reveal itself. It will also call for courage to bear the tension of not knowing while we are feeling.

As we allow ourselves to feel and gradually release the energy of our feelings, we can become receptive to a more cogent understanding of our emotional experience. We permit strong sentiment to teach us rather than impetuously defining the feeling in order to secure some alleged control over our emotions. Give the heart its time, and the mind will expand its clarity.

I recently had an opportunity to interrupt my tendency to prematurely explain my strong sentiments. My wife and I were enjoying some time at a new health club. A number of the amenities were gender specific, which meant we would be separated for a portion of our visit. We made a plan to meet at 3:00. My wife suggested we meet at the mixed gender hot tub and I mentioned we could meet upstairs, dressed and ready to depart. Both of us heard the recommended time, with neither hearing the suggested meeting place. At 3:00 sharp, I was showered, dressed, standing in the lounge ready to depart. By 3:30, I was angry and feeling quite critical of my wife, who was missing in action as far as I was concerned.

I decided to return to the locker room area, where I asked a young woman to check for someone named Connie in the women's locker room. She returned announcing that my wife would be out in ten minutes. I went back upstairs prepared to interrogate my wife's obvious blunder with my chest tightening like a drum. When she arrived, it took only moments to clarify that neither of us heard the other's designation of a meeting place. However, I could not let go of the energy relentlessly building in my chest.

I told Connie of the mounting tension in my chest and that I was very curious about its intensity. I understood the mishap and yet my emotions were still building. Finally, Connie asked, "Why did you want to leave at 3:00 when you enjoy it here so much?"

"You define me as a gym rat while you like outdoor activities like hiking, so I was attempting to expedite your departure," I explained, assuming a thorough and considerate assessment of my wife's preferences.

"I do like exercising outdoors, and I really like it here," she said.

Was I attempting to be considerate? Did I not want to burden Connie? What was I doing up in that lounge so prepared to leave? The energy burning within me was too intense to reflect a man trying to be considerate. I continued to breathe into my constricted chest. After several hours, I got it that my punctuality for a hasty departure was my attempt to prove that I was a loving person. Connie gently looked at me and said, "I've known that for a long time."

What frightens us so much about being seen either by others or by ourselves as sentimental? I hardly ever hear someone worrying about being too rational, too logical, or too analytical. At the very least we recall where our vulnerability lives, and it's not in our brains. Are we so concerned about unbiased thinking, or are we doing what we can to stay away from potential hurt? We know the difference between a broken heart and a bad idea. The latter does not bleed.

It may be that the balance of body and mind, heart and thought, or soul and spirit needs to ever be corrective. It helps to stay mindful of where we most comfortably live and be willing to step toward the less visited. Our own development coupled with life's exigencies pulls and prods us forward and away from heart. It may be that the more we need to deny the insecurity and pain in life, the more we disallow ourselves to be informed by heart. It is heart that will remind us of our sorrows and fears.

In Jack Kornfield's book *A Path with Heart,* he discusses the impact of fear on our hearts:

> When we let ourselves feel the fear, the discontent, the difficulties we have always avoided, our heart softens. Just as it is a courageous act to face all the difficulties from which we have always run, it is also an act of compassion. According to the Buddhist scriptures, compassion is the "quivering of the pure heart" when we have allowed ourselves to be touched by the pain of life.[27]

One root of the word *soft* is *to yield to the touch* or *to take in the touch.* As Kornfield points out, "when we let ourselves feel the fear, the discontent, the difficulties we have always avoided, our heart softens." Yielding to the harsh realities of our own lives brings us closer to ourselves and closer to life. This may be the birthplace of Sophia's wisdom.

Rather than ask, "What is Sophia's wisdom?" we can ask, "How does Sophia's wisdom come about?"

Sophia's Wisdom

- Refuse to see yourself as a victim of your fate.
- Return again and again to the question "Who am I and where do I come from?"
- Ask, "What is my heart's longing?"
- Remain curious about who in you is asking for forgiveness.
- Ask, "What sorrow, anger, fear, or shame in me is asking for a voice?"
- Be willing to make peace with death.
- Remain curious about what life is asking of you.
- Welcome your gifts and your wounds.
- Ask, "What medicine is my broken heart asking for?"
- Be willing to be lost and hunger for where you belong.
- Be willing to be a fool.
- Be open to being informed by your physical sensations and emotions.

- Accept the impenetrable mystery of life.
- Remain devoted to having an authentic and intimate relationship with life's mystery.
- Commit to truth-telling accompanied by compassion.

Once we have allowed our lives to be touched by heartful energy, we can create a richer personal narrative, allowing life to touch and deepen who we are. In the picture of a twenty-four-day-old fetus, brain cells are emerging from the heart. And so we may be asked to allow our hearts to yield to the touch of life, followed by bringing a mindful curiosity to that touch. It may be the touch that we find frightening, as we feel vulnerable and out of control. Sophia's request is that we view experience (feel, suffer, and undergo) to be the essential informant and not our ego. Therein lies the challenge.

Welcoming the depth of experience will inevitably lead to an opportunity to welcome more of ourselves. We may actually be frightened of integrating or welcoming more of us than we think we can handle.

There are those of us who would find it quite comforting to wrap ourselves in the blanket of sentiment, who would be more than willing to let go of whatever beliefs, values, and decisions would make us more responsible for our own lives. And some of us are prone to taking sanctuary in the disembodied world of abstract thought, comforting ourselves with the illusion that we have shed ourselves of our creatureliness and all the bodily arousals and nudges implied by being a creature. We can continue to ask if the story we presently live in is asking for more heart or more mind. Some act of courage will likely be calling us to greater inner unity.

The Marriage of Sophia (Heart) and Logos (Mind)

The mystic is called to the ever-deepening connection between Sophia and Logos. A photograph on page 84, *A Child Is Born*, by Lennart Nilsson and Lars Hamberger, depicts a twenty-two-day-old embryo with the heart giving rise to a primitive nerve cell, which will give rise to the development of the brain. The photo suggests the intimate link between heart and brain, with the origin of their relationship taking place in the heart. It is likely that such a nuptial bonding is how personal wisdom is fed and nourished. Jung suggested, "At the bottom of the soul we find humanity." Is it possible that in the welcome we offer to the depths of our own souls, we can eventually encounter the soul of humanity? And so we are called to the beginning place over and over again, where our hearts are touched by love, pain, and the sublime. As we allow our hearts to be moved and aroused by our experiences, we can continue to enroll the curiosity of mind to call our hearts into larger stories, welcoming the unexplored territory of ourselves.

Recently, while I was preparing to leave the grocery store, a man in a wheelchair positioned by the exit caught my eye. I immediately looked at the clock on the wall for permission to avoid both his solicitation and my guilt. The clock betrayed me. I had plenty of time and I could not find another excuse to pass him by.

I pulled my shopping cart up to his table and asked what he had going. Rather than responding verbally, he handed me a printed sheet explaining he was a Vietnam vet who was sponsoring a raffle. He was not only paralyzed, but he also could not speak. I felt a wave of shame wash over my face as I thought of my eagerness to avoid him.

He proceeded to type out a message on a keyboard explaining with an automated voice that he had just met a woman in the store whose brother had swum across a river in Vietnam in order to escape a prison camp. As I listened, I filled out the raffle information, which offered me just enough of a needed buffer from this man and his story. I could sense I was just a little too close to some part of myself that I would rather avoid. I handed him the raffle ticket, held out my hand, and said, "Take care, my man," allowing myself a brief moment of eyes with eyes, as I yielded to his touch.

I left the store with my heart softened with compassion for this veteran and more ready to allow the arousal of my curiosity to rest upon my compassion. How do I feel about my own ableness and my own disability? What was I reminded of in the presence of this man? How do I feel about my mortality? How do I feel about my avoidance of going to Vietnam? Do I feel as if I owe this man something? I can either avoid these questions or respond to them, further allowing myself to yield to the touch of the encounter. As we attempt to hold a devotion to deepen the connection between Sophia and Logos it may be helpful to ask: What is a question? and What is an answer?

Questions and Answers

The word *question* has an old meaning *to quest or seek*. When life is naïvely stripped of mystery, we are inclined to believe that our questions are simply ways to acquire answers. The more literal and concrete we make our answers and questions, the more we get to massage our egos with the lure of some kind of secure knowing. However, the mystic remains devoted to honoring the mysteries of self, others, nature, and God.

From that kind of honoring, the mystic's questions are not simply seeking a comforting rejoinder that attempts to subdue the tension caused by life's ambiguities. Rather the questions are attempting to sustain a dynamic relationship with life energized by compassion and curiosity. At the heart of this relationship, our softened hearts (compassion) seek to allow more of life in; we want to move closer to nature, others, God, or to ourselves.

What is an answer? One ancient root of the word *answer* is *to reply to*. We can see our answers as a way of replying to life's mysteries, as a way to remain in dialogue with life. We allow our hearts to be touched, moved, and aroused by some life experience, leading to some question, and then we reply, not as a way to draw closure to our curiosities but rather to remain in the conversation with life. Our answers can also be seen as a temporary respite, offering a rest from our seeking. However, we fracture our relationship with ourselves and with life when we do not allow our grip upon our answers to loosen, realizing that our answer, our response, is but one story we are weaving about reality.

In his book *Finding Inner Courage*, Mark Nepo offers an intriguing view of what it means to hold fast to our opinions or answers: "Mostly, our opinions try to compensate for our failed attempts to order life . . . And so our conclusions are seldom life sustaining." Nepo's suggestion oozes with a quiet voice, "Maybe I can get it right this time. Life won't slip away eluding my attempts to be right, pulling me into more turbulence and confusion." We can relax our striving to order life and rather have a relationship with it, where we are willing to listen and be further informed.

It is critical to accept that we have created one story, which can be embellished as well as joined by other narratives. The ego becomes at the very least restless with such a suggestion and at times rigid, as it attaches to its stories for dear life. It can be humbling to accept that an answer is simply one way of responding to life's impenetrable mystery. We do not need to belittle our stories but simply hold them as a single response among infinite options. Sophia delights in our willingness to indulge in creating endless stories about all she offers us through our worldly experience.

We hold a gentle grip on our answers when we softly place the question "What else is there?" alongside our answers. We see this attitude displayed by Socrates when told by his childhood friend, Chaerephon, that Apollo's Oracle had claimed him to be the wisest in Athens. His reaction was to doubt the Oracle's decree and begin searching for a man wiser than he: "So I left him, saying to myself as I went away: Well, although I do not suppose that either of us knows anything really worth knowing, I am wiser than this fellow—for he knows nothing, and thinks he knows; I neither know nor think that I know. In this one little point, then, I seem to have the advantage of him."[28]

Time and time again, Socrates speaks with a voice indicating a loose grip upon his answers, humbly accepting his limited capacity for wisdom. "O men of Athens that God only is wise; and by his answer he intends to show that the wisdom of men is worth little or nothing."[29] Socrates modeled what it means to invite oneself, as well as others, to remain in conversation with life.

We can imagine a contemporary Socratic conversation infused with the following questions: In regard to the belief you hold most dear, how did you come to align yourself with this thinking? How does this belief serve you? What limiting implications spin off this belief? Does this belief allow you to move closer to yourself? Does this belief support a compassionate vision of humanity? How does the contrary belief impact you emotionally? How tightly do you grasp the need to be right?

The marriage of Sophia and Logos remains vital as heart stimulates the wondering of our minds, and as our minds invite us to hold a vision that allows for a more courageous life of heart. When this takes place we have more clarity about where we may want to serve and what our offering is. We begin to expand taking the kind of risks that allow our loving to live more fully. I continue to learn how impactful deep feeling can be to the formation of our beliefs and ultimately to the choices with which we are willing to live. So often, the refusal to feel our pain constricts the heart as well as our minds, leaving us with a hardness of heart and rigidity of mind.

I recall that the more I refused to acknowledge and feel the pain of my daughter Sarah's disability, the more I generated stories about the world being a hostile and unfriendly place. As I contracted my heart, the more I condensed my stories about the uncooperative nature of people. Eventually, I became more contentious in my interaction with others, especially with the members of Sarah's professional support team. I decided that none of them benefited me or Sarah.

The energy of Sophia is invigorated as we remain curious about our answers, that is, our replies to how life has moved us. This kind of wondering is reflected by the following questions: Do I hold my reply to life either too quickly or with too much rigidity? Do I tend to wait excessively for more information, rather than offer a reply? (Sophia is enlivened when we both allow ourselves to be moved by life and bold enough to offer a reply.) When we see our replies to life as heartful and mindful, the nuptial bond between Sophia and Logos is consummated.

Listening with Our Bodies

Sophia is welcomed into our lives as we accept the Gnostic suggestion that she is *at the heart of matter* and as such, she is at the heart of our bodies, although the Gnostics had a much greater affinity with Logos than with the body. We can live Sophia's energy because we have bodies. For example, living with more heart does not happen without a body. However, our bodies have allowed us to be seen, heard, and accessed, leaving us vulnerable as children to myriad hurts and mistreatments. Our bodies are also the place where we are most prone to experiencing our limits. Illness, fatigue, and injury remind us of our mortality and the inevitability of dying. Our bodies constitute the place where we are most alive and yet, also, closest to death.

It may be no surprise how we have come to favor Logos as a source of reliable information. Anchoring in our minds allows us to temporarily escape the tension of our bodies' reminders of pain and death. It is just a hop and a skip to decide that our bodies are an unfortunate aspect of existence as we invest more and more in the glory of mind.

Before we can really listen with our bodies, we need to give ourselves permission to be bodies. It may call for a vigilant inventory of ways in which we either reject our bodies or mistreat them. Some questions that can help include: Am I willing to accept responsibility to nurture my body, which includes feeding and resting it properly? What criticisms do I readily direct at my body? What frightens me about having a body? Am I prone to punishing my body? What is my body asking of me? Before we can listen to and with our bodies, it will be necessary to continue to make peace with them.

Sophia also comes to us when we see and accept that *the plan for creation* lies within us and with her. Each moment offers the opportunity for us to participate in creation. Our inner worlds lead to action, and that action manifests the plan within us, constructed from our feelings, beliefs, values, and imagination. Similar to a woman in labor, the creation of anything new is ordinarily accompanied by tension. Probably the best example of this tension is being in the presence of someone expressing a vastly different view or ideology from our own, that is, manifesting a different plan for creation from ours.

Carrying Tension

Why does being in the presence of differing or opposing plans commonly produce such tension? So many of us have had little or no validation of our unique vision or plans, leaving us vulnerable to believing there must be something wrong with our offering. If we are not listening with our bodies when we hear a contrary plan, it becomes likely that we will not notice the fear that would have us abandon our own plan or invite others to abandon theirs.

These times of being immersed into differing plans may be one of the mystics' greatest challenges to unity. It is so easy to allow fear to direct us to right/wrong, good/bad, and acceptable/unacceptable, all potentially driving us toward divisiveness. If we are to move beyond holding a discordant attitude in the presence of opposites, we will need to be more mindful of our fear. Fear is at the heart of the matter of diverse plans.

When we are willing to allow our bodies to inform us, we can welcome our fear rather than have it unconsciously driving our reactions. It helps to breathe into our bellies or our hearts, not pushing for a quick, clever response to what we are hearing from others. Our plan for creation, or our Sophia energy, is vitalized when we place ourselves into a relationship with the inner tension. Surrendering to this tension can allow it to both inform us and direct our action.

I recently had an opportunity to practice listening to my body with a full complement of tension. I had just finished working out in the gym when I entered the locker room to hear Louie, an acquaintance of mine, indulging in verbal gay-bashing. He was addressing two other men with sarcastic references to "Don't Ask, Don't Tell."

Well, there I was once again, in a locker room with an alleged straight man, spouting his anti-gay propaganda—a plan for creation directly in opposition to my own. Facing an all-too-familiar challenge, I wondered what to do, as the tension within me continued to build. Do I simply ignore him? Do I vacate the locker room immediately? Do I confront him about behavior I find unaccept-able? I decided to breathe, feeling the tension gripping my chest.

Suddenly, with no forethought, I burst out, "For Christ's sake, Louie, ever since you were five, you've been yelling, 'Don't Ask, Don't Tell!' and nobody has ever known what the hell you've been talking about!"

Everyone, including Louie, began to roar with laughter at a remark that actually made little or no sense. The gay-bashing had been interrupted with no indication that divisiveness had been fostered between us. In fact, we all seemed quite pleased to get a chuckle at Louie's expense, even Louie. I was glad that I did not have to diminish Louie in some way in order to jostle his plan for creation in the moment. In these moments of diversity, Sophia asks, "Is there something for me to feel here?" while Logos looks back in retrospect and asks, "Is there something for me to learn here?"

SOPHIA'S WELCOME

A plan for creating our lives is guided by deep Sophia energy when it is infused with an earnest desire to include or welcome, in support of belonging. Sophia does not want much to be left out of her plan for creation. That does not mean that all discernment is suspended, but rather she prioritizes offerings of welcome before exclusion and banishment. It may be that, when it comes to belonging, we are all naturally mystics, wanting to find where we belong, where to unite.

Our plans for creation are enlarged when our plan possesses some elements of inclusion and welcome. I was recently part of a study group that met weekly at one of the participant's homes. For weeks, nine chairs were arranged in a circle with two chairs positioned inside the circle, placing the folks in those two chairs with their backs to the rest of the group. On one particular day, I arrived early to hear George, one of the participants, ask the home owner if he could reposition the two chairs, making it possible for those folks to maintain eye contact with the rest of the group.

I noticed the participation of the women who typically sat in those chairs substantially increased over the next few weeks. Their plans for creation deepened and expanded. I was thankful for George's simple offering of a plan to modify physical space, which brought more welcome and more creativity. I was also reminded that the welcome of Sophia lives in very simple ways.

We welcome her and she lives when we heighten our mindfulness about the role of inclusion in our lives. The process might even begin with our relationship to ourselves: Is there a part of us that seeks our welcome? We further our consciousness by asking: How can I best offer welcome to whomever is in my presence? Do I know how to offer a welcome while employing the kind of boundaries that define how much I want the other in my life? Who in my life is seeking a welcome from me? How can I best support the inclusion of some member of my family or group with whom I am affiliated?

Lover of Imagination

The touch of Sophia can be felt when we free our imaginations. In *The Wedding of Sophia* Jeffrey Raff states, "Imagination is the crucial element in the process of individuation. It is the means by which the conscious and the unconscious come into union." Raff is suggesting that imagination can be the bridge between what we know and don't know, or who we are and who we are meant to be. One of the ancient meanings of the word *imagination* is *to embellish*, and the word embellish is also a very old meaning for *medicine*. We can say that our imaginations can serve as a very important source of medicine.

Imagination loses its power to embellish, and to heal, when it is reduced to wishful thinking. This loss of power happens when imagination falls under the reign of ego and where embellishment moves in the direction of fame, glory, prestige, notoriety, and other inflated expressions of whatever personal prowess we believe deserves more attention and praise. Imagination sustains its potency when it is energized by the heart of a seeker.

The Seeker

The heartful quest of the seeker can be characterized as a genuine devotion to the offering we are destined to make to humanity, or as an interest in knowing and stewarding the gifts we possess that will generate our offering. It may be a sincere investment in attending to the wounds that separate us from our gifts and therefore our offering. The seeker wants to know how to best serve. It is this service that unfolds into a deep unity with the mystery of life. It is the place where the mystic truly claims deep identity as a mystic. It's what makes a mystic, a mystic.

Sometimes the seeker moves into a crisis of faith, where holding any kind of embellished vision is nearly impossible. At those times, it can be extremely beneficial for a mentor or friend to carry the vision for us until we are able to generate a new plan for creating ourselves.

Such a crisis occurred in my life when I was a sophomore in college. I had flunked off the basketball team, lost my girlfriend, was incapacitated from a motorcycle accident, and the local draft board was eager to send me off to Vietnam. Aware of the malaise that had engulfed me, my roommate announced that I should take a philosophy course and strengthened his argument by suggesting that the people in the philosophy department talked like me. I had no idea what his comment meant.

Sometimes the first step to imaginatively beautifying our stories is to simply respond to the feeling of desperation in which we presently live. So I did. I did not want to face the embarrassment of returning home after flunking out of school or finding myself in Vietnam. I made an appointment with the chairman of the philosophy department and asked him to explain what philosophy was. He laughed and told me to register for a course. I realize now that if he had ventured down the road of an explanation, the odds are high that Sophia would not have been mentioned.

Desperation was energizing my search and my imagining how I might stay in school and avoid being a casualty of war. I entered my first philosophy class having read only one book in my entire nineteen years. I had relied on CliffsNotes for all my previous book reports. I had taken great solace in seeing myself as a jock, with quick hands and a great first step. All of which seemed useless following my accident. I knew myself as body, holding no vision of having a mind that could be appreciated in an academic environment. Besides a loss of faith, I was also experiencing an identity crisis. Somehow I knew that my ability to lead a fast break was not going to help much as we surveyed the thinking of Immanuel Kant in class.

Like so many of us, I drew much from a small, comfortable part of me, my athletic ability. My poor grades and my physical injury were taking that away. Typically, some death precedes the creation of a larger story. It can very difficult to see that a significant loss is the first door to opening a much larger story.

I went to my first philosophy class convinced that although my roommate had been well intentioned, he was dead wrong. I was never going to fit in this class. Maybe I did belong in Vietnam, after losing my girlfriend and flunking off the basketball team. As I sat in the back of the room, which I firmly believed was reserved for athletes, I noticed there were only two dozen students in the class, an anomaly at such a large university. The professor would ask us to read a passage from a philosophical anthology and wait for our responses. And wait he did, for no one appeared eager to engage him. It had always been a jock mandate not to speak in class. Was it possible that the room was filled with university athletes who needed a philosophy class to fulfill some curriculum requirement?

The passages we read seemed as lucid to me as pages from *Sports Illustrated*. Why was everybody in the room holding back? Surely there had to be some goody-two-shoes eager to impress the professor with some smart-ass answer. I began to feel sorry for the professor. I imagined our unresponsiveness making him feel inadequate. My holding back started to feel ridiculous, not so much because I was convinced I knew exactly what the passages were saying, but more because I liked what they said. I was beginning to have a crush on Sophia.

Would I dare open my mouth and run the risk of being confirmed as the jock who was an intellectual klutz? After two weeks of enduring unbearable silences, I decided to say out loud what I appreciated about Kant's categorical imperative. The professor's eyes widened as he leaned forward, asking me more questions, which felt like a deep welcoming rather than a test of my knowledge. Following that day, I participated in every class discussion.

I began to imagine I might be more than quick hands. Seeking energized my imagining. Maybe I would actually major in philosophy! Maybe this was my home, where I belonged. I took almost every philosophy course I could, developing a great fondness for ethics, existentialism, and metaphysics.

At the end of my senior year, I discovered that although I had performed well in my philosophy education, I was still prone to living in a small story characterized by a guy with a quick first step. Once, as I was leaving an ethics seminar, the professor stopped me and asked if I had applied to graduate school. I was stunned by the question because my self-perception continued to place me in a locker room preparing to compete. However, I was being invited to embellish my story, imagining a new vision of myself, offering the seeker an honorable quest.

It took me two years following graduation to finally apply to graduate school. I vividly remember attending a meeting with the department chairperson, who suggested I read a letter from the American Philosophical Association before accepting their invitation to admission. The letter basically explained that most people with a higher degree in philosophy were either driving cabs or working as short-order cooks. I handed the letter back to him, explaining that the scarcity of teaching opportunities was not an issue for me. He pointed out that I had an infant at home and that a heavy academic program with no prospect of work might not be appropriate. I responded by saying that it wasn't really a choice; it was something I had to do. He looked puzzled and welcomed me. My crush on Sophia was turning into a torrid love affair.

I did my best to ignore the possibility that my love of Kierkegaard would lead me directly to the first shift at the local diner. In the past, my academic life had gotten a bit derailed by girls, alcohol, and rock 'n' roll, but my classmates were real scholars. I would imagine myself teaching philosophy, passing on what I loved. It was difficult to hold the vision as thoughts of my classmate's academic superiority regularly interrupted my embellished narrative as a teacher of philosophy. I could hold the vision of teaching because I loved the image, not because I thought I deserved it. Two years later, one of the fifteen of us who started that graduate program was called for a teaching interview. I started teaching two months later.

I did not think I deserved it, but I deeply loved the vision I held of teaching. It was the love that ignited my imagination and embellished my story. I was healing my relationship to myself by honoring what I loved, even in the presence of forces that would suggest I was not fully qualified. My imagination was driven by love and would be an offering of medicine for my soul.

Sophia steps intimately into our lives when we allow our imagination, energized by heart, to be the plan for what we desire to create. It is helpful to see imagination as a guiding energy for the seeker and not as an extravagant Christmas list, nor as a plan for personal improvement. Here are some questions that can help focus our imaginations: Does the embellishment of my story have a path with a heart? Who will benefit in the expanded narrative? Is the development of my talents and gifts incorporated in the larger story? What does this embellishment say about my offering to the world? What is it that I am wanting for myself in this imagined perspective? What forces are operating in opposition to my embellished story? What is the role of my ego in my evolving narrative? Is my imagination calling me to be who I was meant to be?

Ruthless Sophia and Sweet Sophia

When it comes to matters of the heart, Sophia can be ruthless, that is, without care. We respond to early hurt and pain by deciding that we can live comfortably with little or no heart-opening. We construct a belief system suggesting we can live a meaningful life without the inevitable messiness of heart. Then, without warning, the penetrating energy of Sophia blows our hearts open! Sophia does not care how a heart opens. She simply wants it open.

There are endless stories of hearts opening in situations that are clearly unmanageable. Extenuating circumstances bear down on lovers making the price of their loving unbearable as either they or others are deeply hurt by their love. They can either choose to live their love and accept the consequence or walk away from one another, betraying the call of their hearts.

The Italian film *Malena* depicts a teenage boy's fascination with a sensual woman twice his age who is married to a soldier away fighting the war. The weight of the age difference and of wedlock keeps the boy in the role of an admiring voyeur. He persists in living in the grips of impossible love. The villagers turn against Malena because of her dealings with the Germans during the war. Although the boy longs for this woman's attention, he helps renew Malena's relationship with her husband, who returns a wounded war veteran, by writing an anonymous note affirming her faithfulness to him. It may be that when Sophia's interventions are the most ruthless, preventing us from stepping into a full expression of heart, we may be asked to live in a larger love story, characterized by diminished self-interest.

When we refuse to welcome her, we bring on divisiveness, turmoil, emptiness, and estrangement. However, opening our hearts to her invites a sweetness characterized by delight, kindness, and pleasantness. Typically, she will ask for some form of ego reduction, or sacrifice of grandiosity, in exchange for the sublime comfort hidden in simplicity. The task of downsizing our egos may not itself be so pleasant. It quite often means being willing to acknowledge how much we do not have control over, or how many mistakes we have made, or some act of ours that we refuse to forgive, or just how little we know.

I have often described my friend Gary as a sweet man. I have seen him in many situations where he is willing to pause, remaining receptive to the heart of a situation. He neither strives to generate solutions nor makes impetuous offerings of new meanings. His cessation does not feel passive, but rather like an active invitation. His demeanor instills the atmosphere with a softness, a place where a heavy heart could land. My friend carries the grace of Sophia. This softness and grace can be felt in the following poem by Mary Oliver:

Wild Geese

You do not have to be good.
You do not have to walk on your knees
for a hundred miles through the desert repenting.
You only have to let the soft animal of your body
love what it loves.
Tell me about despair, yours, and I will tell you mine.
Meanwhile the world goes on.
Meanwhile the sun and the clear pebbles of the rain
are moving across the landscapes,
over the prairies and the deep trees,

the mountains and the rivers.
Meanwhile the wild geese, high in the clean blue air,
Are heading home again.
Whoever you are, no matter how lonely,
the world offers itself to your imagination,
calls to you like the wild geese, harsh and exciting—
over and over announcing your place
in the family of things.[30]

Sophia abhors victimization. She does not want us withdrawing our plan for creation in the name of life being too big or too unmanageable. She does not want a lover who insists that she's too much to handle. When we do insist upon seeing ourselves as victims of our life experiences, there will be no room for sweetness, no opportunity for delight. How simple an act it is to call to mind kindnesses offered to us throughout the day or some pleasantness exchanged.

The ordeals of life will remain inevitable. Sophia asks that we not excessively protest the plan of creation known as our fate, all those events that lie outside our will, but rather see our fate as desiring to participate in the creation of who we are. The more we turn toward life, willing to remain its student rather than its victim, the more we deepen our capacity for personal wisdom. As we accept ourselves as students, grandiosity subsides. We remain both seekers and the ones whom life is seeking. From this perspective, we have been chosen by life, the universe, God, and the gods to be prodded, pushed, aroused, and agitated. We begin to move beyond holding our lives as unfortunate; we can start to celebrate the journey, allowing for delight and the mystics' quest for unity.

We end this chapter with a prayer imagined as coming from the lips of Sophia.

SOPHIA'S PRAYER

I demand heart. You will know my power by a heart touched, broken, or blown open. Ask the question "Does my path have a heart?" I have no consideration for the uninvolved heart. My imperative is that your heart participates in your plan for creation.

I am not tolerant of your attachment to distraction, your preoccupation with looking good or massaging your ego with clever strategies for attaining illusionary expressions of security. The journey calls for heart or courage.

Learn to pause. Suspend what urgency lies in your chest, as it often is a reaction to some illusion of loss. Your immutable goodness cannot be lost. Let your truth be touched by what I have sent you, not moving so fast that the message can't find you.

A life well lived will reflect the light of your devotion and the ground of the character you craft with that devotion. Allow your devotion to dance with the luminosity of your fate. You will certainly be called time and time again to that for which you are surely unprepared. See your lack of preparation as the heart and mind of a beginner. And you will be touched as never before.

Those times of bewilderment are asking you for a heartful presence. Listen with your whole body, bear the tension of the unknown and you will be offered my welcome. You will not be forgotten. I will remember that you desire my wisdom and from that longing I will reveal myself to you.

I ask that you not trivialize being touched and moved by suggesting it is simply excessive sentiment. Your quick judgment is only a reflection of your fear of feeling out of control. Let me be in control. Feeling touched and moved is simply you being alive! Come with me! See what I touch in you and to where I move you.

LIVING IN LARGER STORIES

*"Wisdom requires a sense of story, a feeling for
where things are headed, a narrative reflecting an
intelligence for what is important and enduring
not what is temporary and most distracting."*
—MICHAEL MEADE

FORGOTTEN ON THE DOCK

James Junior, as his family called him, was attending his first Gathering of Men, an assemblage of men who were willing, at least temporarily, to shed some of the veils of masculinity that take men a long way away from themselves. These men were willing to set aside needs to diminish others in order to aggrandize some achievement or attempt to sweep attention away from a man finding his voice for the first time.

James Junior took a deep breath and began to address the men who were willing to hear him without interruption or an avalanche of advice. He began telling a childhood story that kept him living in a small narrative. "I was raised in Stonington, Connecticut, in a family of lobstermen. My father and grandfather could relate to lobsters with more fervor than they did with their women, or for that matter, any family member. Until now, I could only wait on the dock for the return of the boat and help remove the catch of the day. When we left the dock at 4:00 AM, I felt like I was leaving toy trucks, bicycles, and other childhood accoutrements behind. I wasn't sure what awaited me, but I did know it was larger than the world I had known.

"I had just finished my first day out with my father and grandfather, emptying the traps. It was my tenth birthday, a day I had waited for with great anticipation. I mostly enjoyed how the men worked together, how they reacted to a full trap of lobsters, the smiles of success that washed over their faces. My father turned to me and instructed that I should wait for him on the dock while he went to help old Jack unload his boat.

"It was late May, the waters still holding the chill of winter while the air possessed the warmth of summer. As I sat there on the dock the mixture of these temperatures worked to create a dense fog. A boat moored some one hundred yards away could no longer be seen and the voices of the men where my father had gone grew faint.

"The fog brought a premature ending to daylight and I decided I should start walking home. I wasn't sure how far it was, but I was pretty sure I had never walked that far before. In any case, I knew what direction to head down Route 1. I had thoughts of my father getting busy helping other lobstermen, any thought that supported him as a good man and helped to explain how I had been left on the dock.

"Suddenly, a vehicle slowed down and approached me. It was hard to make out who it was. Then I heard the voice of my mother, 'James Junior, get in this car!'

"She didn't sound happy. 'Where's your father?'

'He went to help old Jack unload his boat,' I explained.

'Yeah, right, he's drinking again with old Jack. And the damn fool forgot his son in the process!'

"Well, I want you all to know that I'm fifty-five and I've been waiting on that dock most of my life. In jobs, friendships, and in a marriage that went bad, I sat on that dock waiting for someone to come, someone who cared, someone who would remember me."

James Junior had been living in a small story. And maybe that's what happens at some pivotal time when we are deeply hurt. That pain longs for its reprieve, waiting for someone on a dock who isn't coming, waiting for someone to prove that we are worth remembering. After listening to James that day, my hope was that by telling the small story he lived in, the narrative would be expanding and he would hopefully be willing to open his heart to the boy waiting on the dock.

It is likely that we all have a "dock" where we were forgotten, a place we must visit and be willing to feel the heartache of being left. So many of us will neither find the courage nor the mindfulness to visit the regions of pain that contract our stories. Those places of hurt and anguish keep our stories small, devoid of vision and creativity. The pain continues to weave the same yarn consisting of a few rigid themes that express our inadequacy and the reasons we are unlovable. If the ego cannot ground its worth in being special in some positive way, it will gladly attach to being special in some negative way, but it will not go on without some degree of being special.

EGO STORIES

I continue to be surprised when I witness someone admiring a person who has taken up residency in a large ego story, a narrative void of depth and meaning. We have been willing to trade off what is enduring for displays of exuberance, dazzle, and distraction. We may have become so pain-avoidant that we settle for any story that brings temporary relief from a life lived genuinely.

Large ego stories are meant to soothe feelings of insecurity, massage self-loathing, and impress others. The ego abhors feelings of apprehension and easily attaches to illusions of invincibility. It insulates through denial. Any reminder of vulnerability can quickly be erased. The ego loves marching to the tune of right and wrong, eager to demonstrate the rightness of any ideology or belief it favors. It also enjoys the sound of comparing and contrasting, which offers the ego an opportunity to walk the high ground, casting a disparaging glance at the less fortunate. The ego delights in attaching to whatever distraction might offer insulation from life's uncertainties.

Large ego stories are typically a compensation for feelings of self-contempt. The telltale sign of this desperate attempt at self-support is falling into self-absorption. In conversation, there is no invitation to the other, just a tally of one's achievements, plans, preferences, beliefs, and anticipated success. The inventory is a kind of balm being applied to a gaping wound. People presenting this way are often identified as confident. An old meaning of the word *confident* is *full of trust*. The irony is that self-absorption suggests little or no trust that individuals will offer love and compassion to themselves.

Increasingly, when I am in the presence of self-absorption, I respond with both disdain and sympathy. I have yet to accept my own self-absorbing tendencies as reflective of a greater need for self-acceptance. My unity with another person is being obstructed because I have not united with myself through compassion.

Large ego stories are energized by pride meant to inflate the narrator, bringing him or her to an unnaturally large size. Brightest, biggest, best, strongest, and longest are the superlatives reflecting inflation and an enslavement to perfectionism. Typically, our ego stories are not simply based upon some perfunctory comparison to others, but they also entail an attachment to idyllic standards that assault our humanity. They do not allow us to accept our limits with some measure of grace. Pride becomes a substitute for genuine self-love, an expression of Agape that can welcome the whole person, not simply what glitters and shines.

The ego narrative focuses upon an attachment to being impressive. The ego is so obsessed with control that it insists upon weighing, measuring, and tabulating its own worth and refuses to succumb to offerings of unconditional love (Agape). The result is that we lose the very power that the ego is preoccupied with, as we depend upon others having a favorable reaction to various displays of our proficiencies.

I recently ran into my own attachment to being impressive that ironically enough, my pride convinces me that I've outgrown. My wife and I were waiting for a flight to Miami and eventually on to Costa Rica. We sat at a restaurant in the airport, where I decided to take my vitamins, enough to support the health of five men, with a glass of orange juice, which I seldom drink. Within minutes, I was struck with a severe case of acid reflux.

I wandered the airport in search of an antacid, confident that my intestinal malady would subside before boarding time. I found an appropriate remedy that appeared to have no effect. My hope to be on the other side of my affliction before boarding the plane was quickly dashed as I entered the plane convinced that my chest was about to explode.

I took some comfort in the fact that I had an aisle seat, which would be helpful in case I needed to make an abrupt move to the restroom. As I began to take my seat, a woman with a window seat in our aisle asked if she could have my seat, since her husband occupied the aisle seat directly across from my seat. I discourteously responded, "No!" fearing that she and my wife might be subjected to regurgitated vitamins and juice.

I immediately realized that my response to the woman did not help me look like the polite, cooperative passenger to which my ego was attached. I began to accept that my condition was only to be remedied by vomiting. I hurled my body out of the seat, headed to the restroom at the back of the plane. As I approached my destination, the flight attendant instructed me to return to my seat since the plane was about to taxi away from the gate.

"I'm sick!" I exclaimed, grabbing the handle to the restroom.

"We can take you back to the gate," she responded, offering an unacceptable solution.

I ignored her and pushed my way into the restroom where I immediately began to vomit. After my immediate physical relief I felt the embarrassment of having obstructed the departure of the flight. I could feel the blows to my ego as I realized there was nothing impressive about my behavior. I exited the restroom and the flight attendant handed me two large trash bags whose purpose temporarily eluded me. Then I got it—if I had to vomit again, she wanted me to remain in my seat and use the bags.

I returned to my seat with my trash bags and everyone around me looked at me as if convinced they were being subjected to a potentially deadly disorder. Any hope at being an impressive passenger was all but destroyed. However, I was convinced that I would not need to use the trash bags, an illusion that was dispelled rather quickly as I spent takeoff with my head in the bag, vomiting what little remained in my stomach. When I finished vomiting, I knew I was experiencing a serious ego reduction as I considered making the rest of the trip with my head in the bag in attempt to avoid disgusting my fellow travelers.

SOUL STORIES

Unlike large ego stories, large soul stories are not invested in soothing feelings of insecurity; rather, they are about allowing us to feel the depth of our experience and attributing meaning to what happens to us. We can think of depth as boundlessness or simply our willingness to be addressed by mystery over and over again. We are asked to be open to uniting with life's mystery, allowing our hearts to be blown open, broken open, or simply touched, which drops us to new levels beneath the surface of things.

An old interpretation of the word *meaning* is *to name*. We rename ourselves over and over again in a large soul story. James renamed himself as he became the man telling the story of being forgotten on the dock, and he trolled his emotional depths as he allowed himself to feel the role that being forgotten had played throughout his life.

Meanings evolve as we become more or less loving, more or less confused, and more or less courageous. We live in large soul stories as we allow life to move and jostle us out of the old names we attributed to ourselves and as we become receptive to seeing ourselves in new and emerging ways. We embrace expanding soul stories as we refuse to take refuge in some old script whose job is to quell the tension we feel in the face of the unknown.

Large soul stories reflect a delight in offerings of compassion and blessings both to the self and others. I recently heard an elderly attorney describe his participation at a conference for contract lawyers. The joy of his eldership shone brightly as he described the delight he took in acknowledging the gifts and accomplishments of his young colleagues.

Soul stories are energized by devotion. These narratives depict a loyalty of heart. We come to understand more fully where heart wants to live. It is devotion that makes a story believable. Although there is no way to accurately determine who or what should be the recipient of my devotion, it is the risk of living with that much heart that makes the narrative soulful. When courage is woven through the fabric of devotion, we escape the marginalization of Hamlet's rumination as he searches for some idealized expression of loyalty. We act courageously rather than think about it. Soul is willing to accept the imperfection and messiness of the human condition and does not strive for some sanitized version of ourselves.

Some years ago I was working with Maria, a young woman suffering from anorexia nervosa. She was considerably underweight with a powerfully adversarial relationship with food. She was clear with me from the start of our work. She wanted to reclaim her life, eat nutritionally, develop meaningful relationships, and offer her daughter a model of empowered femininity. Much of her learning and healing focused on her belief that her body was a contaminant to her spiritual life. I pointed out that she was living by an ancient ascetic principle, which was that the body and material grown in the earth diminished spiritual purity. She was obviously moved and comforted by this nonpathological interpretation of her condition.

We went on to discuss other paradigms regarding spirituality. She became very interested in the thinking that her soul was incarnating, taking on a body so she might attend to what she came to the planet to learn and from those lessons, make some offering to others. Two years later, she had made peace with her carnal nature, accepting her body as a channel for the learning she was willing to undertake. I began to bless her efforts and devotion to remaining a student of life.

"Well, I can remember what did it, when I decided to exercise the courage needed to stop avoiding life and step in fully, ready to remain curious about who I am and what my purpose was," Maria explained.

"Tell me, what happened?" I asked.

"I'll never forget what you did," she responded.

I sat there with ego poised, ready to hear her describe some unique intervention I made that was a catalyst for her recovery.

"Oh yes, I remember it like it was yesterday. I was leaving your office and as I exited, you placed your hand gently on my shoulder."

I sat there dumbfounded with disbelief that some act so innocuous could be so meaningful. Of course, my ego was not prepared to accept such a simple act as possessing any kind of healing power. Plus, that level of simplicity really was not reflective of my ego's need to be offering some grander, restorative intervention. My soul story involved accepting that I am a small part of a person's healing and being okay with that.

Maria's soul story was about letting go of her protest about having a body, and accepting her body as a conduit of her life's purpose. She developed a vision of her body's relationship with the earth and an acceptance for the imperfection of earthly things, including her body. She became increasingly interested in how her body could make choices that reflected her values. She became a mentor for unwed teenage mothers. The focus of what actually fed her body expanded to what genuinely fed her soul and her heart.

Large soul stories are uninterested in being impressive; rather, they are characterized by expressions of integrity. These narratives illustrate how a person's choices reflect personal values and beliefs. The enduring value of integrity is often lost when stories of spiritual leaders and teachers accentuate how nice the main characters are. Was Christ being nice when he did not like what was being sold at the Temple and so decided to knock over the wares of the vendors while hitting them with a stick? Religions could advocate large soul stories by stressing the theme of integrity rather than behavior aimed at being well mannered, adaptive, and oppressive to the soul.

WHY LIVE IN LARGER STORIES

It is important to ask why we should be interested in living in larger stories and what it takes to do such a thing. It is a prayerful act to be willing to step into a larger story. It says that we acknowledge life's exigencies and the depth of the mystery. It declares our unwillingness to shy away from the vastness of life because we are willing to feel more, adventure more, and remain ever more curious. The mystic accepts life on life's terms, understanding there will be the challenge of harsher realities. There is an abiding sacredness when we refuse to pretend that life is simply a repertoire of our ego's fondest pastimes. Once we are open to the possibility of living in a larger story, it will serve us to identify how to approach such a task.

Not to Forget

An old Greek translation for the word *truth* is *Aleithia*, meaning *not to forget*. One starting place, as we make ready to live in a larger story, is not to forget the story of where we come from. We place ourselves in small stories when we either decide that there is no story of our origin worth telling or that our story is either magnificent or dreadful.

Not to be forgotten is the story of our legacies, the gifts and wounds bequeathed to us. In Latin there is the word *captatoris*, translating into *legacy hunter*. The hunt is done justice when we refuse to get stuck on glamorizing our findings, or excessively darkening them, and most important of all, when we refuse to give up the hunt.

My mother was French Canadian and grew up in a small town where ethnicity offered an illusionary feeling of security. If your neighbor was French and Catholic, then they likely could be trusted. If they were also hardworking, then they were considered a valued associate. I was taught that diversity of any kind was threatening, including the ideas that sprouted in my adolescent mind. Classism was rampant in our family. If your possessions indicated in any way that you were financially successful, then your moral fiber was immediately called into question. Your station in life had obviously been attained by unscrupulous means.

The underprivileged were depicted as lazy and irresponsible, while the affluent were easily discredited as unapproachable and unethical. Life was to be lived from a place driven by hard work (hard work being defined as physical labor) and sanitized of anything hinting of either advantage or disadvantage. My socioeconomic place has always felt like a foreign country to which I have yet to gain passage.

Shortly after my seventeenth birthday my mother reminded me of where I belong. The basketball coach of our state university was pulling out of our driveway following a recruiting visit. My mother turned to me and said, "You know, there's nothing wrong with staying home and working in the mill. Your grandfather and uncles did it, and they made out okay." There was no mention of the likelihood that my grandfather died of bladder cancer due to the dyes he worked with daily.

I was being called to a small story, a legacy woven with fear and the illusion that the familiar was always a better place to land. Straying away from what you know is dangerous. All suggestions of innovation were viewed as heretical. What I don't want to forget is that my mother's life was dominated by fear and how deeply she believed that the contract of her story was her only recourse for safety. Anytime I introduced something new into my life—jobs, beliefs, and vacations—she would dismiss it immediately, mocking my alleged indulgence.

My initial maternal narrative was small, woven with threads of ridicule and disdain for the woman who raised me. I resisted noticing how my maternal legacy lived within me. I preferred believing that I could simply walk away from my origins, like giving away clothes that no longer fit and slipping into a more desirable and fashionable self.

There is always some level of deprivation accompanying our legacies. We don't get enough encouragement, affection, love, or discipline. Something will be missing. The ego enjoys either indulging itself in denial, pretending that its roots are pristine, taking solace in a past without blemish, or stripping itself of accountability by being a victim of the past. We only move out of the small stories of our legacies by continuing to ask: Where do I come from?

My maternal accusations were melting away, giving rise to deep pools of consideration. I began to see how much of my mother's fear resulted in a life held in simplicity and how grateful she could be for so little. I began to see how her pride that gave voice to claims such as, "I've never had to apologize to anyone and I'm glad of it!" was a temporary balm for the woe of her self-loathing. I saw how she called me to some semblance of rapport with her, always from an invitation laced with guilt. She could not imagine one of her children wanting to be connected to her.

It took awhile before I was able to see how my pride, carried as vanity, served as a medicinal ointment for my self-loathing. At first, I decided that I carried a typical dose of vanity, which would serve anyone needing an occasional self-esteem boost. However, it became increasingly apparent that my vanity stretched deeply into my psyche, holding me hostage to the admiring glances of others. I knew that I was gifted with enough physical appeal to hold the attention of members of the opposite gender. My aging correctly informed me about who really held the power in those younger years. To my dismay, it became clear that my personal worth had been in the hands of my admirers. And as their numbers dwindled as my body aged, I was left with psychic terrain laid barren with a worn vanity that was no longer able to irrigate my ego.

My father was a great dreamer. Rather than cope with his fear with real action, he expanded his vision to realms of endless story. He took up residence in possibility, leaving reality unattended. Curiously enough, he did allow for his largeness when it came to telling stories and loving men, with the combination reflecting the robust nature of his soulful imagination.

He welcomed men into our home with a resounding timbre, suggesting to the visitor that his coming had been greatly anticipated. He would almost immediately begin to tell stories highlighting somebody's buffoonery, with the implication being that the listener would never have succumbed to such foolishness. There was a kind of enchantment to his telling of a story that invited all who listened to let go of the borders separating imagination from actual events. His words possessed a seamlessness that allowed us to slip from the present to whenever and wherever his narrative called us. The vividness of his delivery generated the illusion of listening to a tour guide who was inviting us to myriad sights and sounds.

In so many other ways he was not destined to step into the larger stories of his love of history that called him to teach and of his passion for travel. His actual story was increasingly condensed, which may be the way of it because our stories are ever expanding or shrinking. My father envied men who received social acknowledgment. He regularly spoke of the importance of receiving public recognition. It took me years to understand that he was waiting for a paternal blessing that never came. Subsequently, his self-loathing and despair were palpable throughout the years leading to his death.

A legacy may haunt us, obstructing our personal empowerment when we unconsciously live out its most debilitating aspects. The alternative is to attempt to prove that we have somehow transcended all aspects of the legacy. The latter is a compensation that typically throws the baby out with the bath water. This latter response reflected my best efforts.

Determined to prove my father wrong, I started my private practice in my basement with no advertisement and no listing of a phone number in the local directory. My practice evolved and so did my fear of any public acknowledgment, as I imagined it to hurl me into the grips of my father's mandate, namely that a man is only as good as the recognition he can produce.

Appreciation and Interruption

Our stories remain infused with meaning and creativity as we recall which themes of our legacies to appreciate, and which deserve to be interrupted. The former continue to remind us of the strengths giving rise to our personalities, while the latter identify our psyche's task. Of course, our perspectives of where we come from are forever changing, depending both upon the grace and the pain we bring to the viewing.

We can employ a variety of curiosities to help build the narrative of our origins: How did my parents hold power? How did they approach the task of loving themselves? Were they able to identify their gifts and develop them? How did they treat their woundedness? How did they approach accessing support? Did they know where they belonged? Did they feel entitled to have a voice? What did they long for? How did they live what they loved? Whom did they love and by whom did they feel loved?

Our narratives continue to enlarge when we are willing to continue to be informed by our pasts. The essential key is not to define ourselves simply as a victim of our origins, even when it is clear we were in some ways victimized. The challenge often is to stop protesting where we come from and to let go of our idyllic vision of a more appealing start. All the ingredients necessary for the development of a unique character lie in our beginnings. However, we must be willing to get honest about where we come from—understanding the struggles, the strengths, and the pain of our origins—to be able to grieve the defeats and celebrate the victories.

MAKING PEACE WITH THE JOURNEY

The mystic is devoted to making peace with the journey, the journey of life. A friend recently asked his colleague, whom he described as bright and competent, what she thought of the idea that life was essentially insecure, unpredictable, and mysterious.

She responded by suggesting, "Anyone who believes such a thing must have had a really disruptive, early family experience."

Our culture will not help us make peace with life. We cannot imagine being on a journey that is way beyond our keenest understandings. We don't like the idea that the nature of life will inevitably elude our ego's finest strategies for reducing life to a task easily defined and accomplished. We are told that there is some product we can purchase that will help us win the war against life's harsher realities.

The latest example of this is the war against "erectile dysfunction." A pharmaceutical company identifies some physiological or emotional aggravation, then identifies it as an unwanted malady with a recommended elixir, such as Viagra. This marketing ploy easily gains momentum from the cultural mandate that males must remain perpetually ready to demonstrate their sexual prowess. What a dilemma!

We invite men to be something unattainable and then sell them a product to cope with their defeats. Once we abdicate the responsibility to define ourselves, we become vulnerable to some cultural definition that is aimed at grooming us as consumers.

Men seldom speak with other men honestly about their sexuality, which makes them more susceptible to societal influences, such as a pharmaceutical company telling them who they are and who they ought to be. Men can step into larger sexual stories by attending workshops and seminars on the topic of male sensuality. They can discover how men become more sensual and heartful with age, with less focus on their genitals. The pleasure of sex becomes more whole body and more emotional. Feeling emotionally present and connected to a sexual partner becomes more important than a variety of titillating sexual positions.

We can say we have begun to make peace with the journey by remaining self-referenced, focused upon ourselves, committed to remaining self-examining, and by maintaining our own responsibility to define our self. We begin to make peace with our interior worlds when we remain eager to meet ourselves again and again, offering compassion to the self we find.

If we meet life with a divided inner world, striving to escape from whomever we deem unacceptable, then we encounter the outer world with deep insecurity. We live in fear that others will confirm what we have already judged as unsuitable. We begin to make peace with others by calling for an inner armistice.

With some semblance of an interior truce in place, we can begin to take risks. We might even deepen our tolerance for making mistakes. We might even evolve to the point of seeing mistakes as a reflection of a life well lived, rather than blemished by errors.

We are doomed to live in small stories if we accept the cultural depiction of life as secure and predictable. The illusion is that the right education, right spouse, right neighborhood, and right financial investments all lead to an assured security. Over the years, people have been coming into my office feeling confused by some calamity that has beset their lives even though they have been living by the correct cultural formula. Of course, I am viewed as the bearer of bad news when I inform them that there is no right formula and that life will remain insecure, unpredictable, and essentially mysterious. My office has been the site of countless experiences of disillusionment; fortunately, these often lead to a renewed personal empowerment.

I am often asked, "Is there any source of genuine security?"

I typically respond by saying, "If that means, is there a way to prevent your death or others deciding you're not deserving of their love, then the answer is no!"

Once we begin to accept life as deeply insecure, mysterious, and unpredictable, we can calm down a bit by accepting our inevitable defeat. There is some solace to be had by placing ourselves appropriately amid the vastness of life. When we define ourselves as participating in an impenetrable mystery, we go way beyond the confines of our ego's representations of life.

I told a friend recently that I respected his commitment to live in a larger story. He responded by saying, "Well, I am, but it scares me!"

I replied, "Of course it scares you. It scares all of us."

What's the Fear?

We live in a society only too familiar with large ego stories. If what is coming at us is big enough, loud enough, or strange enough, then we're impressed. We drop back into an adolescent holding pattern when we actually believe there are only large ego stories. It's like saying, "There are only teenagers and no real adults." And when we encourage such narratives, we collude with reinforcing the life of unbridled ego. Then we wonder why financial and political leaders either lie or cheat us. They are simply acting out of stories we have endorsed, stories created from hubris, aggrandizement, and duplicity.

Living in a larger story often calls for a betrayal of the past. It is easy for heartful folks to fear the big-shot syndrome. We tell ourselves it is disloyal to the clan when we live with greater vision, more compassion, and more depth. Sometimes the story is about going somewhere we have never been and where members of our tribe have never been.

I have carried such a narrative for almost fifty years. When I was seventeen, we were playing on our home court against one of the best teams in New

England, or possibly, in the country. It was the beginning of the fourth quarter, and we were down by twelve points. I proceeded to make five consecutive baskets. The last shot was a fifteen-foot jump shot from the right baseline. Their big man came to block my shot, leaving the player he was defending. His hand was some twelve inches above my shooting hand. I instinctively adjusted the arch of my release so the ball cleared his menacing attempt to obstruct my shot. Nothing but net—the ball went sailing through the basket, leaving us only two points behind.

Eight hundred people where cheering madly as the opposing coach called a time-out. As we gathered around our coach, he made it clear that they would counter my recent efforts by defending us with a box and one (a two-two zone with one player watching me). He instructed my teammates to continue to pass the ball to me. Sure enough, I returned to the court to see their fastest player ready to defend against me. I was in a personal zone and he knew it. He looked tight and scared. I had been groomed for this moment since I was seven. One fake and he was going to be removed from the path to the basket.

But I proceeded to pass the ball to my teammates over and over again, not doing what I came there to do, much like Percival, who had been groomed to acquire the Holy Grail and forgot what he was to do upon entering the Grail Castle. We lost by six points.

For years I wondered why I didn't shoot that night. I knew what to do and didn't do it. I had never been afraid of missing a shot. I had enough confidence to shoot under almost any circumstances but not enough faith to go somewhere I had never been before. I had never been at the precipice of taking down such a giant. It meant going somewhere that I and the members of my clan had never been before.

The gift of that fateful evening has been a deep, bodily knowing when I am at the threshold of going somewhere I have never been before. Such a somewhere typically indicates the presence of a larger story asking to unfold. Distractions will inevitably ensue, calling us away from the errand that beckons to us into a larger narrative. There will be enchantments, interruptions, forgetfulness, and myriad unsettling experiences all aimed at attempting to help us cope with the fear of stepping somewhere we've never been.

Walking into an authentic larger story is never done simply for ourselves. A story with heart heightens our interest in what we are giving and receiving from life. We want to know how to have a robust rapport with life-founded, ever-strengthening acts of giving and receiving.

Uncharted Territory

An old meaning of the word *receive* is *to make room for*, which is a non-ego way to understand receiving. We are allowing life to add to us, to help develop and create us. We allow ourselves to collaborate with life when we are never a finished product, nor the sole author of ourselves.

We fear the uncharted territory. Our willingness to step into a larger story means facing new challenges, different responsibilities, and unanticipated defeats. I recall stepping into the narrative of a mentoring community for teenage boys. In late winter of 1992, fourteen men met every Tuesday evening with the goal to create a community. After six months of meeting, our plan was to receive twenty-four teenage boys.

I was calling myself and the men to a larger vision, one that transcended seeing ourselves as delivering a social service aimed at saving high-risk teenagers. I recall the youngest mentor regularly saying to me, "I know we're not here to merely help the boys. Could you tell me again what we are doing?"

I did not tire of responding to his curiosity. He was reminding all of us that we had stepped into a new and larger narrative that needed our attention and articulation. My typical response went something like this: "We are a community of men who extend an invitation to boys to join our community. We understand that boys join gangs because boys know their development happens in a community. However, we have elders in our community where gangs do not.

"We listen to the challenges facing the boys and we tell stories of the perils we faced. We define ourselves as wounded and gifted, similar to the boys. We define ourselves as holding authority for the community and, as such, we establish guidelines for acceptable behavior, holding one another and the boys accountable for violations of these guidelines. We are clear with the boys about the ways decisions will be made. Where appropriate, we engage in a service with the boys in support of the larger community."

I regularly ended my remarks by saying, "I hope no one here thinks I actually know what I'm talking about."

The men would laugh, affectionately making fun of me, graciously accepting my leadership and courageously stepping into a much larger story.

Fate had called us to an offering of stewardship. It was now up to us to decide how we would exercise our will in response to the call by yielding an unknown destiny.

WILL, FATE, AND DESTINY

As we desire to make peace with the journey, it may be helpful to identify the grand dance to which we have all been invited. An old meaning for the word *fate* is *divine utterance*. Fate becomes the stage constructed by the gods and, ultimately, the place where we decide who we will be. Fate involves everything outside of our will, from the genes we inherit to the people, places, and things we encounter along the way.

"Destiny favors the bold," suggested Cicero. We always have the option to either contract our stories in response to the divine utterance or expand them. Why wouldn't the Great Mystery that put all this in motion prefer we jump in rather than recoil in fear! What host takes pleasure in his guests huddling, reluctantly, at the doorway rather than stepping in and partaking of the spread that has been prepared?

Fate is our dance partner. We can either position ourselves across the ballroom, mesmerized in a cautious gaze, or step out and, as they say, cut a rug. Nonparticipation can be characterized as either protesting our origins or our current stations in life. We simply don't like our dance partner and believe we deserve better! Or we could say we do not appreciate what the gods uttered to us. Why would fate favor those who protest and complain?

The Dance

The dance of our wills and fate does not always move with a desired finesse. People arriving at my office for the first time are eager to tell me how cruel, exploitive, and downright malicious fate has been to them. They are disgusted with the dance and would appreciate some sympathy regarding the terrible misfortune that has befallen them. I typically extend some sympathy and move on, unwilling to collude with their need to define themselves as victims of fate.

David, a forty-four-year-old pilot, came to his first visit seeking confirmation that his wife was certifiable or at the very least, a very insecure woman.

"I can't take it any more! My wife is crazy! She believes that I am perpetually betraying her, at work and on the Internet," he exclaimed, soliciting my understanding.

"It sounds like life can be challenging with the woman you chose," I responded.

"Challenging? It's damn right miserable!" he insisted.

"I hear you've been having a rough time. So tell me, how do you handle her accusations?"

"Well, I try to explain to her that I've done nothing wrong. But nothing works."

"I want to hear what would happen if something did work," I said.

"I guess she would stop accusing me of infidelity and she would stop feeling so damn insecure."

"So, let me see if I get this. You want to do or say something that eliminates your wife's insecurity and her propensity to accuse you. Well, are you doing anything that warrants her distrust?"

"Well, I did deceive her while we were engaged. I dated a couple of other women and she found out."

"Did she find out because of her own investigation or because you told her?"

"She found out on her own."

"That kind of violation of trust, where the perpetrator does not come forward voluntarily, often entails more time for healing," I suggested.

"You mean, if I had fessed up, she might not be carrying on like this?"

"Fate placed a couple of attractive women on your path and you chose to break an agreement of monogamy with your fiancée and deceive her. The deception is typically experienced as the core of the violation," I pointed out.

"Okay, I guess I see that I contributed to all this when I deceived her. But when is she going to get over it?"

"I want to hear more about the guy who wants her to get over it."

"It's just not very enjoyable being the constant object of suspicion."

"You thought you could deceptively violate her trust and not be the object of her suspicion, and you don't like how long it's taking her to get over it," I reflected.

"You make it sound like there's something wrong with me feeling oppressed!"

"No, there's nothing wrong with you feeling oppressed, and if you insist on remaining focused there, there's not much you will be able to do about your situation," I suggested.

"I'm doing everything she asked me to do. I'm not flirting with other women and I'm not into porn on the Internet."

"I don't think doing everything she requests is such a good idea," I said, and David moved to the edge of his seat in eager anticipation of what I was to offer next.

"What do you suggest?"

"Your choices and fate have placed a suspicious woman in your life. I strongly recommend you respond to her suspicions by describing your values and expectations of yourself regarding other women. Your values may or may not be compatible with hers. In either case, it's a good starting point."

"I'm fine having one woman in my life. But what do I do when she continues to doubt me?"

"What happens to you when she doubts you?"

"I don't feel seen and appreciated for who I am."

"For now, you might need to diminish your investment in her seeing you the way you want her to, and work on seeing yourself."

David was willing to learn about the dance between his will and fate that presented him with a distrusting wife. He accepted how his will had contributed to her distrust and what choices presently sat in the domain of his will. Her perceptions of him to a great extent were beyond the scope of his will.

The first step for him was to find integrity in himself by identifying his values and how he was going to implement those values. That choice moved him out of the "good boy/bad boy" dynamic created when he received an unfavorable response from his wife. Also, his resentment of her began to diminish.

David was learning to dance fluidly with fate. He began to accept that it was his investment in being seen as devoted and trustworthy by his wife that was the source of his oppression. His investment was certainly honorable, but it was the cause of his oppression. The issue was that his wife was not ready to offer what he wanted. David was learning about the limits of his will and the most creative direction in which to focus his willfulness.

Fate holds a divine call to us. We can deny the call, distract ourselves from it, or become receptive and curious. This divine utterance may be the closest we ever get to the Great Mystery. The call will commonly stimulate our fear of death and/or our fear of life. David's fear of death was expressed as a fear of losing love by being defined as untrustworthy and therefore unlovable.

How can you know that a call to a larger story is happening? We will know because we will likely be experiencing a disturbance, which can be happening around us or within us. The natural reaction is to search for a way to subdue the disruption, rather than to welcome it. Only too often, the medical community, in conjunction with pharmaceutical companies, is more than willing to help us numb ourselves to the call. The thinking is that we simply have to eradicate some symptom and we are back to life as usual.

The ego delights in the illusion that there is nowhere to go, no fear to face, no lesson to learn, and certainly nothing of which to let go. Ego is gratified to immerse itself in the belief that it will be status quo forever.

Each time we deny a call or do our best to anesthetize the ensuing disturbance, the ego returns to rudimentary ways of guarding itself, and fear wins. There is no status quo for the authentic self. We are either fortifying ourselves against the call, all the while declaring how wonderful our lives are, or accepting the invitation to a new pilgrimage, one we are likely unprepared for. The call coming from fate is not interested in whether or not we are ready, that is, whether our emotional bags are properly packed.

The Call

The pilgrimage into a larger story often begins with some longing or desire. An old mentor of mine would often say, "There's no greater insult to the gods than to want little or nothing from life."

Sometimes the pilgrimage to a larger story calls us to a distant land and sometimes to remain in our neighborhoods. As pilgrims we are seekers, and what we seek is something we lost or denied within ourselves. The journey helps bring us into a more authentic relationship with ourselves. There is no geographic blueprint for deepening authenticity.

In some spiritual circles, I have heard the sacredness of longing diminished as more ego rhetoric. I suggest that desire is the actual boldness that fate favors. There is more to mature longing than a child running about in a candy shop. We can offer seasoned questions: Will this desire help me to live my gifts more fully and make a larger offering to others? Who will benefit from my desire? Is this desire compatible with my values? Does this desire reflect who I am meant to be? Does this desire call me into a larger story where it appears I belong?

In the end, we may not have neat, concise responses to these questions. What is important is the devotion and fervor with which we carry these questions. When I left the business world I was much too naïve to ask important questions. I only knew I was forty pounds overweight, drinking and smoking too much, and depressed and empty. The only call I heard I was "Leave this place!" So I did. I was driven more by vanity, in the hope of reclaiming my youthful athletic body, rather than by a creative vision of my destiny.

Somehow, my past had gifted me with the following imperative: If it feels awful, move on—figure the rest out later. I would later discover that the predicament may be somewhat more complicated, needing a level of discernment to test whether character is best forged by facing the prevailing challenge or by retreating and redirecting our energies. In either case, our wills are dancing with fate, moving us toward an awaiting destiny.

Our Destiny

An old meaning for the word *destiny* is *lot* or *portion*. How our wills dance with fate determines our portion of life. I am inclined to believe that vision becomes more fine-tuned in retrospect. There are a number of questions that I call *questions for the last hour*. That is, questions to be asked when we are close to being granted our last breath. These questions are meant to help guide our will as we step into the dance with fate. Some clarity regarding how we want to die, that is, who we want to be at our death, can shed light upon how we want to live now.

What did I come here to give? Did I give it? What did I receive? What did I learn? Did I live what I love? Did I remain curious about what life was asking of me? Did I avoid being a victim of fate?

If Cicero was right and fate does favor the bold, then destiny favors those willing to get lost again and again.

Getting Lost

We make peace with the journey, allowing ourselves to live in ever-larger stories if we are willing to get lost. The ego shudders at the thought, while the novice mystic accepts that a pilgrimage into impenetrable mystery guarantees getting lost again and again. If we are creating a meaningful relationship with life, uniting with it, then we are willing to make peace with getting lost.

For sure, getting lost will not feel good; however, we can deepen an appreciation for it as a necessary condition of the soulful sojourn. It is the in-between place, neither here nor there. The lost place or the in-between place scares us because it reminds us of the evolving and ever-changing nature of the journey and of our own identities. The ego appreciates continuity and consistency and therefore resists the ever-shifting nature of our walk through life. The ego believes it is destined to arrive somewhere, somewhere it can claim its completeness, celebrating itself as a finished product.

The following poem by C.P. Cavafy reflects Homer's account of Ulysses' trip home to Ithaka and captures the gift of the voyage and not arriving at some destination:

Ithaka

As you set out for Ithaka
Hope the voyage is a long one,
full of adventure, full of discovery
Laistrygonians and Cyclops,
angry Poseidon—don't be afraid of them,
you'll never find things like that on your way
as long as you keep your thoughts raised high,
as long as a rare excitement
stirs your spirit and your body.
Laistrygonians and Cyclops,
wild Poseidon—you won't encounter them
unless you bring them along inside your soul,
unless your soul set them up in front of you.

Hope the voyage is a long one.
May there be many summer mornings when,
with what pleasure, what joy,
you come into harbors seen for the first time;
may you stop at Phoenician trading stations
to buy fine things,
mother of pearl and coral, amber and ebony,
sensual perfume of every kind—
as many sensual perfumes as you can;
and may you visit many Egyptian cities
to gather stores of knowledge from their scholars.

Keep Ithaka always in your mind.
Arriving there is what you are destined for.
But do not hurry the journey at all.
Better if it lasts for years,
so you are old by the time you reach the island,
wealthy with all you have gained on the way,

not expecting Ithaka to make you rich.
Ithaka gave you the marvelous journey.
Without her you would not have set out.
She has nothing left to give you now.
And if you find her poor, Ithaka won't have fooled you.
Wise as you will have become, so full of experience,
you will have understood by then what these Ithakas mean.[31]

The poem suggests that all places are in-between places. Our destinations offer us a large vision and some respite from the anxiety of the journey. Our ports of call give us some reason to initiate the journey and some reason to believe we will know how to get there. The only component we have some control over is the desire to get somewhere. The gift of the destination is the story supplied by the journey that the soul needs in order to get closer to itself and to life. The eventual arrival offers some validation of the original desire to sojourn and the effort exercised along the way, for the gift was the journey.

Getting lost is inevitable when traveling a deeply mysterious journey. Nothing suggests a willingness to step into a larger story more than getting lost. It is an incredible assault upon soul when we attach ourselves to gathering data and information about the most innocuous events of life. We attempt to trick ourselves into believing that if we inundate ourselves with what is mundane and meaningless, we will not have to worry about getting lost. Such a strategy attempts to sidestep the mystery of the journey, which will inevitably result in our being truly lost.

Only by surrendering to the mystery and taking responsibility for what is in our control, like the level of truth we are speaking, the quality of compassion we are offering and receiving, and the status of our integrity, will we not be living at a great distance from ourselves. The dilemma is that it takes a great deal of courage to get lost and, likely, more courage to know where we are.

We came to the planet to experience change. The word *change* is a euphemism for dying and birthing; every change involves something dying and something being born. When we are at the dying place of change or in between the death and what is emerging, we inevitably get lost. Because our culture idolizes exaggerated ego, getting lost is typically shamed. We are supposed to have an ironclad grip on knowing exactly where we are, and our culture is fine with us pretending when we don't know. However, pretending only gets us really lost.

The novice mystic honors his or her own evolving nature by accepting the inevitability of getting lost. Nothing ushers us into a larger story more than getting lost. When we are lost, it is likely that some belief, relationship, job, or way of living no longer works for us. We have outgrown something and its death will leave us wandering bewildered and confused. If we can find the courage to acknowledge our predicament, there are gifts to receive.

By the nature of my job, people come to me feeling significantly lost. I diminish my enthusiasm about their situation, temporarily concealing that I do not see their feeling lost as unfortunate. They want to find their way if for no other reason than to get a respite from the shame they are pouring all over their experience. My job is to gently welcome them into a more creative perspective about getting lost.

It is an ideal time to rightsize our egos by learning to ask for help, with some level of humility possibly emerging. We can begin to craft a belief in the appropriateness of being lost if we are living authentically and accepting the immensity of mystery surrounding us. It is a time to make a deepened peace with ourselves and with life. Living in larger stories means being willing to be a student of getting lost. If we can hold some devotion as a student, then we may find ourselves awakening in a larger story.

The Awakening

What does it mean to not be awake, to be asleep? To be nocturnally asleep means to be defined by the other world, the dream world. When we are asleep during the light of day, with our eyes open, we are also defined by the other world through societal conventions, mores, and mandates. We look to "father" society for some legitimization of our beliefs and choices, a confirmation that we are on the right path. And of course, like our sister Eve, we fear the father's wrath and the possibility of banishment.

What does it mean to wake up? One understanding is that we experience enough pain or enough inner disturbances in order to shake the unyielding grip we have on some societal protocol that has not delivered on its promise. It may be the role of provider, spouse, or housewife that begins shredding at the seams, no longer able to hold some soul's longing, or the vision of our spirits evolve, which points us to a larger story.

Roles keep us in small stories when they are aimed at insulating us from mystery by keeping us defined by societal expectations. They can be paths leading to mystery when we, as seekers, define them, unwilling to allow ourselves to slip into a complacency lacking personal vision. Roles then become conduits for our inner worlds to be expressed and created in the outer world.

In the film *The King's Speech,* the character of Lionel Logue lives in the role of a speech therapist, although he belongs to no appropriate professional organizations. His gift as a healer flows through his role with a sharpness and adroitness, creating a rapport with his patient that is renewing and empowering. In the film, it is the duke preparing to become the king of England who benefits from Logue's services as he addresses the impediment of his stammering.

Awakening by its nature is heretical and, typically, heresy is driven by adolescent energy. It is a time of dissent, carrying enough disturbances to call cultural icons, especially those we have allowed to define us, into question. One old meaning of the word *awakening* is *disease*, indicating a lack of balance. This suggests that the beliefs, values, and choices that once brought order to our personal worlds are losing their efficacy. Our personal worlds are being shaken. It may be the status of a marriage, a family, some religious affiliation, a friendship, or the nature of our employment. We have lost a customary ease with calling a certain way of being our own. Hence, awakenings involve loss. Something that offered security, identity, and balance must be sacrificed.

The word *sacrifice* comes from an Old Latin word meaning *to make sacred.* Whenever we sacrifice beliefs and values that do not belong to us, especially those beliefs and values that obstruct our vision of our gifts and wounds, we are making the pilgrim's path sacred. As mystics, we unite with the Great Mystery by stepping closer and closer to our own mystery, especially our gifts and our wounds.

When we let go of whatever is getting in the way of our seeing and addressing our gifts and wounds, we are in the midst of a rich awakening. Gifts and wounds of the soul remain our deepest mystery. We are anointed as mystics when we live a devotion to identifying and stewarding our gifts, healing, and learning from our wounds. This process deepens when we experience the gold or the gift that accompanies the injury.

The benefits of healing are typically portrayed as results occurring from some successful therapeutic intervention. However, there is some positive advantage that comes with the wounding. To unearth this gold, some heartful devotion will likely be necessary. In the movie *Buck,* a horse whisperer who was physically battered by an alcoholic father carries a profound sensitivity to horses' fear, with an even deeper wisdom guiding his rapport with horses. The courage to open our hearts in spite of the wounding, to become devotional in some way, seems to offer the opportunity to garnish the positive offering of the wound.

Our woundedness calls us further into the mystery by offering an evolving set of requests. We may be asked to rename our wounds. If we felt abused emotionally, physically, and/or sexually, then we can understand this injury as abuse of power and violation of trust and boundaries. The story is now larger and can be expanded by the following curiosities: Am I presently abusing power in some way? Am I feeling abused by someone else's power? What do I want to do about an abuse of power, whether I am the perpetrator or victim? Is it difficult for me to trust myself or others? What do I need to do in order to trust in a discerning fashion? What do I need to learn about employing more effective boundaries?

If we felt neglected we can understand our wounding as feeling alone, powerless, and unlovable. The narrative grows with these questions: Who are my genuine allies today? What do I need from them? Do I allow myself to receive from them? Am I able to distinguish what is in my control and what isn't? Do I take appropriate action regarding those situations where I have some control? Do I surrender where I have no control? Can I readily identify who loves me and allow their love in?

The story of our wounds is embellished by acknowledging any resistance we have to accepting our wounds by identifying what healing is being asked for, identifying any hurt being perpetuated by the wound, and ultimately identifying any teaching offered by a wound.

Our gifts or talents continue to ask something from us. We may be asked to understand them with more depth, identify some fuller expression of them, or acknowledge some group or place where they are needed. Sometimes the gift is requiring some training or instruction for further development. We make greater peace with the journey and live in a larger narrative when we accept that our life's purpose includes bringing our gifts to our people or family.

Another old meaning for the word *awakening* is *watchful*. This suggests that an awakening, like an ongoing consciousness, may be larger than a grand epiphany. Recently, I was reminded of this aspect of awakening. While in conversation with a man I noticed a strong attachment to being right rising up within me. I later decided it was a fluke, feeling I had moved beyond such an unevolved way of relating. However, the following week, while talking with the same man, my need to be right again roared to the surface with a vengeance.

I was comfortable with my need to be right coming to the surface. I was not content with actually speaking to someone from that need. Once that happened, I was no longer listening to the speaker, I was not available to be cocreative, and more important, my need to be right suggested that I had drifted away from my essential goodness. Once we are in the position of needing to prove something, our tolerance for diverse thinking will diminish rapidly.

My initial assessment was that there must be something about this guy making me react in this way. I then decided that blaming him was not going to deepen any awakening about who I was. I decided to tell the gentleman about my need to be right in his presence and remain watchful of my need gaining momentum so that I would not allow the need to continue to inform me.

Risks

No action possesses more potential to move us into a larger story than taking risks, especially those we believe in. Old meanings of the word *risk* are *venturesome* and *bold*. These interpretations suggest making choices that relocate us away from the familiar. Although it is easy to talk about fearing risks, I would offer we don't really fear them at all.

What we do fear is twofold. First, we fear how we will likely treat ourselves if the risk we take bears unfavorable consequences. We shame, ridicule, and hold disdain for ourselves when some desired outcome appears unattainable. The second fear is that of going where neither we nor our ancestors have ever been.

Neither success nor failure plays a significant role in regard to this second fear. The issue is rather about breaking a barrier and moving onto ground where our people (family) have not trodden. This fear can be experienced as a kind of betrayal as we separate from the clan, going where none have gone before. This fear powers us back into small stories, postponing venturing into a larger narrative.

Interrupting legacies that contract our vision, longing, and choosing opens the way to stepping into larger stories. It may be a primitive loyalty that keeps us living in a constricted legacy and a small story. These loyalties reflect threatened egos, as we feel the security of our loved ones being shaken by new ideas and novel dreams. That time comes to an end. Our ancestors rejoice in our willingness to step out of some compressed story. My best intuition tells me that those who have passed to the other side, as well as future generations, benefit from our letting go of stories that may have bound and confined the soul of many of our people.

In the film *The Help*, the character Skeeter, played by Emma Stone, is blessed by her mother, played by Allison Janney, after the two worked through considerable mother-daughter tension. She says, "Sometimes, courage skips a generation." It is a special offering when the older generation can witness and acknowledge the interruption of a legacy by their offspring.

6

LIFE AFTER EGO

"Our task is to be defeated by ever larger things."
—RAINER MARIA RILKE

This quote from the Austrian poet Rilke has been hanging on my refrigerator door for the past year. I felt called to it as if its truth had been looking for me. At first, I naïvely decided it was simply an appropriate mantra for a sixty-three-year-old man.

Before long, I discovered I had asked life to show me just how puny my will was compared to the immensity of fate. My ego immediately protested as the veil of illusion faded, revealing how little was under my command.

The voice of life's exigencies became louder. The support in place for my disabled daughter crumbled, leaving our family in crisis. An organization to which I belonged became polarized and divisive, with the expectation that I address the issues. Friends faded away, while enemies appeared to advance.

My disenchantment included how much of my life I had credited with my alleged potency, leaving me with a frayed sense of self-worth. However, I was receiving an arduous course in rightsizing my ego.

More will be said about Rilke's suggestion and its support for the unity sought by the mystic. For now, our story of ego properly begins with acknowledging its contributions to our development. From the Latin, the word *ego* translated into *I*, which references the identity we call ourselves. We will explore what it means to build an I and allow for transcending the I.

THE GIFTS OF EGO

A number of years ago I had just entered my mentor George's office for our scheduled meeting. Our sessions usually began with my setting an initial focus. On this particular morning, George leaned forward and said, "There's something I've been meaning to tell you. Would it be okay if I started the meeting?"

"Sure, go ahead," I replied, noticing a note of seriousness in George's demeanor.

"You know, I have mentored many men through the years. You and I have been together for three years."

"Yes, it's been about that," I agreed.

"Well, I want you to know that during our time together, I have never once witnessed you attempting to impress me," said George, with softness in his voice that I received as affection.

"Thanks, George, but you've got to admit, that's damn impressive!" I said, which made the two of us roar with laughter.

George and I sat there appreciating the clever maneuvers of ego insidiously finding its way into any human dynamic. Our exchange reminded me that ego renders a great service to our identities and will always be with us. Our spiritual goal may not be to eradicate ego but rather to develop one, be conscious of its benefits and the presence of its voice, while creating the option of a *life beyond ego*.

Desire

The force of ego constellates around our desire. Starting around age two, our ego begins to express itself as desire that is not necessarily compatible with the wishes of parents and authority figures. The ego's desire is the energy that drives a child's unwillingness simply to conform to prevailing expectations. We then begin to explore what it means to be separate and pressed by desire. However, the importance of knowing and valuing what we want during these early days does not go unobstructed.

Typically, parents want their children to be aware of the parents' desires and do not encourage children to know their own desires. The child figures out early that being loved and approved of is often associated with knowing and responding favorably to parental wishes and not with remaining loyal to one's own desires. Hence, a tension is created that will likely be a lifelong challenge: Adapt and allegedly get approval, or follow our own desire.

This is especially true of girls, who are supposed to be aware of the desires and needs of others while neglecting their own. Girls run a higher risk of being tagged as selfish when they attempt to follow the lead of their own desire.

Recently, I was at the supermarket as casually moving my cart down the aisle behind a young mother and her toddler. The child pointed at almost every item on the shelves, saying repeatedly, "I want that." The mother responded by saying, "No, you don't."

The child turned his head toward his mother with a befuddled look, suggesting that what his mother said had no connection to what he was actually feeling. The mother may have been simply annoyed by the ceaseless demands of her son. Or maybe something a bit more sophisticated may have been occurring. The mother, like so many of us, may not have known how to acknowledge the reality of the child's desires while employing a simple boundary—"I get that you want a bunch of stuff but you can't have all that right now."

When ego development falls short, we run a high risk of living someone else's life, guided by their wishes, beliefs, and values. Our desires give direction to our lives. They tell us where we belong. They confirm our preferences. They determine how we will work and play. They define how we love and want to be loved. Our desires give rise to the intentions that are the plans of how we want to live.

Intentions

We can think of our intentions as the bridge from our inner world to the outer world. They take us from the privacy of the dressing room to the world stage. Intentions reflect the ego's desire to manifest itself, to make something happen, to be creative, productive, or destructive in some way. Intentions are ideas incubating.

Our intentions reflect our will's plan to meet fate and engage life in a way that reflects the uniqueness of our desires, beliefs, and values. Sometimes life graciously supports our intentions and other times it obstructs and challenges what we intend. Egos typically do not relish fate offering impediments to its intentions. Making peace with the power of fate is not an attribute of ego, because ego easily succumbs to pouting, complaining, feeling like a victim, protesting, catastrophizing, and indulging in intolerance.

Ego typically does not take some frustration to its intentions as a possible call to something larger than its plan. It will not ask: What is life asking of me here? Is there something for me to learn here? To what am I being asked to surrender? For ten years, I protested being the father of a disabled child, convinced that the gods had simply forsaken me, ignoring my hallowed intentions.

Entitlement

Entitlement to live our intentions is a significant characteristic of ego strength. Entitlement is synonymous with holding an inner authority that grants us the right to voice our intentions and take action directed at implementing our intentions. Similar to other ego strengths, entitlement can become inflated. We can find ourselves interrupting others while they are speaking, ignoring their boundaries, becoming demanding, or simply taking up an exaggerated amount of psychic space.

Entitlement can also be deflated and in need of strengthening. When this happens, we unnecessarily sacrifice rights and privileges. This commonly is expressed by losing our voices and not speaking up for what we need or want. It may be expressed as an act of deference, where we capitulate to the preferences of others.

When my wife and I were first dating, I noticed a significant difference in how we oriented ourselves in restaurants. She would ask how I felt about the temperature of the room, the sound of the music, and the view from my seat. I was initially bewildered by the questions. She entered the restaurant with a level of entitlement completely unfamiliar to me. My attitude reflected a desire not to appear too demanding to the waiter and to find enough inner authority to speak up if my meal wasn't anywhere near what I expected. I couldn't imagine having the right to express an opinion regarding the temperature and music.

Over time, I have learned that I can be a gracious patron while remaining entitled to receiving a service commensurate with the cost involved. It is common to experience a varying degree of entitlement in different settings and with different people. For example, I often hear reports of folks feeling entitled at the Department of Motor Vehicles where they typically issue their complaints and criticisms, but they don't feel very entitled to registering dissatisfaction when it is related to their physician.

Entitlement calls for a willingness to remain vigilant, evaluating where we may have either inflated entitlement or deflated entitlement. Rightsizing our egos is a lifelong endeavor, which invites us to remain self-examining. We can become curious about our entitlement by asking questions like: Where is life asking us to have more voice? Or are we being asked to create more space for the voices of others?

Choice

Ego prizes itself as a free agent that chooses or causes events to happen, rather than just being influenced by the effect of external events or the choices of others. Choice is an action; it is a lived intention. Many of our choices simply reflect our basic needs for shelter, food, and comfort. However, our choices can also reflect our strongest desires and values.

When we live a devotional life of self-examination, our choices become opportunities to move closer to the uniqueness of our beliefs and priorities. Such devotion often calls for the courage to be willing to separate from convention. The choice to authentically be ourselves, standing alone if necessary, is a reflection of ego strength. And when our choices deeply reflect our values, we are in the realm of ethical choice and integrity. Contrary to the beliefs held in many personal growth circles, strength of ego supports our capacity to be ethical. We are able to know what we value and remain curious about how our values impact our lives and the lives of others.

Integrity

When ego supports choices that are compatible with our values, we are acting with integrity. We act outside of integrity when our behavior is incongruent with our values or when our actions reflect the values borrowed from family, society, or from our own cravings.

How do we know that the values we purport are actually ours? That is actually a great ego question. The ego wants to know what belongs to it. We're probably never going to be completely immune to cultural forces. However, with enough ego strength, we can continue to remain curious about which values truly belong to us.

The drive to determine our values is a great gift of ego. More than any other human endeavor, the search for our personal values marks our devotion to creating ourselves and renewing our authorship of our lives. Clarifying personal values gets an important jump start when we live close to our desire. Desire is the seed capable of germinating into a value. We move from wanting something to having what is desired become a guiding principle for how we want to live.

Initially, we may want to be loved, and as we pay attention to how love lives in our lives, we may begin to value compassion. The process of being clear about what we want and what we value calls for a devotion to living a self-examining life, where questions of desire and value are always close. Forsaking self-examination can lead us into a haze where we do not really know what we value or the true impact our choices have upon us and others.

Our desire may drive us toward abuses of power as we attempt to compensate for feelings of self-loathing and past failures. Rather than focusing on what might benefit the greater good, we become obsessed with simply satisfying our own cravings. Wondering about what we want, identifying it, and pursuing it allows us to be informed by those unique stirrings of the soul. How we hold longing and the nature of what brings us fulfillment creates the fertile ground where we decide what will guide the direction of our lives. This direction may be reflected by enlightened ethical insight or possessed by fixations aimed at self-gratification.

There are questions that can help clarify what we value: Would I advocate this value to others? Does this value promote life? What belief is violated when I feel guilt or shame? To what human endeavor do I devote much of my time and energy? What would others say about me regarding what I hold important? Does compassion play any role in the expression of this value?

Boundaries

One of the ego's greatest gifts is the need for boundaries. In a number of spiritual circles, separation receives a disparaging notoriety, as if it diminishes the human condition. Yet ancient alchemists suggested that when a compound was separated into its composing elements, the molecular bond was stronger when these elements were brought back together.

Boundaries separate us from others, helping us to refine and clarify what is and is not us. Effective boundaries are not meant to isolate and dissociate us, but rather to keep us moving in the direction of our unique desires and values. Then and only then can the coming together with others reflect an authentic connection, where people are not pretending to be alike. This is when they allow their unique individuality to call one another to a larger life orientation than would be possible alone. There is an ongoing invitation to live in a larger story.

Boundary ego strength means being able and willing to say "yes" and "no" authentically. People-pleasing can easily drive us into compulsive replies of "yes" that inevitably lead to resentment. Learning to say "no" is the ego helping us remain loyal to ourselves. It means growing a resiliency to being in the presence of another's disappointment or anger. It means developing a capacity to hold tension. Hearing unfavorable feedback from others especially calls for a suppleness of ego. Strong ego allows us to hear perceptions about us that differ from the ones we hold about ourselves.

Being able to hear someone say "no" to us also involves holding tension that was created by other people's differing preferences and needs. The more tension we can hold, the more an ego can let go of attempts at recruiting the other to some shared vision. Ego strength is exhibited by supporting our separateness from others as well as allowing others to be separate and unique from us.

One of the valuable offerings of good boundaries is clarity about where and to whom we will bring our love. There is something naïve and dangerous about believing we can or should open our hearts regardless of the recipients. With solid ego strength we can create boundaries from a refined sense of discernment. Our discretion can be crafted from questions like: Who appreciates my loving? Whom do I respect? Am I fulfilled by my own acts of generosity? Do my offerings of love result in the creation of genuine rapport? Who experiences my loving as a blessing of their uniqueness? With whom do I feel free to speak my truth? Are those whom I love genuinely curious about who I am?

The Observing Ego

The ego can develop its own capacity to observe itself, which can significantly add to its options and deepen its capacity to choose. The observational benefit is that we can become less reactionary. When that happens, our interactions with others will likely be guided by more grace, compassion, and discretion. Hence, there is the acting ego and a developing observing ego that strengthens the ego's capacity to inform itself.

Because the ego has the propensity to contract or expand when it is scared, keeping the ego rightsized often depends on compassion accompanying the ego's observations of itself. Without compassion, the ego is prone to either moving into hubris or launching an attack on itself. The move into hubris would be characterized by aggrandizement and pretense, while attacks upon self would be launched by shame, self-ridicule, and disdain.

EGO IMBALANCE

It may be important to see how the ego strengths we just reviewed get unbalanced when they are held by either undersized or oversized egos.

UNDERSIZED EGOS	OVERSIZED EGOS
Don't know what I want	Obsessed with my own desires
Mostly know what others are intending	Only know what I intend
Little or no entitlement to live my intentions and desires	Excessive entitlement
See my life as defined by the choices of others	Focused only on my choices
Live adaptively to the values of others	Obsessed with my own values
Poor boundaries resulting in being easily influenced by others	Poor boundaries resulting in being highly attached to influencing others
Compromised integrity due to an over-attachment to the values of others	Comprised integrity due to an inability to explore diverse values
Limited self-observation due to diminished self-compassion	Limited self-observation due to arrogance compensating for genuine self-compassion

Compromised Integrity

Most of the items in this table appear to be self-explanatory. However, it may help to clarify the references to values. "Compromised integrity due to an overattachment to the values of others" means that it is literally impossible to hold to our integrity while we live the values of others. Integrity means our actual choices directly reflect our personal values, not someone else's values. Our choices and our values are integrated.

Under the heading of Oversized Egos, the condition of being obsessed with my own values typically leaves me rigidly attached to what is important for me, with little or no openness to possibility. Under a different title, I explored the notion of *ethical engagement,* where we remain deeply curious about what values might best apply to a given situation. The price of this kind of curiosity can be a willingness to let go of some value that previously meant a good deal to us.

If we are not open to considering new and different value perspectives the experience of living in integrity may be left a bit suspect. Valuing needs to remain organic, reflecting our emotional maturing, the changing circumstances, and the demands of the times. When we are rigid about our values, we are not allowing ourselves to be moved, inspired, and informed by conditions that call for a deep sensibility to suffering and need. It is not the kind of integrity we would call growthful or in keeping with ethical maturity. The exhortation of this kind of integrity might sound like "I'm going to act this way because I'm right and that's all there is to it."

We compromise our integrity when the values guiding our choices are not open to review and examination. Integrity calls for a discretion that moves us away from being wishy-washy or uncompromising. The price of rigidity is not only an inhibition to our own deepening but also is typically debilitating to building and maintaining rapport with people whose values are different from ours. We lose a curiosity about who we are and who we want to be, and we lose friends and acquaintances by communicating to others that there is our way and their willingness to get with our way.

Trouble with Self-Love

An unbalanced ego remains absorbed in the task of attempting to demonstrate its worth. Typically this happens by getting caught in a relentless obsession with proving we are right. It is as much preoccupied with controlling the process of acquiring temporary relief from self-loathing as it is with getting the relief. It is fixated upon accessing any degree of self-stroking and demonstrating its prowess to do so.

An oversized ego clings to grandiose demonstrations of our alleged greatness. The typical strategies in support of this end include striving to achieve, accompanied by the appropriate opportunities for boasting and soliciting the admiration of others. Other tactics include being highly attached to looking good, sounding good, being impressive, and being special. Of course, the ego fools itself into believing it has the control over these schemes coming to fruition. The truth is that the ego is placing its worth in everyone's hands but our own. After our plans to be impressive are duly implemented, we stand there helplessly waiting for the applause or some other favorable response that we desperately need.

An undersized ego can easily cling to an inner voice echoing sounds of negative self-valuing. This happens when we embrace self-pity, obsessed with self-flagellation and fixated on identifying ourselves as victims. If the ego can't generate positive attention, then it will do its best to secure pernicious attention. The undersized ego will attempt to define itself as *negatively special*. This typically expresses itself in several distinct ways.

The undersized ego gets to be negatively special by:

- **Suffering excessively.** This shows up by defining ourselves as victims of life where we see the choices of others as the force creating our lives. The ego feels entitled to whine and complain about all the awful things happening to it. Victimhood is the first cousin to martyrdom. The martyr ego denies its limits, suffering the consequences of self-neglect.

- **Indulging in being burdened by the attention given to others' needs.** For the martyr, self-neglect becomes a hallmark of dark value. The ego abhors seeing itself as ordinary and will gladly shower itself in negative energy. "Get control" is the imperative of the ego, meaning get control of any form of self-absorption, positive or negative.

- **Describing transgressions in grandiose terms.** The wrongs of the undersized ego are too large to be forgiven, for they are exceptional in nature. This same grand posturing often occurs when an undersized ego becomes psychologically wounded. "I'm damaged goods!" "I'll never be able to heal the atrocities enacted upon me!" "What happened to me has left me incapable of leading a meaningful life!" These reflect a few of the cries of the undersized ego as it views its childhood injuries.

- **Practicing false modesty.** This is another negative strategy of the undersized ego attempting to generate worth. The voice of false modesty incessantly minimizes its contributions, talents, and importance. "I'm not sure I can do this." (When in reality the person possesses some real expertise in the area.) "It was nothing. Anyone could have done what I did." (The truth being that the person made a uniquely valuable offering.) These self-diminishing utterances are often accompanied by excessive praise of others. The falsely modest are susceptible to deferring acknowledgment of their gifts to others, as they wait patiently for people to see their skills and their contributions. Of course, the falsely modest are prone to resentment as their expected recognition is delayed.

Before exploring how we can creatively approach downsizing our egos, it may be helpful to cite how our culture interferes with ego downsizing.

MANDATING OVERSIZED EGOS

There are at least seven significant ways in which our culture interferes with downsizing the ego, therefore providing us with several severe hazards regarding the downsizing process.

Preoccupation with Heroism

Our culture adores heroic efforts that help us to maintain the illusion that life can be conquered in a single bound. We get obsessed with identifying with sports heroes, movie stars, entertainers, and television celebrities. We vault ourselves into a magical relationship with these enchanting figures, hoping to gain some reprieve from the insecurities of everyday life. Recently, while checking into a local airport, a clerk announced that Susan Sheridan and Robert De Niro were spotted heading to a nearby movie set. The clerk looked like a child who had seen Santa, wearing an exuberant smile on her face that seemed to reaffirm her faith in life itself.

Attachment to Living in the Future or Past, Not in the Present

Our culture's favorite time zone is the future, and that is typically where an oversized ego wants to reside. Our culture has a thing for busyness and speed and an attachment to the thinking that we do not have to experience the inherent insecurities of life. Of course, all emotions are felt in the moment, hence the hope that rushing, moving quickly in any way will usher us out of our encounters with frightening emotions. Also, the only place we can be really moved and hurt is in the present where fate (all that is out of our control) can have its way with us.

Intolerance of Mystery

Culture adheres to the belief that science and technology can penetrate all mystery, insulating us from our fears of the unknown. This thinking encourages us to puff up our intellect, blanketing us in the illusion that our anxieties can be put to rest, reassuring us that there is no need to feel lost and bewildered. Answers are on their way. Of course, the dilemma is that a rightsized ego is devoted to making real peace with being lost.

PATH OF THE NOVICE MYSTIC

Promotion of Pretense

Our culture appreciates good theater and anyone effectively masquerading with an oversized ego gets the applause. Authenticity is not valued. To be in the presence of what's authentic might place pressure upon us to also get real when we have to face some insecurity or sadness. We accept the masquerade of inflated ego because it exempts us from having to face life on life's terms or getting straight with ourselves. We comfort ourselves with pretentious displays of bravado, cleverness, and flamboyant spectacles that help run adrenaline through our veins, which distracts us from whatever we deem uncomfortable.

Encouraging Protesting Life

A persistent social invitation is that life is supposed to be happy, painless, and fun. And when it's not, we should posture ourselves as children who are not getting their way, pouting and brooding about the unfavorable circumstances that have descended upon us. If things are not going our way, feel free to protest the situation and get on the Internet for a product or service that will restore tranquility to your life. This kind of guidance reinforces the belief that our egos are certainly larger than life and if fate is presenting something troublesome, we can choose to forget the possibility that acceptance may not only serve us, but possibly empower us as well.

Idolizing Satisfaction

A popular cultural credo is that we should be constantly satisfied, with our every desire and wish being met. If satisfaction is eluding us, then society's voice suggests that our dissatisfaction or longing is due to our ignorance, weakness, or our simply not being good enough to get what we want. Delayed gratification allegedly reflects a loser who is not capable of dealing with life effectively. Longing has no place among the finer components of one's psychological repertoire. However, the following poem on longing from John O'Donohue may help to deepen our understanding of the role of longing in rightsizing our egos:

For Longing

Blessed be the longing that brought you here
and quickens your soul with wonder.

May you have the courage to listen to the voice of desire
that disturbs you when you have settled for something safe.

May you have the wisdom to enter generously into your own unease.
To discover the new direction your longing wants you to take.

May the forms of your belonging—in love, creativity, and friendship—
be equal to the grandeur and the call of your soul.

May the one you long for long for you.

May your dreams gradually reveal the destination of your desire.

May a secret Providence guide your thought and nurture your feeling.

May your mind inhabit your life with the sureness with which your
body inhabits the world.

May your heart never be haunted by ghost-structures of old damage.
May you come to accept your longing as divine urgency.

May you know the urgency with which God longs for you.[32]

"May you have the courage to listen to the voice of desire that disturbs you when you have settled for something safe. May you have the wisdom to enter generously into your own unease." O'Donohue invites us into a deeper story of desire, one not burdened by an attachment to immediate gratification. It will likely be disturbing when we are called to where we have never been before. The unease experienced by the distance separating us from satisfaction may possess a voice that tells us who we were meant to be. This unease may be a herald summoning us away from the comfort of convention that no longer feeds our evolving uniqueness.

We may have been living much smaller than we are. This can be especially true for an ego that has been taking up residency in a very small house. As we begin to hold a vision of possibility, living life more adventurously, taking more risks, being clearer about what we want and what we want to offer others, the tension of holding longing may be contractions of the soul preparing to birth itself in a new way.

Skewed Vision of Confidence

Our culture reveres an ego obsessed with declaring its own grandeur. That is, we live with a fundamental confusion about what constitutes ego strength. We believe an ego that compulsively parades its colors indicates real confidence. An old meaning of the word *confidence* is *trustful*. An ego preoccupied with self-renewal is not energized by trust, but rather energized by compensation. Outside of an attachment to its own preeminence, it holds little or no trust in its essential worth or a deservedness to be loved by others. Hence, the ego can be condemned to compensating for authentic self-valuing by either inflating its positive or its negative traits.

Self-Trust

It may be that the cultural norm for undertaking confidence is so skewed that our thinking has drifted far from an authentic undertaking of developing self-trust. We can say that we trust ourselves when we hold two beliefs:

1. We believe that we allow ourselves to know our own truths.

2. We believe that we will be kind to ourselves, offering compassion for our choices, especially our mistakes.

Creating self-trust is a lifetime work. Knowing our own truths is a challenging undertaking. It encompasses knowing what we believe, what we feel, what we value, and what we perceive is going on around us. Knowing what we believe calls for the effort of separating from the beliefs and values that impacted and influenced us along the way.

The toil involved in this endeavor is also caused by beliefs and values that are evolving and changing over time. Knowing our feelings or emotions can be difficult because of family and societal criticism about emotions such as fear and anger. Typically, females call their feminine identity into question if they are angry and males jeopardize their identity if they feel scared.

Making consistent offerings of kindness to ourselves is also demanding because we tend to treat ourselves the way we were treated by our parents and other authority figures, with abuse and neglect almost a guarantee. Not only is being kind to ourselves challenging, but also it can be difficult to be mindful of the times we are unkind. Kindness can be expressed in simple acts such as resting when we're tired, eating when we are hungry, asking for support when we need help, and granting ourselves permission to feel the whole range of our emotional lives.

Deepening our capacity for self-trust may be a natural result of committing to rightsizing our egos. In order to move beyond our culture's confusion about grandiosity reflecting strength of ego, we need to introduce a new paradigm regarding the nature of ego. We can think of egos as undersized, oversized, and rightsized, with rightsizing being an honorable life's work. Humility can deepen as we continue to accept our incompleteness with rightsizing, remembering that we are not here to become finished products. However, we can stay committed to ego downsizing as we resist cultural invitations to inflate. We now examine suggestions for ego downsizing.

EGO DOWNSIZING

There are a number of ego downsizing practices we can devote ourselves to, which will open us to a deepened relationship with ourselves and with mystery. I would suggest you focus only on one or two of the following and commit to integrating them into your life. Integration occurs by remaining mindful of the practice, talking about it—especially the challenges presented by focusing on the practice, writing about your experience with the practice, praying for the strength to live the practice, exercising compassion when your attempts at integration do not quite meet your expectations, and noticing with gratitude where the practice took hold in your life.

I recently noticed that my own tendency is to catastrophize when I fall short of implementing a particular practice. My ego was eager to make a big deal about me not getting it quite right. My undersized ego was determined to make my choices especially negative, resisting the idea that I simply stumbled while having an ordinary human experience. My encouragement is to be gentle with implementing these practices. On a very basic level, you will be making a significant shift in your identity. Remember, the ego abhors being ordinary and that's just what these practices are aimed at doing.

Downsizing Practices

- Be willing to be vigilant and honoring about what is out of your control as you learn how to let go.
- Commit to deepening humility by accepting personal limits and asking for help.
- Acknowledge and accept feelings of fear and helplessness.
- Remain devoted to the question "What is life asking of me?"
- Be honest about being lost.
- Minimize a life of drama.

- Remain close to the question "What else is there?" (This is especially important with a propensity for self-righteousness or drawing rigid conclusions.)

- Devote yourself to remaining mindful of a need to influence or impress and interrupting where appropriate.

- Take on the guidance of Rilke's suggestion "Our task is to be defeated by ever larger things."

- Be willing to remain a student of your own vanity and greed. (We can understand vanity as "If I look good enough, then I will be enough" and greed as "If I have enough, then I will be enough.")

- Commit to being a highly effective listener.

- Pray and meditate. (As the Danish philosopher Kierkegaard pointed out, prayer says more about the person praying than the prayer itself—being willing to ask for help. Meditation helps develop an observing ego that deepens our awareness of our ego activity.)

- Develop a faith that the moment is where we are supposed to be.

- Devote to accepting life as insecure, unpredictable, and mysterious.

- Allow for the experience of longing.

- Offer authentic blessings to others.

- Offer genuine expressions of gratitude.

- Resist comparing and contrasting yourself with others.

- Expand mindfulness regarding a need to protest life and learn to interrupt the protest. (This practice is especially important when what is protested is out of your control or the protest simply deepens your feelings of victimhood.)

The Dishwasher

Some thirty-five years ago, I was offered a sizable opportunity to begin learning about protest versus acceptance. My mentor John and I were driving east out of the Genesee Valley where we had just celebrated our friend Henri Nouwen's twentieth anniversary as a priest. The celebration had been held at the Trappist Monastery in the valley. It was a moving time for me as the contemplative energy of the monastery had washed over me for several days. As I gazed out the rear window of our vehicle, the sun was setting behind the bell tower of the monastery.

John and I both carried an abiding respect for the abbott, whom we had finally met after becoming acquainted with him through Henri's letters. I turned to John and said, "If I were a member of that monastery, I think the abbott would make me an adviser to the other monks."

"Oh, I don't think so," roared John.

"Well, what do you think he would have me do?" I asked, hoping his response would remain in keeping with some exalted position.

"He would make you the dishwasher," responded John, with no hint of doubt in his voice.

Convinced that he was simply humoring himself with my inflated vision, I changed the subject, hoping to focus on some topic less injurious to my ego.

Several days after our return home, the dean of the college where I had been teaching philosophy for ten years called me for a meeting with him. Somewhat sheepishly, he pointed out that some budgetary adjustments needed to be made that would impact my position. He went on to explain that I would only be teaching half of my normal class assignment and would become the night administrator. I quickly asked what a night administrator was, and he said the duties included answering the college phone and running any messages to students in classes. He went on to say that it would only be a six-hour schedule, from 4:00 PM to 10:00 PM, four evenings per week, in an attempt to buffer the impact of his news.

I sat there stunned and ready to point out that my philosophy classes typically filled up only fifteen minutes after registration began. I stopped myself from pointing out the popularity of my courses because he was well aware. He made it clear that the decision to alter my job description was not negotiable.

Two weeks later, I reported for duty at the switchboard of the college with my entire being protesting what life had presented to me. How could I go so unappreciated? Didn't the administration understand the value of my teaching? Didn't they understand the loss to students? My ego reeled with cries at the injustice being inflicted upon me as my years of service seemed to go ignored.

I recall taking a message to a student in a literature class who was dumbfounded by the messenger being her philosophy professor. One evening the janitor wandered up to the office where I was stationed. He asked me if I knew how to play backgammon. I told him I did not know how to play and he said he would gladly teach me in the back room, where I could still hear the phone. He added that calls seldom came in after 8:30 PM. And so, every evening at 8:30, I was under the backgammon tutelage of Mike the janitor.

I gradually loosened my grip on feeling like a victim of the system as I recalled John declaring that the abbott would have made me the dishwasher. Two days after his comment, I was basically made the dishwasher. Had John's comment been a precursor of what life had in store for me? Had the dean operated in the abbott's absence? Was I to simply hone my backgammon skills?

I decided that the college had indeed made me the dishwasher, and that my challenge was to be a student of my dishwashing experience over the next nine months. My first awareness was that my ego had taken refuge in my role as philosophy professor. I was allowing that role to define my worth, which was no longer working as I ran messages to students and lost at backgammon to Mike almost every evening.

I felt called to more simplicity as I greeted evening visitors to the college and listened to Mike's concerns about his daughter. Our gaming became an opportunity for two men, who appeared to have taken two very different paths, to discover the fathering and the loving that they had in common. I saw how much I lived from an attitude of compare and contrast, always evaluating my worth by measuring my accomplishments against other people's. Gradually, I let go of placing my professorial status in some elevated place compared to Mike's. I could see that we were unique men facing similar lessons. For now, Mike was the backgammon guru and I was his student.

And so it went. I learned a bit about letting go of protesting, accepting what life had presented, becoming less attached to a role defining my worth, living with more simplicity, and finally beating Mike at backgammon. Nine months later I left the switchboard and left the college, aware that I had been initiated into learnings that would need to be revisited again and again.

EGO RIGHTSIZING

The psychological task of the mystic is to remain devoted to rightsizing the ego. Egos do not ever get completely rightsized; rather, we can remain devoted to the process with the outcome being an immense arousal of spirit, where we own our gifts and limits while holding a vision of who we can become. The list that follows encompasses the different states of ego that result from interventions made both upon undersized as well as oversized egos. Typically, we all need to make both kinds of adjustments:

- Remaining curious about our own desires and the desires of others.

- Preparing our desires for expression through the development of our intentions as well as remaining curious about the intentions of others.

- Developing feelings of entitlement with discretion, while discerningly supporting the entitlement of others.

- Remaining curious about our own values and the values of others.

- Learning to employ boundaries that support our individuality and safety, while remaining aware of our tendency to try to influence others rather than honor their individuality.

- Living with increased integrity as our choices remain congruent with our values, while remaining open to other perspectives of values.

- Maintaining a devotion to ego observation accompanied by a compassion for what is observed.

The devotion of the novice mystic is to attend to the life of ego, recognizing a need for either inflation or deflation, which opens us to a spiritual path.

IGNITING THE LIGHT

Spirituality eludes us if we insist on pursuing it. Intending such a quest will typically move us farther and farther away from a spiritual path as the needs of a rightsized ego go ignored. If the demands of the undersized ego are neglected, then excessive flights into self-neglect are likely. These self-effacing tendencies will likely be accompanied by a variety of compensatory strategies in order to get needs for recognition and affiliation met.

The undersized ego can spend a lifetime citing examples of how specially negative it is, or constantly trying to get life right, never learning to hold a mistake with a grain of grace. If the distortions of the oversized ego go unattended, then spiritual exhortations of piety will be laced with hypocrisy and self-righteousness. Doomed to a path of perfectionism, limits are denied and rebuked, resulting in emotional exhaustion, which does not allow for a meaningful connection to ourselves or others.

When we are willing to remain gently vigilant about the needs of our egos, we lose the urgency to demonstrate our worth at every turn with either some grandiose accomplishment or by aggrandizing our failures. There is a soft welcome extended to our humanity and a deep arousal of our spiritual lives.

Our culture has wandered a long way from what the authentic spiritual life might look like. We cannot capture such a life by formulating seven steps to the authentic spiritual life. Of course, oversized egos typically like any suggestion that lacks ambiguity. However, it may be an immense injustice to the spiritual life when we reduce it to a recipe aimed at comforting us, rather opening us to the depths of mystery, evoking awe and wonder. I recommend that the following be viewed as bursts of light that can occur when we are willing to attend to rightsizing our egos; an illumination comes from within when we are not excessively burdened by imbalanced egos.

Protest Your Life Less

One of the great gifts we receive from remaining devotional to rightsizing our egos is that we fight with life less and reduce our protests. I want to suggest a particular lens we might use to view our relationship with life. This lens is composed of our will, fate, and our destiny. Our will manifests as intention and action driven by our desire. Fate is everything that is out of our control (i.e., the will of others and all natural phenomena, including what happens in the heavens and on earth). Destiny is the outcome of the dance occurring between our will and fate. For example, our response to how someone treats us constitutes the dance of our will with fate. The outcome of this dance, or the quality of the ensuing rapport with the person, constitutes our destiny.

Typically, the undersized ego brings too little will to the dance with fate, while the oversized ego brings too much will. The undersized ego commonly echoes a protest of life as it feels victimized by fate. This reaction can be seen when we allow the will of others to govern our lives and then complain that we feel controlled by them. The oversized ego launches a protest as it demands more control over the uncontrollable. It refuses to surrender to what is out of its control. Protest begins to subside as the undersized ego exercises more intention, more entitlement, and more will in its affairs. In contrast, the oversized ego protests less as it accepts what is out of its control, which normally shows up as letting go of the lives of others.

It can be helpful to get honest with ourselves about life as presented by fate. Life is insecure, unpredictable, and mysterious. Of course, any acceptance of that definition of life dashes all the heroic gestures of the oversized ego upon the rocks. However, it may be the most authentic account of the journey, an odyssey that calls us to courage, love, humility, and community. Life can be seen as a pilgrimage filled with opportunity to introduce us to ourselves over and over again. We are not meant to get life right, but rather to learn to accept what it shows us, with our eyes wide open, able to see more clearly as the ducking and swinging fists of the fight drop away.

Increase Your Curiosity about Self and Life

Devotion to ego rightsizing frees curiosity. We can risk living the self-examined life when we trust that we will not turn our backs on ourselves when we come across some personal shortcoming. Self-awareness can deepen at an accelerated rate within a context of Agape love.

This offers us a renewed courage to face life on life's terms. With an ego that does not need to portray itself as larger than life, we become more accepting of the immensity of life's mystery. We can face our unknowing with more grace, becoming less demanding of an immediate expertise. We can take our rightful place as students of our own natures and students of life.

Curiosity is a form of longing. It is the way of the seeker. When constricted to our intellects, our egos will likely be the driving force as we affirm ourselves in our knowledge. When it is infused with heart, the rightsized ego frees us to live intimately, living closer to our suffering, our longing, and the love that flows from us and to us. When living intimately, life is experienced as a passionate and demanding lover, arousing Eros at every turn. Nothing affords the novice mystic more opportunity for unity than living intimately.

Knowing and not knowing become so much more than either the acquisition of or the failure to acquire certain information. An inquiry becomes a moment of opportunity to be touched and moved, brought to depths not before traveled. Ego rightsizing moves us away from feeling victimized by life, and like a demanding lover, it wants us to both receive and give as much as possible.

Practice Greater Equanimity

Devotion to rightsizing yields a peace and calm as we spend less time feeling victimized by life or angry about not having more control over our fate. Dramatic reactions are replaced by an ease as we relax into a simplicity that welcomes spiritual awakening. We become more accepting of our unknowing and therefore gifted with questions and eager to breathe in new life: Who am I? Where am I going? Where do I belong? Where is my home? Who accompanies me?

We rest into our curiosities when we remain seekers while still holding faith in the sacredness of the moment. When the present is disturbing, provoking us out of some comfort, we can be mindful that there will inevitably be an opportunity to exercise our will or move into deeper acceptance of what is out of our control. In either case, we will be learning how to be ourselves and live life. Equanimity is preserved when we can say, "I did what I could or I let go and accepted what I could not do."

Heighten Your Peace with Making Mistakes

This peace happens as we move away from the tendency of the undersized ego to make high drama because of a mistake, and let go of the oversized ego's investment to prove it can live a life mistake-free. The devotion to rightsizing ego yields a deepened acceptance of making mistakes and a compassionate recognition of our inevitable incompleteness. Our blunders are not so much experienced as a measure of our disgraceful natures, but simply as a reflection of our humanity. Mistakes become true teachers of not only how to approach certain tasks but also how to treat ourselves and others.

Laugh at Your Own Ego Activity

Rightsizing diminishes the seriousness and the severity of our choices. We are not alive in order to *demonstrate* something, but rather to *be* something. Moving from proving to being is an immense spiritual shift. Proving is not an authentic gift of self-love. It demands that we suit up and prove our worth over and over again, with no respite from the labor of demonstrating our value, rather than simply making an unconditional offering of welcome to ourselves. Permission to be suggests that we are making an offering of Agape love to ourselves.

Offer Agape Love to Yourself and to Others

One of the most unfortunate precepts of contemporary psychotherapy and religious denominations is the incessant encouragement to become better people. Devotion to rightsizing the ego allows us to hold the blessedness of who we are while growing toward becoming who we are meant to be, not who we should be. Sheldon Kopp captures this well in his book *The Hanged Man: Psychotherapy and the Forces of Darkness* when he states, "I am no longer interested in character development as long as that implies in any way that my Buddhahood is not already at hand." Kopp is insisting that his development should not be an expression of pressing on for improvement, but rather a devotion to allow what is already in him to seek to live more fully.

Another way of saying this is that the very best expression of you is here now and you can commit to dropping into deeper levels of yourself—not necessarily better versions of you, but fuller versions of your uniqueness. The refusal to offer unconditional love (Agape) to ourselves may be due to where we come from. Could it be that parents, surrogate parents, and authority figures taught us that their love must be earned? Was such a lesson driven by the fear of elders that they would lose control over us if their love was simply given? It may serve us to remember that our resistance to offer ourselves Agape love is not a statement about our deservedness but rather the result of what we may have been taught.

What we offer ourselves may not necessarily be a prerequisite for what we can offer others. However, what we offer ourselves greatly hastens what we can offer to those around us. If we are trapped in a web of proving our worth, then it is likely that we will invite others to join such a web. It is appropriate for genuine friendship to be crafted from the conditional love of Philia. However, within the context of having chosen a friend for particular character traits, we will have the opportunity to offer Agape love as they fail themselves and us. Unconditional love may be what deepens our capacity to forgive.

Find Your Deepened Capacity to Forgive

With a larger tolerance for making mistakes comes a stronger faculty to forgive ourselves. As we saw earlier, one old meaning of the prefix *for* is *away.* We can think of the word forgive as *away giving* or *giving away*, giving away sin or transgressions. Giving away our own sins is especially important to the undersized ego that wants to make its sins really big. When we forgive ourselves, we are not defining ourselves by our sins. We acknowledge them and step into a larger story involving our gifts and our essential goodness.

With the trust that we are devoted to forgiving ourselves, we will take more risks, we will become more adventurous, live more authentically, ask for what we want, and live with less fear of making a mistake. We are more willing to live with uncertainty and not chastise ourselves for failing to live with a steadfast assuredness, which results in diminished pretense.

When we delay forgiving ourselves or giving away our sins, we run the risk of slipping into overcompensating or working harder at proving we are okay. The key here is to remember that proving our worth is a full-time job that severely hampers our authenticity and our capacity to create a meaningful life. And it is a task that cannot be fully satisfied.

When we arbitrarily refuse to forgive others, we carry toxic energy as resentment, revenge, and hatred. We also more easily fall prey to defining ourselves as someone's victim, as well as succumb to the hold of self-righteousness. More will be said about forgiveness in Chapter 8.

Years ago, an old friend fell in love with a beautiful Parisian woman who was visiting the States. Their relationship flourished and my friend wanted them to exercise a strong commitment to one another with a vision of a common future. The woman resisted entering into such an arrangement, although she appeared to deeply enjoy the company of my friend. Finally, she made it quite clear that she was not available for such a relationship and asked him to bring her to Boston so that she could fly home.

Brokenhearted, my friend was standing next to a viewing window at the airport when suddenly he noticed the plane interrupting its taxi and returning to its original gate. He immediately wondered if the plane was returning his love to him. Filled with hope, he stared at the runway leading to the gate door, and his dreams appeared to come to fruition as she emerged into the terminal. Exuberantly he ran to her with open arms, only to receive a straight arm as she explained how she had decided to fly to Canada, which would allow her to reenter the U.S. with a renewed visa. My friend left the airport with his desperation in tow.

Shortly after this incident occurred, I was telling the story to my mentor, who commented about the amount of disgust he could hear in my voice. I reacted by affirming his perception and my disbelief that a man could act with so much desperation. The elder looked at me and said, "Do you know of anything more human than desperation?"

I sighed, fully aware that I was neither forgiving my friend for his humanity, nor had I ever forgiven myself for my own desperation. In this story, I was not forgiving my friend for what he was doing to himself, rather than for some transgression enacted upon me. But I could not avoid seeing in him a part of me that I strived to banish. My own desperation awaited my forgiveness.

Increase Your Receptivity to Diversity

As our devotion to rightsizing deepens, our need to compare and contrast ourselves to others diminishes, leaving us more accepting of diverse beliefs and values. The undersized ego often fears running into someone with different convictions and life experience, since it easily becomes data supporting one's inferiority. Conversely, the oversized ego can easily slip into a need to dominate and influence anyone who holds different views. The former is obsessively attached to proving its unworthiness, and the latter is locked into demonstrating that its beliefs are the way to go.

Diverse ideologies are frightening because we create the story that only one position is true or correct and that somehow we are more secure by demonstrating that ours is the right one. When this thinking is pushed, we can create the story that the differing ideology will have to prove its superiority by destroying ours, which only results in greater fear and suspicion.

Our commitment to rightsizing strengthens our capacity to witness differing worldviews as representing the same needs as our own. We simply see different ways of making meaning out of life, varying ways for people to feel good about themselves and to protect what they love. The capacity to create community greatly deepens as we experience the ability to welcome difference. We can grow an ability to greet diversity with more grace, stepping into a chance to further understand ourselves and life.

Be More Willing to Take Risks

The best reason to come to this planet is to give a lot and get a lot. Our job is to figure out what we came here to give and what is it we want a lot of. Figuring this out, as well as giving and getting a lot, will mean taking risks. Taking a risk typically means making a choice where consequences are more uncertain than the choices we commonly make. Of course, the ego enjoys taking refuge in the illusion that the consequences of familiar choices are clear and obvious.

The oversized ego also wants to anchor the issue of taking a risk to be simply about figuring out the likely results of a particular decision. Ego comforts itself in believing the only real issue is to be smart enough to accurately assess the likely outcome of a specific choice. As we saw earlier, no one is afraid of taking a risk. What we fear is the harsh treatment we likely will level against ourselves when things don't quite work out. Devotion to ego rightsizing offers us some reassurance that we can take a risk and make a mistake without the fear of launching severe punishment upon ourselves.

Find Less Denial and Drama in Your Emotional Life

Imbalanced egos struggle to have a clear and grounded emotional life. The emotional theme of the oversized ego is denial, with a heavy attachment to not feeling vulnerable, weak, or out of control. The oversized ego is prone to pretending it simply is not having any feelings, because emotions create a sense of feeling out of control, which leads to disassociated states. The undersized ego can also get into denial, especially in the midst of martyrdom. However, under-sizing is prone to dramatization, where emotions swell disproportionately to human experience and lack grounding. Sometimes a tendency to be a victim inflates an emotional experience in order to make a case for the intolerable nature of one's predicament.

Devotion to rightsizing brings more peace with oneself and with life as we struggle less to prove our worth. We indulge less in either large positive or negative testimonies of who we are. Moving toward rightsizing we acquire permission to feel helpless and scared as expressions of our humanity, rather than denying these primitive urges. We come home to the human condition.

Dramatization of our emotions happens as we get caught in the stories of our feelings. If we are hurt by someone, then we can create a story about the wickedness of that person and our need be on guard in their presence. We can easily embellish the story by adding a cosmic dimension whereby we decide that life itself is not trustworthy because of the inevitable hurt that happens. It would be easy to then add a theme of anger as a response to having been placed in this awful predicament.

Dramatization of our emotional lives subsides when we focus on our emo-tions in several specific ways. We can begin a fuller relationship with our emo-tional lives by fostering the belief that having emotions is about being fully alive as a human being. First, it is important to exercise some emotional creativity by being able to feel our emotions, by allowing our breath to connect us to the emotional energy and to bodily sensations of tightness, fluttering, or ache. Secondly, we need to be able to name emotions (e.g., hurt, sadness, fear, anger, joy, guilt, etc.). Thirdly, we should acknowledge the story that is either creating the emotion or being generated by the emotion. The process can run either way. The key here is not to be stuck in some story that either amplifies the feeling or allows us to drift away from feeling. Finally, we need to offer ourselves enough internal and/or external support to feel safe in feeling our emotions.

Internal support might come in the way of committing to deshaming our emotions. Shame is typically an early primitive defense prohibiting our own emotions before someone else ridicules or diminishes us in some way for expressing them. We are talking about deepening our entitlement to being fully human. External support happens as we call for support from those we trust who are also committed to rightsizing and living full emotional lives. Developing internal and external support for an emotional life is especially challenging for the oversized ego, since it enjoys pretending it is never feeling overwhelmed, indulging in the illusion of being comfortably self-reliant.

Experience Sensitivity as a Strength

One of the great offerings received by walking the rightsizing path is that sensitivity is transformed from being a liability to being a strength. The undersized ego typically sees its hurt and pain as a result of its excessive sensitivity rather than mistreatment perpetrated by another. The oversized ego either denies its sensitivity or blames others for its own irritability.

Rightsizing sees sensitivity as a measure of our involvement with life. Our sensitivity then moves out of numb and anesthetized states to being touched and moved. In order to be alive we must allow what is on the outside to penetrate us, such as air and water. And so it is with our hearts. In order to be heartfully alive, we must allow ourselves to be penetrated or touched by love, kindness, cruelty, and innocence. In fact, we might need to allow our hearts to be so touched that we experience a broken heart—a heart that lived with so much that when its contents fell, the heart broke.

When we are moved we lose our identity as stone. We become water flowing eager to move over sloping terrain, finding that place where we will be held. Through our sensitivity we know where the holding happens; we are not confused by seductive overtures or driven to some new place simply because we have not been there before. We flow, become still, and flow again, knowing our belonging, and our belonging knows us. We move with some grace because we are the movement.

Sensitivity reveals the range of texture and hues in our experience. Grays lose their translucent quality and become brightly opalescent. Sensitivity is a herald announcing what is most precious to us. Sensitivity moves us toward ourselves when we have drifted away. It allows us to shed whatever inoculation of numbness we employed to survive the perils of childhood. We know our hurt, we know our likes and dislikes, we know our love, and therefore we know how to live.

Hold Faith and Give Witness to the Sacred Ordinary

The ordinary can become another opportunity for the undersized ego to feel bad about itself, while the inflated ego can experience the ordinary as a call to perform, demonstrate personal value, or be irritated with the boredom of life. For both, the sweetness of life is easily lost. Devotion to rightsizing minimizes comparing ourselves to others or being driven to perform some heroic act. Rightsizing holds a faith in the possibility that the moment may offer the sweetness of the sacred ordinary.

It may be helpful to mention some expressions of the sacred ordinary and its accompanying sweetness: witnessing beauty, creating beauty, offering or receiving an authentic blessing, expressing gratitude, being involved in some tenderness, getting lost in making love, enacting generosity, getting lost in play, having an experience of authentic belonging, being struck with delight, loving and feeling loved, participating in a genuine ritual, living some passion, being present to ourselves, and allowing our imaginations to take us to some form of comfort. A friend recently described his experience of the sacred ordinary's sweetness: "I was baking an apple pie listening to music from the Grateful Dead, and suddenly I began dancing around the kitchen, delighted by my baking and the music."

A key to our relationship with the sacred ordinary is our willingness to cultivate the faith in its sweetness. I recently heard a woman describe her loss as laced with sweetness: "My husband is presently working a long way from home. When I pause, calling to mind and heart his absence, I feel the deep loss of him and the sweetness of our heart connection. On one occasion, I actually could smell him, defying the barrier of the miles."

The deeper the reverence for simplicity, the greater our chances are to experience the sacred ordinary. The moment becomes pregnant with possibility, rather than barren of excitement and distraction. It may be that the present offers us an opportunity to move closer to ourselves, discovering what we feel and want. The appreciation for a single breath may reflect the simplicity guiding us to the sacred ordinary.

Open to Shadow Material

As the ego's exertion to demonstrate and prove its worth subsides, we can open to Shadow Material. It critical to shed any abstraction associated with the idea of Shadow Material. We can think of it as any trait or characteristic of ours that we deem as unacceptable. These features may be what we think of as darker, such as arrogance, lust, jealousy, selfishness, and sloth. However, if we believe someone's acceptance of us may be jeopardized by some positive trait like intelligence, leadership, or ingenuity, then that attribute becomes Shadow Material.

We can see the ever-present shadow in the following excerpt from T.S. Eliot's poem *The Hollow Men*:

Between the idea
And the reality
Between the motion
And the act
Falls the Shadow

Between the conception
And the creation
Between the emotion
And the response
Falls the Shadow

Between the desire
And the spasm
Between the potency
And the existence
Between the essence
And the descent
Falls the Shadow[33]

To say that a characteristic becomes Shadow Material means we deny it by pretending we simply do not possess such a quality. We will typically consider ourselves as not being in possession of any trait that we believe threatens our ability to be accepted and loved. When these denied traits are assigned residence in some forgotten corner of our unconscious, they become restless, seeking the light of day. These unclaimed find their way out of the basement of the unconscious and into the world as we begin seeing others as insensitive, selfish, and judgmental. With self-righteousness on the rise, we separate from others as our criticism and ridicule of them accelerates.

With the ego not so bent upon sanitizing itself, we have more strength to own both the darker and brighter qualities of ourselves. Devotion to rightsizing frees us to let go of possessing an impeccable nature, allowing for a deeper connection to ourselves and others.

Become More Welcoming of the Unknown

The undersized ego runs the risk of depending upon some allegedly authoritative source for clarity as it faces the unknown, while the oversized ego can easily enjoy pretending it knows when it doesn't and dismissing as trivial what it admits it doesn't know. The commitment to rightsizing holds the capacity to delay the gratification of knowing. It takes solace in being a student of life's larger questions, such as one the mythologist Michael Meade asked, "What spiritual errand have I been sent on?"

Meade's question is supported by other curiosities: What do I love? What is life asking of me? What deserves my devotion? What offering do I wish to make and to whom? What sources of light are in my life? How do I relate to good and evil? Maintaining authentic curiosity allows us to maintain an intimate and creative relationship with the unknown.

THE GROUND OF GOOD
AND EVIL

"The spirit of evil is the negation of the life force by fear.
Only boldness can deliver us from fear.
If the risk is not taken, the meaning of life is violated."

—C.G. JUNG

Nothing has plagued, baffled, and gnawed at our human experience as much as our attempts to understand good and evil. We banish, maim, and kill in the name of what is right and wrong. The attitude of the mystic steers clear of either minimizing the challenge of living with the forces of good and evil, or falling prey to clinging to rules and dogma aimed at easing the responsibility and tension of the task. The mystic is called into the mystery of good and evil, understanding the task is not to reveal the essence of these energies, but rather to enter into a kinship with them. Developing such a rapport with these energies hopefully yields deeper levels of peace, reconciliation, and acceptance.

The boldness Jung refers to in the quote suggests that in order to shed some light on good and evil will we need enough courage to allow ourselves to be touched by fears and also to understand our fears while striving to create safety without violence. The greatest fear may be seeing who we really are by noticing where our own darkness dwells.

The mystic accepts the responsibility to respond heartfully when called to life's deeper considerations, such as wondering about where good and evil live. It is the path to greater unity with life and the way to living in larger stories. It may be helpful to review some devoted attempts to journey with the mystery of good and evil.

THE BIBLICAL JOURNEY

Prior to 600 BC, Satan is mentioned only a couple of times in the Old Testament because he plays a trivial role in the human experience. In keeping with the meaning of his name, he is a minor adversary, offering trivial impediments to virtuous living. The name Lucifer means *bringer of light*. How can the darkness of Lucifer bring light? Do we come into a deeper appreciation and understanding of the light because we come to know darkness? Is there a way in which the very existence of darkness calls for light? Does the transformation of darkness happen because we learn to carry it with light? Lastly, does the tension of these two forces actually act as the creative force behind our spiritual development? Is darkness necessary for the death of innocence and the deepening of maturity?

The God of the Israelites, Yahweh, is the Old Testament's source of good and evil. Isaiah 45:5–7: "I am the Lord, and there is no one else . . . I form the light and create darkness: I make peace and create evil; I, the Lord, do all these things." Not until the Book of Job does God begin to release his domain over evil and we see Satan beginning to play a greater role as a member of God's Divine Court as a source of evil. Likewise in Persia, about the same time, the religion of Zorastrianism has the god Ahura Mazda relinquishing his ability to generate evil to his evil brother Angra Mainyu.

What actually led to this split of the holders of good and evil in both cultures? How did it come about that monotheism containing both light and dark discontinued? There are several ways to respond to these curiosities that may help us understand ourselves better.

We can understand the culture of the Israelites as deeply patriarchal, which would likely have a strong influence over their theology, resulting in a strong paternal relationship with Yahweh. Were they no longer willing to tolerate a potentially ruthless father who could rain harm down on them? Were they striving to create a more secure existence with a benevolent God dedicated to the safety and care of his children? Would their struggle against evil now be augmented by an all-powerful and good God? Were they attempting to purify their own lives by placing themselves in association with a completely good God? These questions reflect just how deeply our emotional needs can impact our vision of where good and evil live.

Satan's power appears to grow in the New Testament with the Holy Trinity of the Christians being completely exempt from any form of evil. Did the followers of the all-good Yahweh and the Holy Trinity not only divest their deities, but also themselves, of evil? As exemplified by the Crusades, a kind of sacred Manifest Destiny becomes the norm, whereby we and our God reflect the good, while others and their God are evil. Again, we see this tendency to divorce ourselves and our God from evil while projecting evil onto others.

THE MYSTIC AND THE MYSTERIES OF GOOD AND EVIL

The mystic is asked to remain devotional to the essential mysteries of life, which may include God, love, freedom, beauty, truth, personal power, and good and evil. These ideas or principles maintain a level of secrecy but their essences remain hidden; hence, exercising a devotion to them calls for curiosity, wonder, humility, and courage.

Why should we maintain a devotional relationship to the mysteries of good and evil? One response to the question is that our beliefs about good and evil drive our decisions and actions when we ask: What's the best thing to do? What is the worst alternative? What should I do? What feels right? These are just some of the ways the energies of good and evil live in us. Whether we are actually promoting something good or courting evil, we seem to be built to wonder about what will really serve us.

The more we remain curious about good and evil, the greater the likelihood that we will leave behind our childhood orientations about them, reflected in our obedience, compliance, and denial. It is also less likely that we will act in a cavalier manner about issues of good and evil, which affords us the opportunity to be sensitive to the fertile grounds where goodness and evil each grow. It appears that to some degree our emotional maturation depends upon the development and interest in creating our own values. Under a different title, I have defined *ethical engagement* as the willingness to remain curious about our values and sustain wonder about good and evil and their composting.

Some questions reflecting ethical engagement include: Who will benefit from my action? Will anyone be harmed? What am I willing to sacrifice to make this action happen? Am I willing to explore fears that may have pulled me toward certain values? Am I willing to remain in conversation with those who hold different values from me?

Sustaining a curious and exploratory relationship with our values is a significant way to relate to the inscrutable nature of good and evil. We can think of our values as cherished principles that we believe will bring about the greatest amount of good.

The decision to keep our disabled daughter Sarah home with us for twenty years powerfully impacted my family. My marriage was affected, as were her siblings when they did not receive the attention they needed and deserved. Our moral quandary reflected the predicament of the depth of so many values. Should we institutionalize our child, facing the inevitable drawbacks of institutionalized living? Should we keep her at home with the support and safety of home life, guaranteeing obvious losses for her siblings?

In situations where there is no apparent right answer, we step into the depth of the mystery of goodness. At that point, it takes more courage than knowledge to make a decision. We will not have adequate information in order to make the right decision. Unfortunately, we cannot rely on the facts to support our moral decisions. It will take some opening of heart, possibly an act of compassion, stretching us beyond what is in our personal self-interest.

Finally, being willing to continue to relate to the mysteries of good and evil may be our greatest responsibility. The larger the vision we hold of goodness the more we likely escape the moral confines of personal gain and immediate gratification. The large view may include stewardship for those who come after us. Our choice reflects a reverence for the mystery of unborn generations as we hold the unborn in our hearts.

COMPOSTING THE GROUND OF EVIL

How does the ground of evil grow? What composting yields greater darkness and destruction? Composting happens as microorganisms break down waste into a fiber-rich material composed of nitrogen, phosphorus, and potassium, yielding a natural fertilizer that can enhance growth. We will explore what compost (thinking, feeling, and acting) contributes to the ground where evil can flourish. For example, compost involving the breakdown of deep emotion, empathy, remorse, humility, and the decay of love may fertilize the ground of evil. We think of this fertilizer as darkness, with some examples including divisiveness, the denial of death, self-aggrandizement, extreme narcissism, deceit, and denied anger.

We can understand evil as an energy that invigorates our thinking, our intentions, and our actions toward antilife or the destruction of life. We cannot penetrate the mystery of evil. However, as mystics we can remain curious. In his book *Evil: The Shadow Side of Reality*, John Sanford reminds us: "The worst thing in the world might be to suppose that the problem of evil had been solved on either an intellectual or emotional level. It is better for us to be left wondering . . ."

If we take Sanford's suggestion seriously, then we devote ourselves to allowing various images of dark and light to move our hearts and minds. Again, the challenge may be to avoid either ignoring the issue of darkness or reducing our thinking to a preestablished recipe given to us by some institution. It may be that our most fervent human endeavor is to not eliminate our responsibility to step closer to the mystery of these energies.

In his book *Facing the Dragon*, Robert L. Moore offers some images of evil: "Evil is very much antilife. It is full of hate. It tries to destroy relatedness. It uses deceit, lying, and illusion. In fact, almost all folklore presents evil as deceit and lying and a master of illusion. Evil hates the light, and even loses its power when light is around. Evil cannot stand to be exposed, and it hates human community for that reason. Evil wants to get you alone and isolate you. It also wants to get you in the dark."[34] We will track our progress toward unearthing the ground of evil by employing Moore's images of antilife, deceit, darkness, and illusion.

Denial of Death

In his book, *Escape from Evil* Ernest Becker cites the dilemma:

> That man wants above all to endure and prosper, to achieve
> immortality in some way. Because he knows he is mortal, the
> thing he wants to do most is to deny this mortality. Mortality
> is connected to the natural, animal side of his existence; and
> so man reaches beyond and away from that side. So much so
> that he tries to deny it completely. As soon as man reached
> new historical forms of power, he turned against the animals
> with whom he had previously identified—with a vengeance,
> we now see, because animals embodied what man feared most,
> a nameless and faceless death.[35]

Becker identifies both the intensity of our fear of death and its mystery ("nameless and faceless"). It may help to look further at the relationship between denying our mortality and evil.

Becker suggests that our denial of our mortality separates us from animals and therefore from nature. However, our own bodies are part of nature and therefore we separate from our own bodies. And it is in our bodies that we feel deep sentiment, empathy, sympathy, and compassion. These bodily sensibilities connect us to nature, to others, and to ourselves. And when we go numb in response to our bodies, apathy, disdain, and contempt easily take the place of those warmer energies.

A master of illusion, our fear of mortality typically does not present itself directly, but rather it comes dressed in more insidious attire. I recently experienced a vitreal tear in my left eye. My optometrist suggested I see a retina specialist to make sure there was no retinal involvement in the injury.

I took a seat in an ornamental and spacious waiting room, experiencing some low-grade anxiety regarding the outcome of the upcoming eye exam. Two gentlemen my age sat some fifteen feet behind me, engaged in superficial chat. As they doled out dull bits of innocuous information, my inclination to be silently critical grew exponentially. My review of their gab began to reveal a palpable feeling of self-righteousness.

There was no pause in their conversation and they did not skip a beat, adding one insipid detail after another. I was convinced that they had collaborated to annoy me. As much as I tried to distract myself from my smugness, I was eventually overcome by the conspicuous nature of my puffed-up position. It did not take an unusual act of introspection in order for me to see how my self-righteousness was working hard to separate me from these men.

I began to wonder: Why did I need to distance myself from these men? Was I sitting in a waiting room with an injured eye attempting to be larger than the man I was? Settling into myself with several abdominal breaths, I began to feel the fear of my mortality quivering in my gut as pangs of vulnerability and fragility. I wanted to transcend my status as a fragile man with a damaged eye. I began to understand my need to distance myself from others with eye impairments.

My lack of acceptance of my fragility vaulted me to a more auspicious station where I was allegedly more articulate and brighter than the gentlemen behind me. Fear of mortality, cloaked in feelings of vulnerability and fragility, were driving me away from my fellow man and from myself. I was willing to take refuge in the illusion that I was not feeling fragile, lying about my vulnerability, and sitting with an antilife attitude toward my fellow injured eye sojourners.

Physical, emotional, and sexual hurt in childhood can be toxic material contributing to the ground of evil. The human psyche is amazingly resolute, giving it a tenacious capacity to persevere. The psyche's fragile vulnerability shows itself it its intolerance of feeling powerless, unable to do anything about the hurt being inflicted. It is the psyche's loss of power that is deeply wounding. In *Power and Innocence* Rolo May says, "The need for potency, which is another way of phrasing the struggle for self-esteem, is common to us all."

Deep early injuries created by abuse or neglect have the ability to influence our construction of a belief system in regard to power. Two major themes can be: 1) Love and kindness will not come my way and 2) I must not allow myself to be vulnerable and victimized. A subtler corollary to these themes is "It is too dangerous to offer compassion to others because I will need to open my heart to do so, which leaves me vulnerable." The only power alternative left is to be the perpetrator of injury. From that position, we are neither excessively vulnerable nor are we impotent. We can at least create harm! Being destructive allows us to attach to the illusion that we are not powerless and to lie about our helplessness.

Untethered Anger

Uncontrolled anger easily slips into being expressed violently. The violation generated by this anger can happen physically and/or emotionally. Anytime a person experiences his or her physical boundaries being encroached upon, some level of physical boundary violation is taking place. This can happen with everything from tickling to producing bodily injury. Emotional violations occur when the verbal content of a message demeans, ridicules, and diminishes the character of the recipient. Emotional violations also happen when the intensity or loudness of the message carries an energy of disgust and belittlement.

Uncontrolled anger typically transpires when we deny feelings of frustration, hurt, or fear, favoring the more comfortable feeling of unleashed anger or rage. The fire and ferocity of this kind of anger is meant to circumvent the more vulnerable feelings mentioned earlier. The message from the person raging is "Somebody here is going to feel vulnerable and it's not going to be me."

However, uncontrolled anger easily morphs into violence. The fire of untethered anger can be seen as another component of the compost where evil can grow.

Denied Anger

In an attempt to cope with uncontrolled anger, a natural response is to deny its existence. Anger is also a natural response to feeling violated. However, it is common to compensate when we attempt to prevent violent expressions of anger, which can result in repression. Denied anger can easily become rich compost for the germination of evil and is much more subtle and difficult to identify.

According to James Hollis, author of *Why Good People Do Bad Things*, "Although each person, and each society, is charged with how anger is to be appropriately channeled, the denial of anger, or its continuous repression, is a deep source of our psychopathology and will invariably seek its expression in a less healthful fashion."[36]

There are numerous examples of serial killers who when captured are described by family members and neighbors as "soft spoken," "quiet," "no trouble," or "cooperative." Could such descriptions describe individuals who are experiencing repressed anger bubbling like molten lava preparing to erupt? The explosion of repressed anger could have a less violent expression, and yet still be harmful, especially to those closest to us. Many acts of abuse likely result from repressed anger.

Another common expression of denied anger is passive aggression where anger is expressed unconsciously. No less hurtful to the recipient, acts such as procrastination, broken agreements, forgetting promises, withholding sex and love, and withholding valuable information are common expressions of passive aggression. Another manifestation of passive aggression is the act of inviting others into a liaison or relationship where they either do not belong or there is no real intention to consummate.

Jennifer, a teacher of second graders, returned from her high school reunion reporting that she had met a really nice guy whom she had dated several times.

"I met Jim at the reunion and we went out a couple of times. He called me almost every day. I really enjoyed his company and we appeared to be getting along quite well. When I explained that my parents were coming to town and I wanted him to meet them, he explained sheepishly, 'I won't be able to do that; I'm married.'"

These cold, quiet demonstrations of anger often leave recipients feeling frustrated, angry, hurt, and taken hostage. When we are not in touch with our anger, we are lying about who we are, deceiving others, living in the illusion that all is harmonious with us, while fostering antilife or destructive behavior.

Steve, a forty-five-year-old engineer who is quiet, polite, considerate, and sensitive, was struggling with his sexuality. He came with his wife, Nancy, to a number of consecutive sessions lamenting his anxiety about pursuing his wife sexually.

"I just can't imagine feeling comfortable pursuing Nancy," he reported with a sigh of regret.

"Sounds like it is difficult for you to get beyond the anxiety and make contact with Nancy," I reflected.

"Yeah, it's just too much, and I don't have a good body image," he said with a note of complete defeat.

"How are you doing with your sexual life being on pause?" I asked Nancy.

"Well, it's really frustrating. I can take care of my own needs, but I would really like a normal sex life," she added.

"Is there any other impact that Steve's sexual inertia might have on you?"

"Well, I don't feel desirable or lovable. I certainly don't feel pretty," Nancy said, with tears streaming down her cheeks.

I encouraged Steve to note the impact his sexual withholding was having on his wife. It took a number of sessions before he began to address his anger at women. He detailed being mistreated by two older sisters and a mother who did nothing about it. Steve discovered that he wasn't as anxious as he was angry.

Forgetting About the Journey

When we forget about the journey, we inevitably forget who we are and envelop ourselves in illusion. We forget about the journey when we generate the deception that life is secure, predictable, and fundamentally understandable. We then believe we can create some formula that will make us immune to life's challenges. These recipes tend to inflate the intellect, as we convince ourselves that earnest reflection will inevitably penetrate the mysteries of life. Unfortunately, one way our culture colludes with our illusion is by promising security and happiness by purchasing some product. Typically, more technologically advanced commodities hold the promise of greater protection from life's hardships.

When we live by embracing the illusion that life is secure based on our latest purchase, we begin masquerading as someone traveling such a journey. There are several significant implications of turning life into a costume party.

The first is that we will likely modify our beliefs and perceptions in order to accommodate our skewed understanding of life. We run the risk of generating an evolving set of distortions. No longer living on life's terms, we pretend life will actually be willing to cooperate with our scripting it. Such a move reminds me of a statement I heard from a colleague: "I didn't stop playing God until I was sixty," which suggested that he erroneously believed that he had understanding of and control over much more than he actually did.

The most popular set of beliefs is a contraction of reality, where we make life much smaller than it is, willing to sacrifice depth and meaning. Fear of life being too insecure, too mysterious, and too big typically guides the contracted script. Reality is reduced to innocuous data and rigid roles that are easily discernable. The superficiality of this approach to life can be palpable to the listener as endless descriptions of what was said, what was done, and what was experienced are reduced to perfunctory information signifying little or nothing. When I listen closely to the unsaid, I hear, "Life is too big and overwhelming; I'll make it smaller."

Here is an example of the use of a contracted script. Marie is a fifty-two-year-old social worker who was exploring being a first-time home buyer.

"I recently visited this really neat, old Victorian house that is for sale. It has lots of windows and was built in 1910. The original owner was a physician who had his office in the house. The office space isn't as warm as the rest of the house but it would provide me with the space I need. I think that room faces north, or maybe northeast. When I went out on the porch, I saw hundreds of grasshoppers. One was on my shoe. I didn't know what to make of the grasshoppers but I knew it meant something. The house needs some work and I can't tell if the owner is willing to address what needs attention. He said we might be able to do something together in order to address the draining issue in back of the house."

More data filled the airways in this conversation. After exercising some tolerance, I said, "Marie, is your truth that you are feeling anxious as a first-time home buyer?"

She emphatically confirmed my perception and I could see she was attempting to take sanctuary in minutia, hoping her anxiety and the large question about the wisdom of the purchase might go away. The reduction of the contracted lens is meant to avoid big feelings like fear, anxiety, grief, and hurt, as well as eliminate big questions related to change, freedom, failure, success, risk, courage, accountability, death, love, and myriad other agendas reflecting the mystery and immensity of life. Our scaled-down versions of life place us at great risk to collude with acts of cruelty and brutality. When we define ourselves as unwilling to acknowledge the actual size of human events, we contribute to the compost of evil by denying that such things are possible.

However, this psychic downsizing typically generates anxiety as the psyche protests being forced into distorted accounts of reality. When we undersize ourselves by taking sanctuary in minutia, we can end up living with an unbearable tension that contracts and contorts our creative energies. The response to this tension is typically some form of depression as an attempt to quell the endless vibrations.

We may also cling to an expanded set of beliefs in which we strive to sanitize life's challenges by inflating ourselves and our beliefs to magical proportions. Here we live in the dream hoping to avoid the utter insecurity of life, where we are immune to life's harshness. Some examples might include: "I know it's just a matter of time before I win the lottery." "When I meet the right person, I'll know true happiness." "If I exercise regularly and take my supplements, I won't get sick." "I just need to love people right and they won't hurt me." "As long as I keep working hard, everything will be fine." "As long as I continue to contribute to my investment fund, my family and I will be in good shape." "Now that we live in the right neighborhood, my kid will turn out all right."

Whether living from a contracted set of beliefs or an expanded set, we inevitably run into impediments. As C.G. Jung suggested, "Life will present many hidden perils." Once we refuse to believe that we are folks traveling a journey with many hidden perils, several significant elements of compost are added to the ground of evil. The first is that we may turn against ourselves, with critical judgments for not getting life right—as if that were possible. Our self-abuse can easily wash over to mistreating others. A second component of compost is denial, where we simply do not accept anything that does not correspond to our beliefs. It becomes quite easy to dismiss the beliefs and values of others when they present some threat to our views. The dismissal can even translate into war.

A third ingredient is scapegoating others. This reaction is guided by the need to blame someone or some group for our script not working out. Per author M. Scott Peck in his book *People of the Lie: The Hope for Healing Human Evil*, "Evil was defined as the use of power to destroy the spiritual growth of others for the purpose of defending and preserving the integrity of our own sick selves. In short, it is scapegoating." We entitle ourselves to cruelly treat some designated person or group, blaming them for the mayhem in our lives due to the distortions created by contracted and expanded scripts of reality.

Finally, if our denial fails to hold back the incongruity between reality and our versions of reality, we may lose faith in life. When our resolve to cope creatively with disillusionment and disappointment erodes because of being hurt or betrayed, our loss of faith may be the result. Sometimes the loss is temporary as we grieve the death of some loyalty or trust we held for someone. As Erich Fromm points out in *The Heart of Man*, "But it doesn't make much difference whether it is faith in a person or God, which is shattered. It is always the faith in life, in the possibility of trusting it, of having confidence in it, which is broken." This broken faith and confidence can easily breed irreverence for others and for nature.

As our faith in life is ruptured, we turn away from loving, productive ways of relating to life. The ego abhors powerlessness. We can readily turn to destructive ways to empower ourselves. A loss of faith easily transforms into *necro-philia* or an attachment to death, as we seek to dominate and control. The love of death is facilitated by an ability to inhibit and destroy life. This necro-philia orientation does not have to be expressed in grandiose proportions as reflected by Hitler and Stalin.

We often offer one another subtle invitations to step away from life: "I know you really love horseback riding, but you might get hurt." "You spend a lot of time writing that manuscript; do you really think a publisher will pick it up?" "What will you ever do with a degree in philosophy?" "Do you really want to get into having to write a dissertation?" "Do you actually believe she will want to go out with you?" "Are sure you are qualified enough to apply for that job?" "How will you ever fit in taking dance classes when you have three kids?"

Necro-philia is alive and well in the many invitations we offer one another to step away from some risk, to ignore some undeveloped skill, to let go of deepening our knowledge base, and to stop planning to embark on some adventure. We beckon one another to fall back on ourselves in fear of failing, acting foolish, or wasting time and energy.

Denied Shame

As a culture, we are quite confused about the difference between shame and accountability. Shame strips us of our essential worth. We typically employ shame as a way to approach issues of responsibility. When we shame we attack a person's character. Examples of shaming voices include "You're very stupid!" "You're very insensitive!" "You never think of others!" "You're incredibly selfish."

When children are raised with these shaming voices of authority figures, the external voices become internalized. We may not know we are feeling shame, but the coping mechanisms aimed at helping us deal with the shame are activated. In his seminal work, *Shame*, Gershen Kaufman explains a series of strategies aimed at helping us to avoid feeling shame. Rage, blame, and contempt are ways to distance and criticize others before they have the opportunity to hurl disparaging remarks in our direction.

Kaufman says, "Striving for power or control is another defense employed in an attempt to compensate for the defensiveness which underlies internalized shame." He goes on to point out that "internal withdrawal" is another way to distance, where we are hoping to gain some immunity from the critical gaze of others, which cannot be tolerated while living in the suffocating grip of shame. However, internal withdrawal inhibits and can sabotage collaborative problem solving, decision making, and emotional intimacy. Kaufman suggests that "perfectionism" is a compensation for shame, as we attempt to exonerate our debilitating sense of self with grandiose expectations. However, such striving is doomed to failure and contributes to a feeling of self-loathing.

When cloaked in shame, our self-worth is quickly eroded. When accountability has traveled in tandem with shame, the ability to be accountable quickly erodes. This debilitation prevents us from offering a shameless account of our actions. Such an account would include our motivation, any anticipation regarding possible outcomes, an awareness of who might be adversely impacted, how we feel in retrospect, and a willingness to offer restitution where possible. Denied shame leads to excuses, blame for others, distraction from the action in question, and denial that anything unfavorable has occurred.

Once denial of shame is a cornerstone of our psyches, it can hurl us into a life of pretense. Denial of shame weaves its way into denying other aspects of our character. We can begin pretending we know certain information or make believe we are in possession of certain competencies that we never acquired. When we deem it appropriate, we can even feign experiencing certain positive feeling states. A serious price of denied shame can be the erosion of our authenticity. M. Scott Peck notes, "Naturally, since it is designed to hide its opposite, the pretense chosen by evil is most commonly the pretense of love."

The more we run from the diminishing impact of our denied shame, the more we run the risk of attempting to shine by pretending to carry a host of applaudable characteristics. The greater our attachment to pretense the more counterfeit our personalities become. We can easily become so comfortable with our fraudulence that we no longer can easily distinguish our shine from our reality, with a growing insensitivity to the impact our façade has upon others. Internal withdrawal, rage, contempt, blame, perfectionism, domination, diminished capacity for accountability, and pretense are rich compost for the expansion of evil.

James, a forty-two-year-old landscaper, initially came to see me because of marital difficulty. Our relationship had reached a comfortable rapport and James was willing to disclose an array of life challenges he faced in childhood, as well as currently.

"I don't know why I keep thinking about my membership in this motorcycle club, which I never really wanted to belong to anyway," he recounted, tilting his head, lifting his eyebrows and shrugging his shoulders.

"Tell me what happened."

"Well, I joined this motorcycle club several months ago. I was the least-experienced rider in the club, which made me feel like shit."

"How did you handle feeling like that?" I asked, assuming I knew what feeling like shit meant.

"I made up a bunch of stories about my North American trips and even created an international motorcycle trip with wild stories about my adventures in North Africa," he said, with both a shyness and a gleam in his eyes suggesting some pride in the creative nature of his narratives.

"How did your stories go over with the guys in the club?"

"Initially great, but after my third accident and the guys noticing how I felt tentative on wet pavement, they began harassing me about my stories."

"How did you feel about their reaction?"

"I started feeling bad. Then I decided they were a bunch of jerks anyway."

"Did you stay in the club?"

"No, I left. I had no interest in hanging out with those guys. What do they know about motorcycling anyway?" he added, lifting his chin and closing his eyes.

There are several noteworthy aspects of James's story. The first is the shame he felt about being a novice motorcyclist. He deals with his shame through pretense and lying about his experience. He begins relating the story about his membership in the club saying he is confused about why he would still be thinking about an experience that is not worthy of further consideration.

It took some significant commitment on James's part to finally own his shame and understand the pretense, deceit, and illusion resulting from denied shame. He was eventually able to see that his castigation of the members of the club added to the illusion of their incompetency, which he'd needed in order to massage the shame produced by his lying.

ARRESTED DEVELOPMENT

In *Dare to Grow Up: Learn to Become Who You Are Meant to Be*, I discussed the ancient meaning of the word *maturity*, which means *at its proper time*. Our development is not entirely natural because we depend greatly upon nurturance, encouragement, and guidance at key times in order to grow. The good news is that the psyche is malleable enough to acquire, along the way, what it did not originally receive. We can think of our development as a lifelong task, marked by a devotion to remain self-examining. A lack of such devotion leads to arrested development.

There are a number of significant benchmarks indicating that our development is being ignored. Not taking responsibility for our emotional intelligence is one example. When this is happening, we do not possess an evolving competency to feel emotional energy in our bodies, such as tightness, aches, and forms of aroused energy moving through us like excitement and disgust. We cannot name energies such as sadness, anger, hurt, joy, and fear and are unable to talk about them. We do not know how to modulate these energies. We either inflate them into some melodramatic presentation or repress them, in an attempt to deny their existence.

Arrested development is often reflected by the ineffective employment of emotional boundaries, in which we disable our attempts at keeping our individual beliefs, feelings, and preferences while allowing for the unique views of others. The most significant emotional skill we lack may be the ability to offer compassion to ourselves and to others, because we are unable to track our tendencies toward self-loathing and self-righteousness and their consequences. Living in integrity, where our behaviors reflect our values and our heart's desire, can be significantly diminished or lost in delayed development.

It would be only too easy to ascribe arrested development to some marginalized segment of the population whose psychological brokenness appears to prohibit the deepening of emotional maturation. The devoted mystic remains mindful of being regularly visited by the depths of the unknown. When we can summon an acceptance of how limited our comprehension is in the face of life's mystery, we may be able to grasp the need to vigilantly renew our development. Hence, we are not developed; we are either facilitating our development or resisting it. It may be more accurate to say that arrested self-examination leads to arrested development, which contributes to the compost of evil.

Family and society will inevitably call us into small stories of self-accountability, love, generosity, personal empowerment, freedom, and forgiveness. When we do not receive such invitations, our development has been impeded. Key to this discussion is how these impediments can separate us from the light and move us toward the ground of evil. In his book *Why Good People Do Bad Things*, James Hollis notes:

> While it is true that we occasionally reach that high promontory, we are not strong enough to remain there. For example, who among us can consistently address our own emotional needs in a mature way? Who among us can fully assume the task of self-worth and not expect our partners to be an uncritical cheering section? Who among us will not retaliate when the Other lets us down? Who among us can really take responsibility for our emotional well-being and wholly lift it off of our partners? And yet, those are the tasks of maturity, from whence comes the quality of all our relationships.[37]

As Hollis points out, we do not attain a state of full development; rather, we are condemned to developing. Our only choice is whether we will remain apprentices of the human condition and be willing to live a self-examined life.

When we suspend our devotion to remain self-examining, it can become exceedingly difficult to understand who we are and how our behavior impacts others. We run a higher risk of reacting, rather than responding in ways that enable us to take care of ourselves as well as build our rapport with others. Only when there is some understanding of our emotions, desires, and the stories we create about others are we able to remain relatively intimate with others and ourselves.

The more we feel confused about our own authentic needs, the less able we are to generate meaningful relationships, and the more we tend to withdraw into isolation. When we are emotionally separated, we lose a capacity for empathy, the ability to be collaborative, solve problems, and make decisions with others. It is only too easy at that point to fall prey to cynicism and a loss of faith in life. The more disconnected we become from others, the easier it is to objectify them, forgetting they are part of a family, longing to be loved, dreaming their own dream, and walking this journey of life and death with us.

Another serious danger of not paying attention to our development is amorality, a state typically ascribed to children, where personal values have not yet been constructed. However, if we do not take the clarification of our own values seriously, we can neither understand their impact upon our behavior nor enter into a meaningful conversation about right and wrong. The most significant implication of amorality is the ease it presents in colluding with evil. If we do not know our values, it becomes difficult to identify insidious expressions of darkness that may be close by. We miss subtle forms of manipulation, deceit, rationalization, scapegoating, bullying, sexism, and racism. We may even miss gross acts of darkness such as our neighbors disappearing, similar to what happened in Jewish neighborhoods in Germany during the reign of the Third Reich.

The unexamined life tends to keep the corrosive impact of self-loathing concealed behind a veil of denial. We do not allow ourselves to know how we really feel about ourselves. As we refuse to accept the ordinariness of our humanity, admonishing our mistakes and shortcomings, we create an adversarial relationship with our own souls. As Robert Moore says in his book *Facing the Dragon*: "The enemy is that unconscious grandiosity within us that constantly tries to persuade us to forget our limits and forget that we need help, to forget that we need others, or as the Native Americans are able to say, to forget that we are all related and all one family."[38]

Moore suggests that it can be easy to wander away from a deep acceptance of who we are. He reminds us that it is only too easy to compensate with an attachment to grandiosity in order to cope with a painful self-deprecation. From the place of alleged grandness, we begin separating from our own limitations and separating from others. We can easily take on the identity of a renegade divested of any responsibility for the family of humanity. It is this kind of divisiveness that diminishes our relatedness to others, contributing to the ground of evil.

Emotional Incest

A profound act of arrested development can occur when a man unconsciously lives out an emotionally incestuous relationship with his mother. This kind of maternal relationship typically happens when the mother prioritizes the son as the central resource for her emotional needs. He becomes the person she feels safe giving to, deepening rapport and trust with, and possibly even using as a confidant. If she is emotionally estranged from her spouse or is a single parent, the likelihood of an emotionally incestuous connection to her son rises. The following is a passage by Erich Fromm from his book *The Heart of Man*:

> Yet man also knows more or less clearly that the lost paradise cannot be found; that he is condemned to live with uncertainty and risks; that he has to rely on his own efforts, and that only the full development of his powers can give him a modicum of strength and fearlessness. Thus he is torn between two tendencies since the moment of his birth: one, to emerge to the light and the other to regress to the womb; one for adventure and the other for protection and dependence.[39]

Emotionally incestuous messages include: "A long as you are connected to me, you'll be loved and safe." "I will make sure your needs are met." "You don't need to take risks." "Connected to me you are immune from failure." "When you have questions, I will provide answers." "You are my world, the source of my fulfillment and happiness."

Being caught in the web of emotional incest can leave a man emotionally disabled. The disability shows itself in several important ways, some of which will likely be more obvious. The first is a deep level of passivity as a man waits to be saved by another maternal figure. This lack of action can wrongly be diagnosed as depression. However, this passivity is symbolic of womb-life where there is no need to summon one's own life forces.

This inertia is commonly accompanied by a belief in one's own incompetence and impotency. Again, deep feelings of powerlessness can easily lead to abuses of power, where acting destructively is preferred to the feeling of unbearable helplessness. The womb-like existence has an antilife flavor or necro-philia. This death orientation can deeply inhibit a man from getting behind the promotion of life and creativity.

The second impairment is a level of narcissism, coming from "My mother told me I was central to her life. She was happiest when we were interacting. I know I'm okay when I'm treated as central." A heavy dose of narcissism obstructs the development of empathy and a general ability to relate to the diverse values and beliefs of others. Narcissism is isolating with an excessive preoccupation with self. It separates us from the rest of the world.

The third debilitating impact of emotional incest is a dependency that can easily generate anger toward women. This anger can express itself as domestic violence, sarcasm, ridicule, withholding affection and sex, condescension, or a cold passive distancing that emotionally isolates a woman. The anger and accompanying hostility are a compensation for a revolting sense of impotency.

Cultural Definition of Manhood

The most striking expression of arrested development is our culture's definition of manhood, which is alarmingly similar to Robert Hare's description of psychopaths. In his book *Without Conscience,* Hare outlines a number of characteristics that point toward the possibility of a psychopathic diagnosis. The suggestion here is not that all men are psychopaths, but rather that we need to clarify how our culture envisions manhood and the contribution of that version of manhood to the ground of evil.

In 1976, in his book *Hazards of Being Male*, Herb Goldberg warned of a cultural undermining of male development:

> Unlike some of the problems of women, the problems of men
> are not readily changed through legislation. The male has no
> apparent and clearly defined targets against which he can vent
> his rage. Yet he is oppressed by the cultural pressures that have
> denied him his feelings, by the mythology of the woman and
> the distorted and self-destructive way he sees and relates to her,
> by the urgency for him to "act like a man" which blocks his
> ability to respond to his inner promptings both emotionally
> and physiologically, and by a generalized self-hate that causes
> him to feel comfortable only when he is functioning well in
> harness, not when he lives for joy and for personal growth.[40]

Unfortunately, Goldberg's insightful admonition mostly went unheeded.

"Psychopaths seem to suffer a kind of emotional poverty that limits the range and depth of their feeling."[41] We live with a strong societal injunction against men expressing a depth and range of feeling. Real men, as our culture has it, can either be angry or leap with excitement and jubilance—but only at athletic events. This withering of range and depth has numerous implications when we're attempting to understand the ground of evil.

"Psychopaths have an ongoing and excessive need for excitement—they long to live in the fast lane or on the edge where the action is. In many cases this involves breaking the rules."[42] Similarly, when a man's emotional life is limited to anger and excitement, he runs a high risk of indulging in acts of aggression and unlawful behaviors as a way to live out the compressed nature of his feelings. We ask, "How could Bernie Madoff abscond with millions of dollars from the retirement funds belonging to many families?"

"Psychopaths are often witty and articulate. They can be amusing and entertaining conversationalists, ready with a quick and clever comeback, and can tell unlikely but convincing stories that cast them in a good light."[43] He describes the psychopath as glib and superficial. I recall a conversation—or a monologue—that was taking place among six people at a social event I attended. A man was meticulously outlining a series of his collegiate athletic accomplishments when I intervened with an invitation to one of the women to comment on her past experiences. I received a look of disdain from her, with the group's immediate attention returning to the original speaker, who continued strutting his stuff. Does listening to a boastful ego ease our social tensions? Do we believe that real men parade their achievements to the exclusion of others?

"Psychopaths often come across as arrogant, shameless, domineering and cocky."[44] A constricted emotional life blocks a man from developing a deep feeling of loving kindness for himself. A compensation for authentic self-acceptance can be egocentricity and grandiosity. We seem to be so accustomed to our understanding of manhood including some measure of pompous revelry, that we often confuse it with authentic confidence. We can think of genuine self-confidence as holding trust in ourselves that we will manage the trials and challenges of life and call upon real support from others wherever needed. We seem to no longer be able to distinguish gracious, self-accepting confidence from inflated, raucous pronouncements of grandiosity.

"They [psychopaths] seem unable to get into the skin or to walk in the shoes of others, except in a purely intellectual sense. The feelings of other people are of no concern to psychopaths."[45] The most dangerous and frightening outcome of a "shallow emotional life" is a lack of empathy. The word empathy comes from the Greek meaning *in suffering* or *the capacity to feel into the suffering of others*. In order to exercise that ability, a man needs to feel into his own suffering, which is not allowed by a shallow emotional life. When a man's empathic facility is disabled, several other psychopathic traits naturally follow. Hare describes a lack of remorse and guilt, deceitfulness and manipulation, and a lack of responsibility as hallmarks of the psychopathic personality.

"Psychopaths' lack of remorse and guilt is associated with a remarkable ability to rationalize their behavior and to shrug off personal responsibility for actions that cause shock and disappointment to family, friends, associates, and others who have played by the rules."[46] Remorse and guilt happen because of an ability to feel into the suffering and pain a man may have caused. Unless there is a strong proclivity to sadism, feeling into another's agony may illuminate those values that stand against such violation. When a man's empathy is truly bankrupt, a common rationalization for his inappropriate behavior is a reference to someone else's impropriety by depicting himself as the real victim in the story.

Hare describes deceit and manipulation as common characteristics of the psychopath. Yet I am often amazed at the popularity and endorsement of a man's capacity for deceit and manipulation shown in the media. Two television commercials come to mind. One shows a couple in a fast-food restaurant with the female complaining about her sister's boyfriend, who prioritizes watching football over spending time with her sister. The male pauses, contemplating his options, aware of his attraction to viewing football, and says, "What a jerk!" allegedly describing the sister's boyfriend. The male clearly understands what statement is in his best interest regardless of its dishonesty.

In a cell phone commercial, a couple is dining, with the male tracking sports scores on his smartphone that is sitting in his lap. When the female confronts his lack of attention to her, he lies about his phone activity. I have noticed that females are never depicted in some unscrupulous fashion; we reserve it for males, and then wonder why they act so immaturely.

Hare goes on to point out that psychopaths spend very little time weighing the pros and cons of their actions. Because injurious consequences are not a consideration, psychopaths tend to be impulsive, and we tend to label such men as bold and decisive. In actuality, such behavior often reflects an emptiness of spirit and conscience.

When drawing a parallel between classic psychopathic traits and a contemporary definition of manhood, we are not depicting the soul of men. We are merely capturing images of a deeply unfortunate portrait of our culture's view of manhood. I have worked with hundreds of men seeking to cast off these cultural mandates of manhood, eager to reclaim who they really are. These men struggle to honor their hearts, the depth of their sensitivity, and their ability to love, in fear of being perceived as something less than real men. One of my greatest professional joys is the opportunity to bless the wholeness of these men. My hope is that more men will find the courage to oppose cultural violations of their souls and discover their way back to the light.

DISTRACTED INTO DARKNESS

We live in a time driven by the supreme distraction—speed. We adore fast phones, fast computers, fast communication, and generally a fast life. Speed hurls us into the future, constantly nudging us out of the present, where deep emotion is experienced. We cling to the illusion that speed somehow equals being fully alive as we leave the moment, the only place where life can really take place.

A recent television commercial for the iPhone has a young man asking a group of children what's better—fast or slow? The children answer in unison, "fast." The children are then asked to identify things that are fast, and they name a rocket ship and a cheetah. The man then asks the children to name something that is slow. One boy says his grandmother, and the man asks what would make her fast. The boy says, "Tying a cheetah to her back." The ad offers unequivocal praise for speed with talk about slowness quickly slipping into absurdity.

Living in the moment requires slow movement, so we have at least the chance to experience what is happening around us as well as within us. As we prolong our encounter with the moment, we can activate our senses, take in sense data, spark our intuition, unfold our analytical reflection, and have time to feel deep emotion. It may be the encounter with the inner world that we are urgently attempting to escape. We hope to sanitize life of the difficult emotions such as fear, sadness, hurt, and desperation. We attempt to outrun these emotional nuisances, in the hope of happily-ever-aftering.

In her book *So Far From Home*, Margaret Wheatley explains: "Distracted people don't notice they are in danger. Ignorant of their vulnerability, they discount warnings or evidence that they are about to perish." As Wheatley points out, not only are we not fully alive when distracted, but we can likely be in danger and not know it. Living close to our vulnerability can be extremely informative, letting us know our losses, possible dangers, what we need, what we value, what we cherish, and possibly what we might die for.

Our strong sentiments can deepen our capacity for bio-philia (love of life) and ultimately give rise to our values. People with a heart that is touched and moved will likely live in kinship with life. In contrast, those possessing a speeding heart, likely a closed heart, move into isolation, unable to remember who they are and removed from the family of humanity. Speed blurs our vision, allowing only slivers of light to enter; we are distracted into the darkness of necro-philia, a loss of life.

Sin

So many of us think of sin as evil expressing itself through the actions of humans. From the German, the word *sin* means *separated* and from the Greek, it means *to miss the mark*.

Immediately noteworthy is that the German meaning, *separated*, is the antithesis of the mystic's devotion to *unity*. Separation is not always a bad thing. Boundaries that support safety and individuality can be wonderful expressions of bio-philia. Such boundaries allow us to trust our ability to protect ourselves from myriad dangers. They also allow our personal beliefs, preferences, and aspirations to have some shelter from the influence of others. We need to consider those acts of separation that divide us from ourselves and others and promote necro-philia.

Missing the mark can be interfaced with *separated*, helping us to deepen our understanding of the ground of evil. We miss the mark by failing to grasp whether or not some act of separation moves us toward necro-philia, contributing to the compost of evil by engaging in an antilife experience. Sin may happen when we unconsciously or wrongly understand the role of our separations. Separations resulting from bigotry, hatred, unfounded fear, unconscious competition, bullying, ignorance, and narcissism may be examples of separation generating darkness. There are a number of traditional sins that can be looked at through the lens of missing the mark or a misguided separation. We can explore how these sins contribute to the compost of the ground of evil.

Greed

Greed misses the mark by missing the true nature of our hunger, leaving us confused about what actually satisfies. Greed separates us from the reality of our hunger and therefore separates us from ourselves. We do not know our actual desire, which often is to be loved. We fall prey to substituting the power to make acquisitions for the deep well of unconditional self-acceptance. When we are separated from ourselves by substituting power for love, we inevitably separate from others. Compassion, collaboration, and cooperation are sacrificed for domination, control, and competition.

Because we are confused about our hunger and what it is asking for, we become obsessed, vulnerable to being caught in an insatiable feeding frenzy. In the grip of such an obsession, empathy for the needs of others can be at best a distant blur.

Greed can manifest beyond the typical compulsion to acquire money and things. Similar to gluttony, greed may attempt to devour attention, power, desire, excitement, admiration, and popularity. So often when I have asked clients who are caught in a greed obsession, "Who loves you?" they either lift their chins in a quiet defiance or gently weep. The acquisition of stuff may be an attempt to exercise control over being fed rather than face the unpredictable and tedious tasks of feeling loved and acquiring meaning.

The ego abhors that our souls may be requiring us to attend to lifelong learnings. Our culture ridicules the state of being hungry or unsatisfied, which condemns us to a fast-food psychological diet, in which we attempt to exercise control over the cotton candy of popularity and attention. There is little or no support to delay immediate gratification, in pursuit of genuine meaning. Our cultural mandate is to take in anything, don't tolerate being hungry, and do it preferably by being impressive.

Vanity

An old meaning for the word *vanity* is *empty*. We can say that vanity is empty of authentic self-love or misses the mark of genuine love for the self. The energies of vanity are an attachment to looking good with the outcome being that our appearance impresses others. It operates under the illusion that we can control how much others love us by presenting ourselves in some impressive fashion. The ego abhors the truth that being loved cannot be controlled. Vanity separates us from both love and genuine personal empowerment because we remain dependent upon the favorable reactions of others. We miss the mark of a true understanding of what unites us to ourselves.

How we present ourselves can replace an abiding compassion for who we are. We no longer offer ourselves genuine acceptance; we are condemned to enter the world having to prove our value. We live with the illusion of being in control of impressing others, when the reality is that they are in control of whether to offer us a favorable or unfavorable response to our presentation.

When vanity becomes an obsession, we not only separate from ourselves but we also separate from others. A young woman once reported to me that she did not feel understood by her mother. "My mother takes an hour to attend to her hair and makeup before venturing out to the convenience store. She says that I need to be more conscious of how I look, and sometimes her glares have a louder demeaning voice. I wish she knew who I really was."

We can understand vanity as a hunger for love, a love that can only ultimately come from ourselves. Of course, getting to that kind of love takes work,

work that extends way beyond a rendezvous with the mirror. It means being willing to learn to interrupt the shaming and diminishing thoughts we have about ourselves and learning to forgive ourselves.

Envy

Envy is getting stuck in coveting the favorable situations of others. It misses the mark because it brings our attention to the good fortune of others rather than to our own hunger and to how we might genuinely address that hunger. Envy also separates us from real personal empowerment because it moves us into being a victim of the favorable situation of others.

We live with a sense of being incomplete but do not take on the task of our completeness or wholeness. Envy allows us to avoid some important questions: What do I need in order to feel whole? What skill or competency is asking to be developed? Is there some personal ambition needing my support? What's missing in my life?

Envy easily finds comfort in comparing and contrasting ourselves to others. As outlined earlier, the ego rejects being ordinary. It is content to be positively or negatively special, and envy has us being negatively special, because we just are not quite good enough. Again, envy's real hunger may be for love.

Sloth

Sloth is an attachment to passivity. Sloth or lethargy separates us from our passions and from a lived life. We miss the mark by believing it is easier not to fully participate in life, or that there is more comfort in passivity, reflecting necro-philia. Sloth is attached to the mandate "Life is too big for me." Once our eyes are open to the intellectual and emotional challenges of a mysterious journey, we can fall prey to protesting such a trip. Our psyches can fall under the spell of an infantilism, as we wish to avoid taking risks and our inevitable defeat.

This childlike orientation toward life is commonly laced with magical thinking. Having abdicated responsibility for our lives, it can become easier to live with the fantasy that there are no serious life challenges. And if one should arise, someone or some divine intervention will supply needed resources.

The sloth posture of waiting is not an act of faith in being helped as we participate in life by doing what is in our control. It is a refusal to do our part, waiting to be attended to. Children who suffered from an emotionally incestuous relationship with a parent run a higher risk of falling into sloth since they were encouraged to be excessively dependent.

Envy and self-loathing generally accompany sloth, as we compare ourselves to others who are living courageously. The energy of sloth can also greatly hinder clarification of our values and our beliefs. It is difficult to grow up when we suspend our psychological tasks and no longer live a self-examined life. From this posture, we no longer seek the depth unearthed by curiosities related to our freedom and our capacity to love, to create, to be generous, to steward our communities, and to guide the development of our children. Instead, we await the arrival of some benevolent parent, spouse, friend, or boss who will allow for our excessive dependency. Typically, anyone obsessed with being needed will do.

Pride

We can think of pride or hubris as a reflection of an oversized ego, a separation from the rightsized ego. Pride misses the mark of genuine self-love and operates as a compensation for the loss of love. Pride seeks to be excused from the natural limits of being human; a world constructed upon hubris is allegedly special, which is commonly a compensation for self-loathing. Of course, a great deal of energy is typically needed in order to demonstrate how special we are.

The ego is easily seduced by the temptation to show how special we can be. Our alleged exceptional status is accompanied by strategies aimed at gaining the admiration and applause of others. We believe we have control over the responses of others, which comforts the ego. After all, isn't everyone impressed with someone special? The alleged payoff is being exempt from the insecurity and unpredictability of whether we will be loved by others, which remains out of our control.

Striving to be special typically breeds strong shoots of narcissism as our cherished features separate us from the commonness of our humanity. Pride dims our vision of what creates life around us as our attention becomes rigidly focused on fortifying our privileged position, which only condemns us to emotional isolation. Once we are duly distanced, being provocative or violent seems like the only way to make contact. The vulnerability of living with an open heart fades away.

THE GROUND OF GOODNESS— SOURCES OF LIGHT

"On the human level it means that if a human being is centered, and related to the Self, there is a certain protection against evil; and when the center of the personality is established, such a person is supported by a more-than-human strength to resist and overcome the evil powers."[47]

It may be that the centering and relatedness to the Self to which Sanford refers can generate a light that serves us in three important ways. First, having enough centering may allow us to come out of denial about the presence of darkness. Similar to noticing we are in a dark room, we have a chance to turn on the light. Second, it may be a discerning light helping us to better ascertain the ground of good from that place where evil grows. Third, to beget such light also illuminates and draws us to other sources of light. This light will not penetrate the essence of the mystery of goodness. However, our familiarity with the light may ignite wonder and curiosity about how we might access more light.

Before moving on, I want to pause and offer a blessing to the light.

A BLESSING OF LIGHT

Only darkness can hold true welcome of the light.
All other illumination is satisfied with itself.

May a gentle, golden autumn light guide you out of darkness,
allowing your eyes time to see fully, like the vision
of a newborn child shedding the vernix from its eyes.

May a soft candlelight invite your attention to false desire
seeing clearly that wanting may lack the ability
to enlarge your heart and your mind.
When you lose your way, may you hold a knowing
of a forgotten light, a torch eager to find you and assist
you in making your way back to the path.
May your thinking be guided by a dawn light,
announcing the coming of a greater luminescence.
This heralding light invites truth to reveal itself
in tiers turned back slowly in shyness, allowing
the soul to gently greet the unknown stranger.
And when you come to know the inevitable, deep
aloneness of this walk, may a lighter hue point the
way from loneliness to solitude.

May the brightness of a midday, summer's light reveal its shadow,
offering the chance to look back over your shoulder toward
what you have forgotten about yourself. Some piece
of your soul longing to be remembered and welcomed home.

As you come back to yourself again and again,
may the depth of your centering and relatedness
to yourself, to the world, and to the gods be illuminated
by a divine radiance.

· ·

We now explore how we can strengthen our capacity for centering and relating to the self, with the hope of generating a light capable of illuminating the ground of goodness.

Returning to the Moment

The moment is packed with reminders of our vulnerability. In present time we will encounter helplessness and aloneness. We will need to become more aware of how far we have walked away from the present. We can get caught hanging on to sentiment binding us to the past or becoming obsessed with our future plans. We will speed off eagerly racing through our days, as if our advanced velocity signifies a bounty of life, when in actuality we are racing toward our deaths. The mythologist Michael Meade reports being asked on numerous occasions whether the end of the Mayan calendar reflected the end of time. He has offered a profound response, capturing our obsession with racing through life.

Meade tells of a conversation he had with a neighbor child. The exchange went something like this: "I can't talk right now, Mr. Meade. I gotta do my homework, and get ready for swimming lessons, and make sure I pack my shoes for dance class, and then go to the store to buy what I need for my history project, and then I gotta . . ." Meade points out that time has ended for the girl next door, as it has for many of us. Real time only happens in the present, and if we have a large enough itinerary pulling us into the future, then time has truly ended.

Speed numbs us. We are literally dashing past ourselves, attempting to postpone our emotional lives. We race about in the hope that someone might hail us down temporarily to inform us who we are and what we should be doing with our lives.

Centering and developing relatedness to the self can only occur in the moment. If we are willing to pause, breathe—then it is there in the present, in the pause, that we can find our perceptions, sensations, feelings, and the energy likely capable of an illumination cast in the direction of goodness. Living from the future, lost in a frenzy of expectations and plans, we lose the power to choose ourselves. As we step away from the moment, we are no longer able to meaningfully respond to the questions "Who am I now and who do I want to be?" When our own hunger does not drive these questions, someone else's hunger is likely driving our lives. The psyche abhors a vacuum. If we cannot find ourselves in the present, then it is likely that someone else's desires and needs will find us.

Returning to the moment not only reintroduces us to our hunger, but to the inevitable insecurities of illness, a broken heart, and many other fears and losses. Above all, our return to the present offers a palpable reminder of the utter vulnerability inherent to the journey. If we can get honest about this vulnerability, then we might embrace our fragility and let go of aspirations of conquering life and focus instead on making peace with it.

The Power of Vulnerability

An old meaning of the word *vulnerable* is *wounding*. How appropriate it may be that our capacity to receive light is greatly determined by our acceptance of life as including a wounding. A wounding can result in an opening, and it is that opening that can generate the light of healing, as well as receive light. Our hearts are opened by being broken. Each time life presents us with some form of distress, we have the opportunity to feel the accompanying feelings and open to learning a bit more about living.

I recently heard the story of a man suffering from the final stages of pancreatic cancer. He had been very committed to his professional life and being a good provider, allowing his professional role to offer some sanctuary from the nagging stubbornness of an ignored heart. His intense work ethic animated his ambition, driving him to the office and away from the emotional challenges of relationships. His connection to family and friends was left to evolve on its own accord, never being brought to life with the warmth of his holding.

The weight of his limited time moved him in ways that this man had not before understood. He began to illuminate a large light that had only flickered as a small flame for years. This new, revived light appeared to draw exception to his tired eyes. The old embers grew brighter, now filling the room with a luminosity to know the people he loved; he eagerly touched their skin, willing to draw his body closer. One day while his aging father napped, he laid his body close to the old man and gently stroked his hair.

This man's impending departure radiated a willingness to forgive past grievances, with a glowing acceptance for the varied ways others chose to live. A distancing self-righteousness began to crumble. The combination of physical pain and the loss of dreams aimed at manifesting in the future left him in the hands of a vulnerability he had never known. And now, accompanying that vulnerability was a power to love and to draw near in ways that unnamed fears had once prevented.

Some light can likely shine depending on how we carry our vulnerability. Our pride can be reduced by suffering. We are humbled by failing. We let go of illusions of certainty by getting lost. We remember what we cherish by experiencing loss. We recall the importance of kindness by being mistreated. Feelings of vulnerability call us to remember our humanity and to remember who we are.

We can think of the opposite of feeling vulnerable as feeling powerful. An ancient meaning of the word *power* is *to be able*. We can say that to feel vulnerable is to feel powerless, or unable. Such a feeling harkens us to our last breath, when we will not be able to continue to draw life in. Hence, feeling vulnerable may be a reminder of how fragile we are, accompanied by a wisp of our mortality. However, the power of vulnerability is far reaching. Before exploring how feeling vulnerable might serve us, let's consider three dimensions of vulnerability.

Dimensions of Vulnerability

The first dimension of vulnerability I call *cosmological* vulnerability. Essentially, this is what was said earlier about life—that it is mysterious, insecure, and unpredictable. In order to cope with this level of vulnerability, we must be able and willing to make peace with life's insecurity, given there is no certainty about whether or not we will make it through the night. Although there are temporary comforts and sanctuary, this level of vulnerability calls for a deep acceptance of life's deep insecurity.

The second dimension can be identified as *circumstantial* vulnerability. This form of vulnerability takes place when a situation possesses the power to injure us physically or emotionally. We cope with physical dangers by learning to defend and protect ourselves to the best of our ability. Coping with emotional threats means learning to employ the kind of boundaries that prevent us from be subjected to unwarranted ridicule and criticism. These boundaries work because we simply refuse to accept accusations aimed at diminishing our characters.

The third dimension I refer to as *restimulation* vulnerability. An example would be that we are in the presence of someone raising his voice and we begin to feel vulnerable because of a past experience where a raised voice led to some level of harm. When experiencing this form of vulnerability, we are safe and need to learn to separate the current loud voice from the historical loud voice.

The experience of vulnerability informs us of external and internal dangers. A middle-aged woman reported to me that she felt extremely anxious every morning and wondered if I would recommend some pharmaceutical help. I suggested that she appeared to be excessively concerned with the protection and support she could offer others, typically neglecting her own needs. I went on to recommend that she consider committing to not allowing herself to be treated unkindly, especially by an emotionally abusive husband. To my surprise, two weeks later she delightfully reported the absence of morning anxiety. She was actively prioritizing her own needs and acting in support of them. I pointed out that she was willing to ask her vulnerability what it was asking for.

Vulnerability has the power to help us craft authentic self-care, as evidenced in the previous example.

Vulnerability can bring us closer to our limits, especially our mortality. If we accept what vulnerability can teach us about life and ourselves, we may be able to release illusions of power aimed at living out the misconception that we can triumph over life. We can sharpen our sensibility about the appropriateness of surrendering to what is out of our control.

George, a fifty-two-year-old construction worker, continued to keep up his youthful pace of nightly drinking, keeping late hours, and working overtime. A heart attack brought him to the realization that if he valued his own life, he would have to live on life's terms, honoring the limits characterized by his aging.

We are inevitably vulnerable when we suffer. Suffering potentially opens us to more light. It means asking, "What does this suffering call me to?" The question invites greater meaning as it points us away from simply being victims of our suffering. Once we take up residency in victimization, we run the likelihood of either compensating for our helplessness by abusing power or losing faith in life. Both of which summon necro-philia.

Vulnerability has the power to awaken our ability to be touched and moved. We can ask, "Touched and moved—away from what and toward what?" When our hearts are touched and moved, we are likely moving away from mediocrity, indifference, sleep, and distraction. We may be touched and moved toward beauty, love, kindness, innocence, brilliance, suffering, and loss. We begin moving toward the fullness of life.

Vulnerability offers an invitation to step closer to the depth and breadth of our humanity. We can be reintroduced to the universal struggle of surviving, failing, healing, growing, grieving, and dying. When we are distant from our vulnerability, we remain distant from the hungry child, from the man on the oncology floor dying alone, from the teenager terrified to step away from gang activity, from the girl trapped in sex trafficking, and from the old woman staring out of the convalescent home window who has forgotten who she is. Vulnerability is the juice of empathy. We can find others and ourselves by the light that is cast by vulnerability. We are touched by others and allow them to be touched by us. We can consider praying in the following manner: *We pray for a heart-opening to what our vulnerability is asking for. Only then will we be able to allow the hollow pillars of our egos to collapse and warmly embrace the self who remains standing in the rubble.*

Devotion to the Examined Life

"We can be redeemed only to the extent to which we see ourselves."[48] The light dims when we forget who we are, making it more difficult to see those parts of us pushed to the recesses of our souls. A self-examined life is a devotional act with no point of completion, contributing greatly to the generation of light, where the good might flourish. It is an ongoing act of welcome, and much of what lives in us will remain unknown. What can happen to those parts of us we forget about and therefore do not welcome?

The first consequence is that these forgotten parts may get acted out unconsciously. We simply react, saying and doing things that may be hurtful to ourselves and/or to others. If our unconscious behavior is accompanied by a lack of empathy, then it is likely we will not even know someone was hurt, as in the case of passive aggression.

As noted earlier, anger is certainly an important emotion to notice and address creatively by talking about it, acting it out in a safe way where no one is harmed, or writing about it. Typically, under the anger lives hurt, fear, or frustration. They too will need our attention. It is the neglect of these more primitive emotional energies that easily results in diminished light, leading to some harmful behavior.

Another outcome of living at a distance from ourselves is that what we do not see and welcome, we will likely see in others. We then perceive other people as angry, petty, insensitive, arrogant, and unkind. When we tenaciously and rigidly hold these views of others, it is likely we have an opportunity to see what lives in us. As long as we continue to describe the darkness of others, conveniently omitting our own, all the energies necessary for scapegoating are in place, and with a sprinkle of fear and self-righteousness, we have permission to act unkindly or even violently.

Could it be that we are being asked to return to old Yahweh, where the dark and light come together and where the darkness is not split off to the devil? If so, we would be taking greater ownership for our darkness rather than separating from it and attributing it to a neighbor or someone of a different religious persuasion. Can moral courage mean taking ownership of our capacity to love and hate, to be generous and selfish, to be compassionate and unkind, to be honest and deceitful, to be forgiving and vindictive, and to be humble and arrogant?

Let's look at what it might take for us to take possession of our shortcomings:

- Acknowledging that the beginning place is a willingness to devote to and accept who we are.

- Acknowledging the enormous nature of the task and asking for help.

- Committing to eliminating blame in our relationships and living with the question "How may I have contributed to the breakdown in this relationship?"

- Viewing our shortcomings as a statement of our participation in the human condition, rather than as an abominable anomaly.

- Practicing taking possession of our shortcomings and learning to forgive ourselves over and over again.

Here are some possible benefits of taking ownership of our shortcomings:

- Living with fewer pretenses and less self-righteousness.

- Living closer to who we actually are and making peace with who we find.

- Living with less hatred and a diminished attachment to scapegoating.

- Becoming more accepting and forgiving of others.

- Diminishing our contribution to the ground of evil with the creation of more light.

We can only imagine what might happen if we claim ownership of these light and dark energies. We would no longer be diminishing and scapegoating others by asking them to carry the burden of our darker attributes. Image what happens when people need to protect and defend themselves less from the darkness we cast upon them.

"The antidote to this evil is psychological honesty, that is, the development of the capacity to be honest with oneself about oneself."[49] One of the great human challenges is to get honest about our hunger. We possess hunger for attention, acknowledgment, love, affection, belonging, and acceptance. If we feel impotent regarding the ability to adequately address our hunger, then we easily begin to lose faith in life. As Erich Fromm reminds us, with a loss of faith in life's capacity to support our needs, we easily turn to darker expressions of potency.

When we are willing to get honest about our hunger, we take the first step toward maintaining our faith in life. We can ask: What do I hunger for? How can I support myself in regard to this hunger? Who can I ask for help as I strive to feed myself?

We can also get honest about the status of our integrity. Living in integrity means our behavior is compatible with our values. It calls for an awareness of our values, a willingness to examine our actions and be honest enough to decide whether our choices actually reflect our values. If we claim to possess values like compassion, honesty, generosity, and tolerance, then we are in or out of integrity when we examine how we are actually living those values. When we are out of integrity, we have the choice to pull our behavior back in alignment with our values or acknowledge a level of hypocrisy.

The goal is not to live perfectly in integrity, but rather to use the lens of integrity as a way to measure how far or near we are living from principles we allegedly cherish. Light is generated not only by the values we live, but also by the commitment to hold ourselves accountable for failing to live those values. Integrity is a way to get honest and get right with ourselves, not a way to aspire toward a pristine moral landscape.

Maintaining Committed Relationships

Martin Buber explains: "Man wishes to be confirmed in his being by man, and wishes to have a presence in the being of the other . . . Secretly and bashfully he watches for a Yes which allows him to be and which can come to him only from one human person to another."[50]

What is this "Yes" coming from another that allows us to be? How does this "Yes" open us to the light? We can say that the "Yes" Buber refers to is an act of choosing, an act of commitment. Others see what we see about ourselves and confirm our self-perceptions, or they see what we cannot see and expand our awareness of ourselves. I make a committed choice by offering my truth and my compassion, while remaining open to hearing your truth and receiving your compassion.

Allowing ourselves to be seen by a significant other has the potential to allow light to temporarily penetrate the opaque veil of goodness. It may be helpful to remember Robert Moore's assertion, "Evil wants to get you alone and isolate you. It wants to get you in the dark." We can say that evil wants you to forget about what you intend and what you do, releasing you from accountability. But the light illuminates who you are, revealing what would otherwise easily slip away into the shadows.

The dedication to my book *Shadow Marriage: A Descent into Intimacy* reads: "To my wife, Connie, who calls me to a place I am inevitably unprepared to go." How difficult it can be to hide from the eyes of the beloved! Areas calling for awareness and development can easily be seen when spouses, relatives, and friends react to neglected areas of our personalities. We have a profound opportunity to create ourselves in a committed relationship and remain self-examining.

Here are some examples of a self-inventory that can be used in a committed relationship:

- **How do I manage conflict?** Do I avoid conflict? Do I attempt to blame and dominate the other?

- **How effectively do I approach problem solving?** Do I deny problems? Do I acquiesce to others, expecting them to take responsibility to solve problems? Do I take all the control and responsibility to address problems? How effectively do I collaborate?

- **How effective do I make decisions with others?** Do I defer to others to make decisions for me? Am I willing to enroll the other in a decision-making process? How negotiable am I in the decision making? Am I able to make clear agreements and remain accountable for those agreements?

- **How effective am I at dealing with diverse needs and values?** Do I cling to a "win-lose" mentality when dealing with differing needs and values? Do I get locked into winning or losing? Can I hold the needs and ideals of the other with equal value to my own?

- **How effective am I at defining and living the role I play in a relationship?** Do I want to be told by the other what role I play? Do I maintain ambiguity about my role? Am I accountable for how effective I am at attaining the intended outcomes of the role?

- **How effective am I at articulating what I want or need?** Do I want the other to meet my needs without voicing them? Do I continually support the needs of the other, neglecting my own?

- **Do I employ effective boundaries?** Do I say "Yes" and "No" honestly? Do I accept the boundaries of others or attempt to talk them out of their boundaries?

- **How effective am I as a giver of what is desired by the other?** Do I take in what the other wants? Are there strings attached to my giving? Do I take joy in my giving? How often is my giving obligatory?

- **How effective am I at opening my heart?** Do I allow myself to feel vulnerable by disclosing tender feelings of fear, hurt, and sadness? Am I able to offer empathy to others when they feel vulnerable? Do I allow myself to join them when they feel slighted or hurt by me? How mindful am I about how I want to be loved? Do I know how to receive love? Do I know how they want to be loved? Does my love contribute to the freedom and empowerment of the other? Does my love call the other to be who she or he is meant to be?

- **How effective am I as a communicator?** Am I able to offer acknowledgment to the speaker? Can I empathically hear where the speaker's deep emotional truth lives? Can I blamelessly express an unmet need? Can I ask for what I want?

It may be that committed relationships are often avoided because of the immense opportunity to see ourselves, see what is pleasing and not so pleasing. If we did nothing else but consciously participate in a committed relationship, we would have a lifetime of opportunity to witness where the light and the dark live in us. Of late, I notice my committed relationships asking me to further let go of my need to be right and listen at a deeper level with my whole body. My apprenticeship continues.

Reenvisioning Manhood

We live in a culture starving for a new understanding of manhood, one that generates a warm and abiding illumination. One cultural definition of manhood invites men to split off from their hearts, which can leave men confused and impotent. As we saw earlier, the prevailing characterization of manhood leaves men off balance, struggling to keep a top-heavy ego in place. This exaggerated ego orientation leaves men emotionally impoverished, isolated, and unable to allow their hearts to lead them to themselves and to others. Unfortunately, a strong pendulum swing in the opposite direction leaves men passionless, unable to live boldly, allowing their hearts' desires and their values to inevitably be disrupted.

The following is one attempt to support men in the reclaiming of their souls and their fire.

A New Vision of Manhood

- A man maintains an openness to the depths of his emotional life and the heights of his intellectual life.

- A man unearths those depths in the form of compassion and empathy in response to the suffering around him.

- A man lives devotionally toward understanding and manifesting his purpose.

- A man strengthens his capacity to live with purpose by responding to what his wounds are asking for and developing his innate gifts.

- A man commits to life lived by following his heart's desire.

- A man remains curious about the strength of his will and exercises it wherever he believes it may contribute to the greater good.

- A man remains curious about the limits of his will, learning to surrender to what lies outside the domain of his will.

- A man knows how to ask for help.

- A man strives to live in integrity, with his behavior compatible with his values.

- A man is willing to be accountable for his behavior, offering amends and restitution wherever possible.

- A man feels remorse and guilt when he violates one of his values.

- A man says "Yes" and "No" genuinely.

- A man delights in supporting the physical, emotional, intellectual, and spiritual development of younger males.

- A man celebrates his manhood by creating meaningful relationships with other males.

- A man actively acknowledges and grieves his losses.

- A man accepts the responsibility to get honest about who he is and to hold what he sees about himself with compassion.

- A man releases his need to conquer life and accepts the responsibility to make peace with the depth of its mystery.

- A man accepts the inevitability of his death.

- A man lives boldly, taking appropriate risks, accompanied by a deep reverence for simplicity.

Prayer

An old meaning of the word *prayer* is an *earnest request* or a *serious request*. All matters of petitions pertaining to acquiring a greater capacity for insight and compassion certainly fall under the heading of earnest. And so when a prayer asks us to be a holder of both light and dark, we can resist our urges to prematurely shy away from either.

HOLDER OF DARKNESS AND LIGHT

What happens to me when I boldly hold opposites?
At first, I can hardly believe all that lives in me.
I may need to cut my way through a thicket of
shame as I behold for the first time how much
darkness dwells in me.

Love and hatred, humility and arrogance,
freedom and bondage, awake and asleep,
generous and self-serving, kind and cruel.
All these have taken up residency in me.

I can't remember choosing to be so much,
taking comfort in the side that looked good.
Now, as I ask to be the holder of these opposites,
I am no longer so kind, so cruel, so humble, or
so arrogant. For I am he who dares carry all
that lives in me. And it is he who deserves my respect.

Slowly, pretending to be one and not the other
loses its drive. I say less in defense of a fragile
self-worth. I attempt to prove less in demonstration
of some alleged prowess. I compare myself to you less,
attempting to secure some fleeting reprieve from the
darkness that I had run from.

I run away from me less.
And as my pace slows, I find a sweet resting place
in my body. Light and darkness are no longer
enemies, but now, members of the same family,
I call myself.

I am he who carries the dark and the light.
As I hold them, the fractured walls of my being
are repaired. Dark and light become kindred spirits
standing in abutment of a whole man.

I carry these opposite forces so they might
rest in me. And as they sit, blanketed in the serenity
of my acceptance, I see you in your light and in your
darkness, no longer needing you to be one without the other.

You are no longer the stranger I intended you to be.
We are no longer standing across from some untraversed chasm.
Your light, my light, your darkness, my darkness—these
opposites stand in testimony of our common humanity.

As we bring this chapter to a close, I am deeply touched and moved by events that recently occurred in a town some seventy miles west of our home. A twenty-year-old male entered an elementary school and shot and killed twenty children between the ages of six and seven. As the days passed, many were asking, "Why?" Suggestions of inadequate parenting and a faulty mental health system were quickly cited as reasons for the darkness of this young man's behavior.

No mention was made of the death of community as a possible explanation of the atrocities occurring at this elementary school. The darker elements of the human condition appear to have a breeding ground when we no longer notice one another's physical and emotional deterioration. Remaining in psychological proximity to one another allows for involvement, acceptance, accountability, and love—all potential sources of great luminosity.

We have been suggesting that the mystic is willing to hold the energies of good and evil within him- or herself and to keep vigil over the outcome of such a holding. The Greek philosopher Heraclitus (527–475 BC) taught, "Opposites come together and from what is different arises the fairest harmony." Until this tragedy, Heraclitus's urgings remained obscure for me.

Twenty innocent children from a quiet community were gunned down. Is this the level of darkness required in order to usher in the light? Will we now take gun control seriously? Is this enough evil to confront the lobbyists representing the National Rifle Association? Can we find the appropriate shame as we have ignored gangbangers killing one another in Chicago and South Los Angeles? Can we find remorse for not responding to the killing of a five-year-old African American girl caught in an exchange of gang violence in New Haven?

It would appear that darkness must touch us closely before we take action that can generate light. May the deaths of the innocent open our hearts to the unnecessary suffering caused by the senseless use of firearms all across our nation. May this violence create the "fairest harmony" with peace and compassion.

RESURRECTION, FORGIVENESS, AND REDEMPTION

*"There is only the fight to recover what has been lost
and found and lost again and again:
and now, under conditions that seem unpropitious.
But perhaps neither gain nor loss. For us,
there is only the trying. The rest is not our business."*
—T.S. ELIOT

Our *resurrection, forgiveness,* and eventual *redemption* will be "found and lost again and again." This quote from Eliot suggests a kind of spiritual resolve whereby we are willing to stay focused not on arriving somewhere but rather on remaining seekers on a path where we are destined to lose our way. Before we resurrect or rise again, or as one ancient meaning suggests, *rise from sleep,* we must break down or go down. The way down is typically reflective of some element in our psyche asking to die. Resurrection or new life presupposes that we are letting go of some belief or attitude that has become somewhat weed-like in preventing new growth. Of course, we have received some comfort from these old weeds, and we might not let go with a great deal of ease.

Hopefully, what becomes apparent is that the relationship between this downward movement and upward motion is simply the inextricable connection between death and life. Because we live in a death-denying culture, it can be somewhat challenging to grasp the essential connection between death and life. Our starting point might be to simply notice that life is about change and every change involves an ending (death) and a beginning (birth) of something else. We say we understand that life is about change, but the mystic devotionally welcomes the vastness of meanings in a journey characterized by profound impermanence.

THE DESCENT

Let's explore this downward movement, what I am calling a *descent*. We'll look at what it involves and its relationship to a resurrection. The purpose of a descent is to allow for some death to take place, casting us into a relationship with loss. Although the loss is typically some distortion inhibiting growth, it will inevitably feel devastating.

I am reminded of several of my own descents, involving the death of a child, the disability of another child, and a divorce. The common announcements of a descent were palpable: "I'm lost, defeated, vulnerable, bewildered, and sad." One of my distortions that unraveled in each case was that I could not get home with my intellect, my good looks, my charm, and my charisma, even though these were characteristics I was convinced would allow me to weather life's harsher realities. After all, our culture had reassured me that these qualities possessed a potency that would arm me appropriately.

Unfortunately, I had been appropriately acculturated with the belief that loss was simply unfortunate and nothing positive came from it. Like the overt bareness of winter, our culture is insensitive to the quiet, hidden life lying below the surface awaiting its spring resurrection. Luckily, I received some countercultural mentoring through each descent. It is difficult to hold that there is some veiled life lying beneath every loss, since a descent is regularly accompanied by a crisis of faith. Hence, it may be the mentor's task to hold a vision of the life we cannot yet see.

A loss of faith can make it extremely difficult to appreciate that the inevitable sense of failure in a descent could hold any value whatsoever. We can see from this poem by John O'Donohue that failure, like all life experience, does have its offering:

For Failure

The will of color loves how light spreads.
Through its diffusions, making textures subtle,
Clothing a landscape in concealment
For color to keep its mysteries
Hidden from the unready eye.

But the light that comes after rain
Is always fierce and clear,
And illuminates the face of everything
Through the transparency of rain.

Despite the initial darkening,
This is the light that failure casts.
Beholden no more to the promise
Of what dream and work would bring.
It shows where roots have withered
And where the source has gone dry.
The light of failure has no mercy
On the affections of the heart;
It emerges from beyond the persona,
A wiry, forthright light that likes to see crevices
Open in the shell of a controlled life.

Though cruel now, it serves a deeper kindness,
Wise to the larger call to growth.

It invites us to humility
And the painstaking work of acceptance

So that one day we may look back
In recognition and appreciation
At the disappointment we now endure.[51]

O'Donohue captures one of the essential sufferings of a descent: "Beholden no more to the promise of what dream and work would bring." Some promise inevitably dies in a descent. These promises are the threads woven into the cloth of our childhood. They keep us from succumbing to unbearable insecurity, toxic cynicism, and a withering hopelessness. And they fall quite short of offering an accurate account of a perilous journey. Such promises include:

"Work hard and good things will come your way."

"Be kind to others and they will treat you kindly."

"Love conquers all."

"Think positively and positive things will come to you."

"Family members will stick by you through thick and thin."

"God only gives you what you can handle."

"If I'm impressive, I can get favorable responses from others."

"If there's a breakdown in one of my relationships, I must not be giving enough."

The purpose of a descent is to unravel these promises meant to shelter us in childhood so that we may move closer to life and closer to ourselves.

"It emerges from beyond the persona, a wiry, forthright light that likes to see crevices open in the shell of a controlled life." Here, O'Donohue reminds us that a descent will inevitably shatter our illusion of having a demanding control over our life experiences. If we are properly mentored, then we neither turn against ourselves nor against life when we begin to embrace how much surrender is being asked of us.

Descent Guidance

We are not meant to endure a descent alone. There is good counsel to be had by a mentor who has some understanding of the terrain. The first wisdom is not to push for premature movement upward. If the helper is attached to rescuing and saving, then there may be some risk of disrupting the descent too soon. The person descending might feel better, but it will be at the price of his or her own deepening and maturing. The mentor must allow for a full expression of grief and disillusionment to accompany the dying experience.

Good counsel blesses the descent and welcomes the grief, holding vigilance for the suffering's gift. The person's descending process is held as a sacred journey. The mentor remains watchful of a tendency for the one going down to shame his or her vulnerability and lack of strength. The mentor can suggest an emotional movement somewhere above shame—maybe appreciation for the courage to go down or the resolve to continue the wayfaring.

The mentor holds the reminder that the trials encountered on a descent reflect someone on a deeply insecure and mysterious journey, which are not indicative of some psychological malady. The mentor can hold a vision of resurrection and redemption while the student struggles in the descent. Finally, the mentor helps in the construction of new narratives to take the place of the ones that are dying. This can take some time since these new stories will be constructed from new values, new understandings, and a new acceptance of life and self.

The mentor understands the following from Rainer Maria Rilke's *Letters to a Young Poet*:

> If it were possible for us to see further than our knowledge
> extends and out a little over the outworks of surmising,
> perhaps we should then bear our sorrows with greater confidence
> than our joys. For they are the moments when something new,
> something unknown, has entered into us; our feelings grow dumb
> with shy confusion, everything in us retires, a stillness supervenes,
> and the new thing that no one knows stands silent there
> in the midst.[52]

Rilke is not promoting a life of sorrow and suffering when he states, "we should then bear our sorrows with greater confidence than our joys. For they are the moments when something new, something unknown, has entered into us." Rather, he is developing the wisdom of where sorrow is capable of bringing us. Sorrow can receive the unknown while joy celebrates the known, taking delight in what is. Sorrow expressed in loss is actively engaged in a quiet movement. What has been so dear to us is quickly slipping away, with the unknown making its way to us. That the unknown "has entered into us" suggests that we have no command over it.

In the descent, "everything in us retires," that is, we feel defeated. What is retiring is not so much what we believe but the tenacity with which we believe it. The very best efforts of the ego to have us shine in some victorious light fall away, giving way to the darkness of the unknown. Now we are one who does not know, old meanings crumble, and unbeknownst to us, we begin to become more hospitable to the stranger knocking at our door. Our receptivity deepens as we allow ourselves to be moved by the water of grief.

The Waters of Grief

The descent is guided and escorted by the water of grief. This water allows us to soften into the death that embraces us, rather than attempting to hang on with a stiffness to some old image of who we are. The tension subsides and we allow ourselves to be penetrated by "the new thing that no one knows" that is standing there silently.

The water moves the gravel and debris of the psyche (e.g., resentment, disgust, and small ways of thinking), often leading to a greater opening of heart. Recently, a protégé of mine felt angry and hurt by my need to renegotiate a plan we had. Initially, she wanted to define me as someone who doesn't follow through. As her grief surfaced, she began to let go of defining me and accepted that our relationship would likely involve a level of disappointment. Her waters brought her to the reality of life's disappointing events.

The water can move us around obstacles that block the flow of life. After receiving numerous rejections of my early writing, I was gradually succumbing to a level of defeat that would have me abandon my writing. My water allowed me to depersonalize the experience and see the rejections as simply part of the publication path, helping me to move back to the flow of my creativity.

George's Water

The water knows how to find the low ground of the psyche where authentic loss and woundedness dwell. George, a sixty-year-old college professor, came to see me in order to explore the possibility of consummating a relationship with a woman thirty years his junior. I listened attentively as he took inventory of how much this young woman enlivened his life and then gingerly approached the challenges accompanying the age difference.

Following hours of processing, he dropped into the waters of the issue. "I'm afraid of growing old. I'm afraid of being confronted by limits I don't want to accept," he said as his tears flowed, announcing the loss he dreaded.

George's water was flowing to the low ground where his demons dwelled. Fortunately, he was willing to place decisions regarding his relationship on hold, while he stepped into the murky waters of his aging.

Grief water has the capacity to diminish the flame of rage, hubris, and excessive attachment driven by desire. When George was finally willing to grieve his lost youth and no longer pretend it could be eternal, his obsessive attachment to the young woman began to subside. His water was diminishing the flame of his infatuation.

Marilyn's Water

The water wants to flow into larger bodies of water (i.e., the psyche sheds some of its narcissism, adopting a larger view of the human condition). Marilyn, a fifty-five-year-old bank teller, had recently fallen in love with Roger. They had been seeing each other for a year when Marilyn decided to tell him how much she loved him. The disclosure set off a series of distancing responses in Roger.

He became less and less available, leaving Marilyn feeling anxious, confused, and lost.

As she and I explored the skills she possessed that could help her build a meaningful relationship with Roger, it became acutely obvious that Roger did not possess a similar skill set. She began to actively grieve the loss of opportunity for the both of them. Her water brought her to a larger vision: "This is not about me! I don't feel unlovable. I feel the loss of an opportunity to build an intimate relationship with him. I know that the same circumstances would have come about if he were in a relationship with another woman."

Marilyn's water moved her into a larger story about her experience. She was able to legitimize the choices she had made in the relationship, including her disclosure of love. She also did not need to reduce Roger's story by deciding there was something inherently wrong with him. She understood that he had survived a very abusive childhood and simply did not possess the healing or the competencies to accompanying her into something deeper.

Maggie's Water

Grief water can quench our thirst for the truth of what we love and how we want to live. Maggie, a high school English teacher, came to me in distress about how she was being treated by an old friend. I noticed that the friend was inclined to define Maggie based on some function that supported that friend's venture. It did not take Maggie long to see how her own mother had defined her as a functionary, when her mother was fostering some task.

"My mother doesn't know me. She has never been curious about my love of literature, or my interest in travel, or my commitment to my students. She only sees me as someone who supports some project of hers. It's the same with my friend," Maggie sobbed, as she expressed the loss of being truly understood by her mother and her friend.

Maggie was closer to the truth of what kind of relationship she wanted with a friend. She wanted her vocation to be seen and appreciated. She wanted her values and beliefs to be understood. She wanted to be visible to a friend. Her grief water brought her closer to what she truly valued in friendship.

Lucy's Descent

Lucy, a fifty-year-old court stenographer, came to see me, curious about the absence of meaningful relationships in her life. She had no interest in a life partner or lover, or for that matter any motivation to have a best friend. Initially, she expressed interest in how she was communicating at work with the staff. After several sessions exploring how she built rapport with coworkers, it became clear that she was living with impenetrable boundaries. It was literally impossible to get close to her. I became very curious about what happened to her boundaries early in her life.

"Do you have any awareness about how your boundaries were treated during childhood?" I asked, hoping the question had some relevancy for her.

"Like what kinds of things might have happened to my boundaries?" she wondered, moving forward toward the edge of her seat.

"Well, they could have been violated emotionally, physically, or sexually," I responded.

"An emotional violation would be like when my parents called me names or said I was a worthless piece of shit?" she said, with a detached tone, suggesting she was describing someone else's life.

"Yes, that certainly is an emotional violation," I said, confirming her insight.

"And I guess what happened with the neighborhood boys might be a physical or sexual violation," she suggested, as her voice trailed off, losing its initial muscle.

"What happened with the boys?"

"They raped me a lot," she responded, with her voice sounding considerably younger than her actual years.

"Tell me what they did to you."

"Three boys raped me every week."

"How long did this go on?" I asked, believing that she was not ready to have the emotions attached to her descent story but very ready to offer details.

"Well, they started when I was twelve, and it stopped when I was eighteen. They raped me several times each week—every week," she explained with a voice carrying the shame of her experience.

I sat quietly, paying attention to my own breath, hoping she would feel the silence offering a deep welcome to her story. I felt confident about remaining grounded as I listened. However, I became uprooted when she said, "Oh yeah, there was the time that I told them I missed my period and that I might be pregnant. They threw me out of the second story of the barn. Luckily, I didn't get very hurt and I wasn't pregnant."

Lucy was embarking on an immense descent that would eventually place her in touch with her grief reflective of her deep losses during adolescence. She had received none of the guidance and protection due a pubescent girl. Instead, she had been the object of cruel and invasive treatment. She soon was ready to grieve and claim her losses. I made sure that our sessions supported her need to both feel and process her grief.

Lucy discovered three significant deaths in her descent. The first was the belief that it was inevitable that she would be the victim of someone abusing power. The second was that she could not supply herself with the necessary boundaries to adequately protect herself. The third was that she could trust neither others nor herself. She slowly began to understand that trusting herself could happen when she allowed herself to know the truth of her perceptions and when she stopped denying her experience. After that she could be committed to treating herself kindly.

Mike's Descent

In a descent, the ego confronts the place where it took up comfort and sanctuary by confronting the losses accrued in these alleged safe harbors. Mike, a forty-two-year-old dentist, came to me already moving downward at a significant pace. Our work together quickly revealed that he hated his work and he resented being a provider and attending to the responsibilities of family life.

When we explored the psychological shelters Mike occupied along the way, we discovered a strong relationship with his mother, one that encouraged excessive dependency accompanied by distortions regarding a sanitized life provided by maternal care. Encouraged to rely on his mother, he gradually relinquished all decision making to the benevolent guidance of his mother. He no longer had to fear making the wrong decision as he lived under his mother's safekeeping.

Upon marrying, Mike transferred his maternal dependence to his young wife in the hope of receiving the same supervision he had had as a child. The goal was to remain in some infantile, idyllic state where he could not be harmed by life's exigencies, immune to the existential struggle of being a man. When his spouse refused to offer some desired instruction, he would collapse into the parental embrace of our culture's mandate to work hard and neglect taking care of himself. The illusion being that self-sacrifice somehow made him okay.

Mike gradually began to see and feel the depths of his losses. His self-trust had been underdeveloped, his heart's desire had been missing for years, with his freedom unraveling, leaving him either appropriately or inappropriately reacting to the expectations of others. If he responded appropriately, then he felt angry, knowing that his life belonged to the other whom he desperately wanted to please. If he was subject to the disapproval of the other, he felt bad about himself since others possessed the power to define him as worthy or unworthy. He was desperate, and in his descent his feet were hitting the ground more quickly with each step.

Mike was shaming himself and his descent, which left him vulnerable and yet close to the very powerlessness that comforted him. Power would mean becoming responsible for his life, which he protested. He was caught in a painful quagmire, wishing to return to the comfort of maternal bliss, with the price being his soul and his manhood. I invited Mike to see himself as a grieving man and as an angry man by reminding him that he had much to be angry at. Mike came from a rigidly religious family in which a pristine persona was a sanctimonious goal. It didn't really matter who you were, what you desired, or what you felt; the family mandate was to look good in praise of the Lord. Life was now asking Mike to befriend something less than pristine, some darkness amid a sacred descent. It would call for a courage he had never known before.

We talked about the word *courage* coming from the French word for *heart*. Mike understood he was being asked to live with more heart, shedding an attachment to what might be appropriate. Before he would befriend his heart's longing, he would need to learn to welcome a broken heart and come to know and feel his losses.

Gradually, Mike called a cease-fire, withdrawing his shame from his grief and allowing the waters to flow freely. Many sessions were spent in deep sorrow, with Mike allowing himself to become fully acquainted with his deprivation. Over time, he stopped waiting for mom or societal mom to tell him who he was or ought to be. He became the author of his own life by discovering and being willing to honor his passion for the outdoors.

He met a gentleman starting an outfitting company in White Horse, Canada, who was seeking a business partner. Mike decided to leave his dental practice and move his family to White Horse. He was deeply supported by a devoted wife who accompanied him in his emerging resurrection.

Dying for Our Sins

The deaths involved in a descent yield new learning and awareness. We can think of the Christian credo "Christ died for our sins" as what we are doing during a descent. We are dying for our sins. We are experiencing a death related to distortions and illusions that we can think of as wrongful acts or sins. Because we are condemned to an approximation of the truth, we are asked to die for our sins in a descent.

Our emerging enlightenment will likely not be some grand epiphany that vaults us into transcendence. No, we move incrementally closer and closer to being able to live what wants to grow in us. Our new self is similar to a stranger who moves into the neighborhood; we gradually become familiar with the person behind the veneer. We might even discover how to best communicate with the new neighbor, how to collaborate and celebrate. We can track our eagerness as well as our resistance to fully include the new person. Our psyches need time to get to know what is taking root in us and to allow us to prepare to welcome the mystery of new life with our newfound courage.

We can see grief as both the energy that releases some old life-form (story, attitude, action) that no longer belongs to a soul aspiring to live in a larger story, and also as the spark of labor seeking new life. The waters of our grief work as a *catharsis,* whose old meaning suggests *vomiting* and *purging,* a letting go, making room for new life. The fluids of grief include nasal discharge, tears, and sweat. During one particular session when Mike was beginning to loosen his resistance and welcome his grief, I turned to him and said, "Aren't these descended fluids so damn trustworthy, completely absent of all pretense?"

I have been fortunate to be in the presence of the sacred grief waters of many people. If it's challenging for you to find your own waters, I highly recommend that you get close to the waters of someone you love and trust. Let their water cascade down your face, allowing your body to be touched by their healing fluids. The next passage calls to the early times in our lives when we lived close to the water and how we might return.

SACRED WATERS

There was a time when the water flowed like those mountain streams carrying melting snows of spring. Those waters moved with urgency, moving with a knowing of some longing, some desired destination.

So it was with my tears, until words and looks of disdain dropped heavily on my heart like piles of debris, little by little, damning the flow of my sacred waters. Words of love, longing, and hurt dried up under stagnant pools of motionless water. My heart's truth submerged like an old shipwreck, no longer knowing its buoyancy.

I lost my way. Waters that had moved me along the river of my uniqueness were no longer there. Still pools lost the radiance of rushing water dancing in the sun. I no longer knew my own light. Now, I walked to the sound of some distant voices which I could not call myself. I was truly lost.

I wandered, pretending each step reflected who I was, until the nausea of my self-deceit brought me to my knees. The sickness grew, as I took refuge in the distraction created by the wails of those suffering from their own want.

Then I saw you, and the sacred pearls of tears moving gently across your face. Stunned, I was drawn to them like a man parched from a desert march. Placing my face near yours, I allowed my thirst to be quenched, drop by drop, as your water washed over me like a gentle spring rain. And then, without warning, a stream of sorrow, joy, and love broke through the dam. My heart danced in welcome of this baptism back to myself.

RESURRECTION

The mythologist Michael Meade suggests, "The Water of Life can only be found by breaking down, by wandering away, by being and feeling lost." We can understand our resurrection as needing a "breaking down," "a wandering away," and "being and feeling lost." The descent was a large opportunity to break down our attachments to familiar belief, stories, and choices and to allow ourselves to wander away from the old neighborhoods of mind and heart that we called ourselves. Every descent involves feeling lost, since the old is dying and the new is not yet born. And in the in-between place, there's nothing to prove or achieve. We can just be with our grief, allowing it to move and touch us. We are no longer living under the illusion of being in command, and that may be the great gift of a descent.

As our grief lessens, we become intrigued by what is asking to be birthed in us. It is common to feel our hearts moving into a deeper level of bio-philia, or love of life. Because some deep disillusionment typically accompanies a descent, we may feel scared about believing and dreaming again in the richness of life. Do we dare once again to open our minds and hearts to possibility? Will we once again be asked to let go of some expression of life we cherish? Will we ever be able to accept the essential impermanence of the journey? Will we ever be able to accept loss as necessary? Will we succumb to the illusion that this rising from sleep is the ultimate awakening, or will we remember that some slumber is waiting for us?

Some belief or some form of distortion is sacrificed in a descent. One of my favorites has been the belief that to repair a breakdown between me and someone I care for, I only need to give more. The mystic is devoted to deepening an acceptance that the release of one distortion does not allow for some ultimate penetration of mystery. Living a deeply mysterious journey means being condemned to an approximation of the truth, with some new distortions asking to be sacrificed.

An old meaning of the word *sacrifice* is *to make sacred*. It may be that our willingness to descend and sacrifice some cherished distortion is a way for us to make ourselves sacred. There may be no greater way to reach the nature of the impermanent self and the impermanent journey than to allow for such sacrifice. It may be the most powerful way to say in our last hours that we fully participated in life. Full participation is ultimately a deeply sacred act.

Each descent and ensuing resurrection hopefully erodes two antilife postures. The first is "Life is much bigger than me and I'm its victim." The second is "I'm bigger than life." The first reflects an undersized ego refusing to meet life and join with one's own will and intention. The second reflects an oversized ego unwilling to accept the immensity and mystery of life with our inevitable defeats. These positions do not allow for a mystical union or intimacy with life. The hope is that over time we can locate ourselves more intimately with the following vision: "Life is much bigger than me and I'm willing to be her/his lover."

Lessons Rising

We can think of a resurrection as *lessons rising*. An old meaning for the word *lesson* is a *reading*, which meant to interpret dreams or stories. When a descent has been properly guided, we bring a larger interpretation to the stories we live in. A resurrection is a rising again into life with some new meanings about who we are and what life is because of the letting go that happened during the descent. It may be helpful to look at some common themes occurring during a resurrection.

Innocence

An old meaning of the word *innocence* is *harmless*. In a typical descent, some quality of innocence dies. As a result, we rise up, seeing ourselves and life itself as less harmless. In this way, the descent and the ensuing resurrection initiate us into new meanings that involve a greater acceptance of harm, not wrapped in cynicism. We can see harm as a reflection of the insecurity and mystery of life, or as Jung pointed out, "a perilous journey." We can also see harm as the acknowledgment of our own destructiveness, as potentially expressed through jealousy, revenge, greed, lethargy, and hubris.

Often, it is our love stories that are being asked to shed some fanciful imaginings of childhood. It is only too easy to have our love stories filled with idyllic themes that have no sustainability in real life. Such themes might include:

"Love conquers all."

"I will be appreciated for my loving."

"Good things will happen because of this love."

"When I love someone, they will let it in and feel loved by me."

"A broken heart won't be a theme in my love story."

"My beloved won't ever feel hurt by me."

"If love comes my way, then I will feel understood and accepted."

It is a significant challenge in a resurrection to accept that the only guarantee of loving is loss. Ultimately, someone will either walk away or die, in addition to all the other possible losses involving promises of happiness, enduring loyalty, and commitment.

My personal resurrections have taught me over and over again that love's only real promise is that if I dare open my heart, I get to live with an open heart. I don't get to be immune from the hurt of a broken heart. My new understandings of harm are not limited to being permanently damaged. With less innocence, living love is understood from the tension and challenges of accountability, honesty, integrity, and sacrifice.

Cowardice

The first line from Mary Oliver's poem *The Kookaburras* reads: "In every heart there is a coward and a procrastinator." An old meaning of the word *cowardice* is *to pause and retreat*. How appropriate it is to exercise the kind of discretion that informs us as to the appropriateness of pausing and retreating. Pausing may allow us to be more effectively informed, while retreating emotionally or physically may render a larger view of what is happening. Of course, we may regret our times of excessive passivity as much as when we acted impetuously.

At its best, a resurrection is rendering an understanding of the proper time for pausing and retreating, and it may call for numerous descents and risings before our bodies possess a sensibility for pausing instead of acting. It can be helpful to know our own propensities to either act or pause and to intentionally practice what is unfamiliar.

However, there are guiding questions that can help us discern whether it serves us to act or pause: If I feel some urgency to act, what is driving the urgency? Does this situation call for immediate action? What emotions are being aroused by this situation, and would premature action be a way to distract from the emotions? What else may be happening here that I have not yet allowed to inform me? What do I fear about this situation? Will some unfavorable consequence result from pausing? Does pausing somehow exempt me from appropriately participating?

Recently, an organization I was instrumental in creating decided to explore the role of elders. One man stepped forward and suggested that we gather in a large circle. When so moved, a man could nonverbally take another man into the center of the circle as an endorsement of that man as an elder. This would continue until thirteen elders stood in the center. The ritual went on as planned, with several men being absent from the event. One man who was not there launched a tirade of criticism of what took place, which led to myriad reactions traveling through cyberspace that questioned everything from the appropriateness of the proceedings to who was an actual elder.

I immediately wanted to react to the disgruntled gentleman, not appreciating his attacks. However, I paused, wondering what else in the situation might be able to inform me. I noticed that the focus of the remarks involved the man leading the ritual, the men chosen as elders, or the disgruntled gentleman. I then switched my focus to a more positive aspect of the situation: the men who did the choosing of each of the thirteen elders. These men were willing to step forward, expressing their respect and admiration for the specific man whom they guided to the center of the circle. I was thankful for where my pause had taken me.

Sensitivity

Time and time again, I have listened to people describe their sensitivity as an unfortunate liability. Stories of sensitivity unfold with themes of pain, hurt, and exploitation. Have we failed to understand the inherent power of sensitivity? Have we neglected to teach people how to effectively carry their sensitivity?

A properly guided resurrection can be rich with new learnings of ways to relate to sensitivity. We can understand sensitivity as an openness to what is around us. It is receptivity to the experiences of others, as well as to nature. Sensitivity is an energy moving us out from the borders of ourselves, allowing us to join others with empathy, sympathy, and understanding.

Sensitivity becomes an encumbrance when we step into the story of someone's adverse situation. This stepping into experience involves feeling responsible to fix, rescue, teach, or save others from the inauspicious conditions of their lives.

A resurrection can teach that sensitivity thrives when it is accompanied by humility in which we accept our limits. We allow the other's story to unfold even amid less than favorable circumstances. The person we are listening to may be embarking on a sacred descent with no need for our interference. We restore sensitivity to its rightful place as a powerful resource when we employ emotional boundaries that allow us to listen, feel, and give witness to the narrative in which the speaker lives.

Suffering

In his book *Dark Nights of the Soul,* Thomas Moore calls our attention to the transformative powers of suffering, reminding us that the goal is neither to be victorious over suffering nor to end it:

> It is a moral development, the result of an initiation in which
> the mysteries of life stamp themselves into you more deeply,
> not necessarily making life easier or happier, but allowing it
> to take place more intensely. You are more fully who you are.
> You engage life more energetically and in that engagement
> discover a level of meaning that dissolves any discontent you
> may have.[53]

A resurrection holds the possibility of a new relationship to suffering. Uninitiated ways to relate to suffering include a protesting attitude toward the existence of suffering. Childhood utopian visions of suffering typically include some hope of its minimization or even eradication. It may take numerous falls and risings before we hold a more creative and realistic view of suffering.

Mainly, we realize that it is here to stay, forcing us to have some form of relationship with it, which isn't a bad place to begin.

We can then acknowledge that it might serve us not to have a relationship with suffering that vaults us into an adversarial relationship with life. Such a relationship would only condemn us to live as victims of life, refusing to walk the mystical path intimately. We can then explore what kind of relationship we do want with suffering. The more creative and healing our relationship to suffering is, the larger our suffering story will be.

There are curiosities that can help infuse our suffering stories with creativity and healing. Is there some action this suffering is asking of me? Is surrender an appropriate response to this suffering? Is there a particular ally who will help bring healing to my suffering story? Is this suffering asking me to make some offering to others? How can I carry this suffering in order to remain on a path with heart? Is this suffering asking for some act of letting go?

An old meaning affiliated with the word *suffering* is *to endure*. We allow ourselves to endure when we remain open to where our suffering may take us. Enduring may be the result of a rightsized ego, where we are neither willing to see ourselves as larger than life's challenges nor succumbing to simply being a victim of life. We can recall the Rilke poem quoted earlier as a way to ground a new understanding of suffering: "For they [our sorrows] are the moments when something new, something unknown, has entered into us; our feelings grow dumb with shy confusion, everything in us retires, a stillness supervenes, and the new thing that no one knows stands silent there in the midst."

As we rise into these new learnings, we may be called to either forgive ourselves or others in order to more fully integrate these budding understandings.

THE OPUS OF FORGIVENESS

The meaning and depth of forgiving and not forgiving may be asking for more exploration beyond what has been offered by traditional religion and New Age psychology. The former group insists that their representatives can act as divine intermediaries, offering forgiveness, while the second group has promoted forgiveness as an energy that promotes general wellness. Unfortunately, both groups tend to emphasize the forgiveness story as something that fundamentally takes place between us and others, rather than an offering we may need to make to ourselves.

We can begin by understanding the word itself. As we discussed earlier, the prefix *for* comes from the High German meaning *away*. We can think of the word *forgive* as *away give* or *give away sins and transgressions*.

We typically speak of either being forgiving or not forgiving. With other human experiences we do not limit our understanding of what takes place by simply describing what is not happening. For example, if we say, "He's not running," we easily can offer some other state of being, such as "He's walking" or "He's sitting." So it is with emotional states. We can say, "She's not lonely," meaning, "She's feeling loved," or "She's enjoys friendship," or "She appreciates solitude." We have not really asked, "What's happening when we're not forgiving?" "What are we actually doing when we are not forgiving?"

Cursing

It may be difficult to swallow, but I would offer that when we are not forgiving, we are likely participating in some level of cursing. The word *curse* can be traced back to an eleventh-century church protocol, where four times annually, the conditions warranting excommunication were read out loud. These conditions would be defined as sins or unacceptable transgressions. We can think of cursing as a way to remain in relationship with someone's sins or what we deem as unacceptable. We stay in relationship to the transgressions rather than letting them go.

There appear to be two levels of cursing. Gossip could be thought of as the more active version, while our thoughts about a person's degenerate nature could be considered a more passive form. Let's note that both forms place us in relationship with the cursed individuals.

There also appear to be two levels of excommunication. The first dimension has us being okay with the person under attack being alive, but simply not in our lives. However, on the second level, we treat the cursed individual as if they were dead. Although this second form of excommunication seems rather harsh, my hunch is that many of us who consider ourselves upstanding folks have leveled this kind of excommunication on those whom we have cursed.

If we desire to deepen our capacity to forgive, then it may be helpful to take responsibility for our cursing and whatever expression of excommunication it may involve. We may also foster a more forgiving attitude by being mindful of how we maintain a state of cursing.

Maintaining a Curse

Jack Kornfield suggests, "Forgiveness means giving up all hope of a better past." Kornfield alludes to one of the ways we maintain a curse, that is, by protesting a life characterized by hurt, betrayal, deceit, and rejection. When we do not accept life as insecure and unpredictable, we fall prey to callow and excessively idealistic expectations of life, which are aimed at making us immune to life's hardships. Such wishing can diminish our acceptance for how life actually is. We believe the violation we suffered was an unfortunate anomaly brought on by a deviation. We lose a suppleness of attitude with an ensuing inflexibility that can easily hold us hostage to a path of cursing.

A second way we can maintain a curse is by holding a victim's mentality, typically accompanied by self-righteousness. From this posture, we insist on remaining focused on the awful things done to us. We dig in by confirming that we are a good person who has been seriously wronged. The cursing continues and we have little room to remember that we too are perpetrators of hurt and betrayal. It is very difficult to access forgiveness when there are two groups, the good guys and the bad guys, and we take up permanent residency in the former group.

The third way to maintain a curse is to deny our anger, which becomes a breeding ground for resentment. Resentment can be a powerful toxic energy holding a curse in place. It is an icy energy that is not easily released. Resentment holds a story in an encasement of rancor, not allowing for change.

A fourth way to maintain a curse is an attachment to revenge. Stepping into a vindictive posture carries an illusion of power. Hence, we allegedly move beyond feeling violated and helpless and we are engaged in the activity of revenge. We're doing something. As we shall see, feeling hurt can be manageable, but the accompanying helplessness may be troublesome.

The fifth way to support cursing is an attachment to a primitive vision of justice. The belief is that justice is achieved by punishing the perpetrator with a curse and some level of excommunication. Of course, the punishment ordinarily exists in our own minds, with the perpetrator feeling no unusual consequences by our curse. In fact, it may be that in carrying a curse to toxicity, we are mostly punishing ourselves.

The sixth way to maintain a curse is by imagining that the curse protects us from further harm. In actuality what we really need is some form of boundary safeguarding us against any potential injury at the hands of a perpetrator. We do not need to remind ourselves of someone's alleged degenerate nature in order to feel safe.

The seventh way we maintain a curse is by needing a connection to the cursed person, keeping that bond by way of a toxic attachment. As long as we continue to curse this individual, we are not letting go of him or her.

The eighth curse-sustaining strategy is our affinity with self-righteousness. The curse identifies who's bad, and by implication, we are the good people. Of course, our goodness may become a bit suspect as we live a life of ongoing cursing.

Learning How to Be Hurt

The last blueprint for a curse can be a deep confusion about how to creatively be hurt. Nothing inhibits a forgiving attitude more than not knowing how to have our feelings hurt. I have met very few people along the way who appear to know how to be hurt, maintain a rapport with the person who hurt them, and then be able to access forgiveness.

What so many of us learned as children is that no one cared about our hurt feelings. We were either left alone or heard reactions such as "I'll give you something to cry about," "Stop being a big baby," "Grow up," or "Stop making such a fuss." Children typically explain that no one seems to care about their hurt because they don't deserve such care, that is, they are unlovable.

Those early feelings of hurt would have been quite manageable if we had not felt so alone and so helpless about enlisting allies who truly wanted to safeguard us against being hurt and who expressed genuine empathy regarding our hurts. The big deal was that we were not simply hurt, we felt alone and helpless and began living in the story that we would be alone and helpless whenever we were hurt.

Cursing becomes a useful strategy to protect against the feelings of aloneness and helplessness when we are hurt. We get to focus on how awful the perpetrator is, rather than feel the hurt, the aloneness, and helplessness that accompanies our hurt feelings. If we're not generating stories about how bad the perpetrator of the hurt is, then we may likely be creating stories about how unlovable we are to explain why we got hurt. Trapped in the cursing paradigm, we avoid creating meaningful relationships, diminish our general life involvement, and live at a distance from ourselves.

Sometimes we can get truly generative and create stories about the perpetrator, about ourselves, and about life. Our life stories commonly carry themes of cynicism aimed at protecting us against the disappointment of future hurts. The trade off is that cursing life hurls us into a victim story where life is constantly abusing us in one way or another. We get to curse the offender, ourselves, and even life itself!

Nothing helps us to sustain a forgiving attitude more than learning how to carry hurt creatively. We can learn to be hurt without living trapped in a grudge shrouded in resentment or turning against life or ourselves. The first step is to give ourselves permission to feel and name our hurt feelings. It can be helpful to remember that this is a tender and vulnerable time. We should also practice locating where and how we experienced the hurt feelings in our bodies (e.g., tightness in our guts or chest). Typically, we survived the hurts of childhood by remaining at a distance from our hurt. Localizing hurt in our bodies helps us remain close to where hurt lives in us.

Second, we should interrupt our tendency to begin creating stories about the perpetrator, ourselves, or life by returning to simply feeling the hurt. A powerful skill involves being able to observe the stories we create and understand that they are not necessarily reflections of reality. Our narratives are typically meant to insulate us from feeling vulnerable and give us a spurious sense of being in control.

The third step is to attend to feelings of aloneness and helplessness. If we believe that the offender will likely be able to hear our hurt, then it can be helpful to go to that person and tell the story of our hurt without indicting them as insensitive or callous. We may ask for their acknowledgment of our hurt and possibly make some request aimed at safeguarding against future injury. If we do not believe it wise to go to the perpetrator with our hurt story, then it can be helpful to bring it to a trusted other.

Fourth is to accept the role of hurt as inevitable when we decide to live with an open heart. We do not get some magical reprieve from hurt when we live heartfully. We are willing to feel and as we saw earlier, to be informed by our feelings. However, our hurt is not a testimony of our being unlovable and deserving of kindness. Rather, it is a reflection of being fully alive and participating in the human condition.

The fifth step involves relinquishing our grip on self-righteousness, whereby we are willing to move beyond seeing ourselves as only victims of hurt and begin to own our capacity to hurt others. A willingness to describe ourselves as possible perpetrators, letting go of any psychological immunity of acting injuriously, goes a long way toward engendering a forgiving spirit.

ENGENDERING A FORGIVING SPIRIT

If we desire to deepen our capacity to forgive, then it will be necessary to remain mindful of the current status of forgiveness and cursing in our lives. We contribute greatly toward a maturing, forgiving spirit when we remain conscious and intentional about either maintaining or suspending cursing.

As I gathered material for a workshop I was about to give, I became aware of the surprising number of people whom I had excommunicated. I was pretending that some were dead, others I perceived as alive and, thankfully, out of my life. I decided to invite two members of the latter group to an event I was sponsoring. They both attended the event and I experienced some loosening of my grip upon excommunicating them.

Another significant contribution to strengthening a forgiving spirit is remaining mindful we have choices regarding how we respond to feeling offended. This does not mean we should quickly move toward the sanitized options of high moral ground where we avoid anger, blame, resentment, and hatred. Rather, we should remain open to simply being curious about a variety of ways to respond, being mindful of our tendency to take up emotional residency in some particular reaction.

A contributing element to embracing our forgiving nature is to be accountable for ways we may have allowed ourselves to be unnecessarily vulnerable to being hurt. Our level of vulnerability becomes self-imposed when our boundaries are ineffective. It became clear to me, in regard to one of the people I had excommunicated, that I had been excessively tolerant of light to moderate levels of mistreatment. Consequently, I owned some of the responsibility for having gotten hurt. In the case of the second person, I had failed to acquire some necessary information, and that left me feeling exploited. In both cases I was culpable for colluding with the mistreatment I suffered.

Our capacity to forgive can be greatly broadened when we remember that we can forgive even without trust. We begin to awaken a forgiving heart as we suspend some curse. However, that does not suggest that the other has earned our trust. They do so when we hold two beliefs about them: We believe they will treat us kindly and we believe they will tell us the truth.

A propensity for forgiveness deepens when we accept life as a deeply insecure and unpredictable journey. An old mentor of mine often said, "Maturing means being willing to dream, become deeply disillusioned, and dream again!" There's much to be said about stopping the protest of pain, mistreatment, and loss inherent to the journey. We can learn to take care of ourselves and stop

protesting. Authentic forgiveness, the elimination of a curse, may be more ben-
eficial to ourselves than to those whom we forgive. And the most challenging
aspect of forgiveness may be to learn to forgive ourselves, which we will address
in our exploration of redemption.

REDEMPTION

There may be nothing more central to the path of the mystic than a devotion
to redemption. An old meaning of the word *redemption* is *to buy back*. What is
it that we are actually buying back? What did we originally pawn and what did
we receive in exchange?

When we forgive ourselves, we are buying back our divine spark or what
might be called our essential goodness. Why would we pawn the essence of
our personal value? What could be so important that we would sacrifice that
which drives our deservedness and entitlement to being alive and loved? One
response to the question would be our belonging and our survival. Imagine
our ancestors some six or seven thousand years ago committing some act that
was deemed unacceptable by the tribe, when banishment would likely lead to
an early demise.

It may be that our DNA carries a very similar fear. Our early attach-
ment needs, satisfied by physical contact, attunement, and warmth, reflect
our need to belong and the safety that accompanies kinship. This would have
been a grand opportunity for anyone holding spiritual leadership to claim
the power and responsibility for an individual's redemption—of course, for
a particular price.

As children, we learn quickly as recipients of shame, blame, and ridicule
that the threads of our connections to others are wispy and very out of our
control. Acceptance and rejection come and go depending on the whim of the
authority figures that reign over us. Our only power is to join them as they
berate us. The separation due to their disapproval is temporarily abated when
we merge with their parental perception. "If my parent says I'm bad, then I am,
and we continue to share the same experience." Ostracism and possible death
are for now postponed. Could it be that we learned to secure a place to belong
by pawning our divine goodness?

Who can actually buy back our goodness for us? One candidate might be
anyone interested in never being out of work and maintaining a hefty cash
flow. However, that keeps us locked in childhood with a new authority figure

holding domain over our goodness. This would be familiar and certainly attractive for many. In fact, it is likely the single most prominent driving force in courtship. We find the one whom we imbue with the power to buy back our goodness. The problem is that the person we give the power to holds possession over our goodness. It is theirs to give and take as they see fit. Our own goodness never really belongs to us.

I recall doing prenuptial counseling with a young couple. I turned to the woman and said, "I get the feeling that you want your fiancé to love you in a way that you are unwilling to offer yourself."

The young woman blushed, dropped her eyes, and let her silence hold the embarrassment of offering a task to her future husband that surely set him up for failure. Only we can give ourselves the kind of love that confirms our essential goodness. Lovers, spouses, friends, spiritual directors, and any other significant other can only be allies in support of our own self-valuing.

Buying back our essential goodness may be our highest spiritual responsibility and is a deeply devotional act. The mystic is willing to take on such responsibility. In doing so, there will be deep primitive stirrings that question the legitimacy of such an endeavor. These primal warnings may reflect those early fears of banishment. "Who do you think you are, deciding you're okay?" "Do you actually believe you don't make mistakes?" "Come on, you know you could be doing a lot better with your life!" "Aren't you being kind of arrogant, deciding that you are a worthwhile human being with all your flaws?"

One important key to maintaining responsibility for our own worth is to appreciate how claiming our goodness calls into question our connection to the clan. Certainly, it helps to travel with a tribe that encourages the devotion of buying back our goodness. Our redemption is very personal and no one is able to do it for us. The decision to open our hearts and offer love to ourselves will inevitably hold some mystery. However, we can identify some actions that reflect such a devotion.

A very helpful analogy is a theoretical intervention being made by a social worker on a parent who physically abuses his or her child. The social worker views all explanations and justifications of the abuse as irrelevant. Of course, the consideration of the child deserving to be treated with kindness is also not open for discussion. It's a matter of a self-evident truth that the child deserves to be treated benevolently. So it is with mistreatment of ourselves; deservedness is not a consideration because compassion is our birthright. Our redemption depends on our willingness to intervene against thoughts and behaviors that are self-abusive. "Stop" becomes our voice of redemption when we do not allow our demeaning thoughts and behaviors to linger.

It can be helpful to recall that all acts of self-loathing are purposeful. They are either aimed at allegedly preventing future mistakes, proving that an authority figure was correct to castigate us, keeping us in the clan, or keeping us small so that we may avoid the challenges and trials of adult life. Hence, it serves us to ask about the purpose of a self-loathing moment, rather than believe that our disparaging thoughts have any credibility.

The second action we employ is to create effective boundaries that protect us from others who mistreat us. An old friend recently told the story of a colleague of his who had attacked his character on several different occasions. What my friend found difficult to believe was that he entered another conversation with the perpetrator, heart open, ready to engage. He had a bit of selective amnesia, which was the coping mechanism in his family of origin. He learned that whenever some family member hurt him, there was no viable recourse or accountability, so he simply forgot the incident. I applauded my friend's new position that let his colleague know that he would not allow himself to express anything tender in the colleague's presence and would be limiting his contact with him.

I am often asked about the New Age technique of reciting affirmations, which are statements confirming our worth. I do not believe they cause any harm. However, the greatest affirmation of someone's lovability is a devotion to protecting that person against all harm. Our redemption, or the buying back of our essential goodness, greatly depends on our willingness to safeguard our person from ourselves and others. Such devotion kindles self-trust when we believe we truly will do our best to protect ourselves and treat ourselves kindly.

Most of us will not move out of the clutches of self-loathing because we do not take on the task to do so with devotion. Even when we exercise enough loyalty to interrupt self-abuse, we will be challenged by the mystery of love. Love asks us to live from the depths of being a mystic. Am I willing to remain accountable one day at a time regarding the status of interrupting self-abuse? Am I willing to let go of guilt that does not reflect a violation of my values? Am I willing to suffer the guilt arising from a breach of my values? Am I willing to attend to my soul's task while carrying compassion for myself?

When we interrupt the toxic residue caused by shaming and ridiculing ourselves, we inevitably carry more light. Increased light leads to a lessening of the likelihood that we will collude with cynicism and gossip, a greater sensitivity to injustice, a lessening of our inclination to be divisive, a readiness to be welcoming, more equanimity and less drama in our lives, and a greater capacity to gently laugh at ourselves.

Our redemption is our personal responsibility. We need not live without our divine spark; we merely need to buy it back. We buy it back when we devotionally interrupt the toxic stories we create about ourselves. We close with a blessing for all who are willing to mystically be betrothed to life.

A BLESSING FOR THE NOVICE MYSTIC

The mysterious journey of life requests your betrothal as a Mystic. Let the enchantment flow as you neither attempt to conquer her nor shrink back into a small place as her victim. The task is to remain mindful of the deep longing life has for your heartful devotion. Like a lover hungry for the caress of the beloved, life yearns for your touch. You will drink in her desire for you when you throw off the shackles of self-loathing, opening to some moment of warmth and kindness making its way to you.

May you come to know a friendship offering you a love that celebrates the uniqueness of your gifts and your wounds. And in that friendship, may you be the recipient of an unconditional love, which calls you back when you have wandered a long distance away from yourself.

All displays of the sublime are her seductive allurements. Her splendor calls to you in the brilliance of a sunset, the power of a crashing ocean, the majesty of a mountain view, and an unexpected kindness handed to you.

She may call to your depths, as she does when you have lost your way. When the familiar fades into a distant memory with new life still incubating, she is calling you to remember that you have been penetrated, inseminated now with new embryonic knowings of who she is. Learn to rest there, where new life is emerging.

In the dark night, you are invited into a large story, a narrative capable of shaking false securities loose. She pushes and even bangs into you, in the hope you will awaken to your desire and your love. From that place you and she can dance. Now, your eyes hold a gaze of her divine radiance less burdened by fear.

You become ready to live devotionally, willing to wonder who in you is seeking your welcome, as you extend a hand to the stranger within. When the forgotten one is warmly received, your redemption is at hand. Then you are in a larger story, where you find yourself able to live with a new tenderness and new boldness enlivening to a new unity. A welcome to the forgotten who lives in you engenders a beginner's heart, and the curiosity of how to live with this stranger animates a beginner's mind.

INTERVIEW
WITH THE AUTHOR

Psychology as a profession is often focused on assessable outcomes, not substantial spiritual influence. How has your work as a psychotherapist affected your path as a novice mystic? Does it help or hinder the progression of your spiritual life, and how so?

My counseling work has supported the deepening of my spiritual life. I began to see an innate longing to understand life and attempt to make peace with it. My appreciation for the depth of mystery surrounding the human condition brought me to a place of greater reverence for all that lies beyond my understanding.

Although I am a Licensed Professional Counselor, I do not see myself as a social scientist. Foremost, I am a philosopher who remains a passionate student of human psychology. The Greek origin of the word *philosophy* means *love of wisdom* and the word *psychology* means *nursing of or caring for the soul*. I live and work with a love for bringing some measure of understanding to what authentic care of the soul looks like. One measure of nursing the soul is a devotion to making peace with life's inherent mystery. I believe that it is my willingness to remain curious while accepting the depth of the unknown that keeps me a novice mystic.

My spiritual life doesn't really progress, it calls me to remain self-examining even when I am seduced in the direction of holding some grandiose cosmic vision. I have come to believe that my deep soul stirrings and a willingness to remain curious about the mystery of the self occasionally gift me with a glimpse of the human condition.

Do you believe that every person could benefit from a devotion to union?

I do believe that each of us can benefit from a devotion to union. There appears to be a spiritual umbilical cord connecting us. The challenge is to first individuate by committing to a self-examined life. It is there we might find our unique values, beliefs, and preferences. The hope is that by unearthing and accepting our uniqueness we can live more authentically and with less pretense.

If we can bring compassion to what we discover about ourselves, we can begin to honor our uniqueness without claims of being special. This compassionate and conscious holding of ourselves allows us to see ourselves in others. Some pseudo hierarchy is dismantled, and with ever-softening eyes, we see ourselves in children, in people who are achieving, those who are defeated, as well as those who are suffering. This kind of unity reaps a rich experience of belonging, with the emptiness of separation being replaced by a heartful sense of connection.

Did you have a defining moment that propelled your desire to help others see the benefits of living with a devotion to union?

I don't believe that I had a defining moment that propelled me to help others to see the benefits of living devotionally to union. It is curious for me that I often don't even see myself as being up to the task of helping others. Rather, I see myself as offering a welcome and invitation to join me in a common endeavor of living the self-examined life accompanied by compassion. Such a welcome is what I received from several mentors and from literature. So I pass the welcome on as an opportunity to unite with the self in a deeper way. This new way includes the wounds and the gifts of the person, with some inevitable demon needing to be encountered, representing what is most feared. Those receiving the welcome typically diminish their self-loathing and draw comfort from the sacredness of being an ordinary person. As I witnessed folks coming home to themselves, I realized that one of my purposes was to offer this welcome. This knowing continues to bring me home to myself.

Your daughter Sarah's disease affects only six hundred people in the world. How has your experience caring for Sarah enhanced your relationship to life's mystery?

My daughter Sarah has been and continues to be one of my great teachers. She came into my life at a time when my ego was stretching to its outer limits.

I was living with a delusional, heroic vision suggesting that I could conquer life. Sarah's disability brought me to my knees. I moved from feeling convinced that I could defeat life to seeing myself as significantly defeated by life.

Creating a relationship with Sarah that worked for Sarah as well as other family members remained an impenetrable mystery. Loss ran deeply in our family story. Keeping Sarah at home meant the needs of others would have to be compromised.

It took years of fathering Sarah before I began to subtly move away from feeling crushed by life. I slowly could see commonality between me and Sarah. Before these perceptions of unity, I separated us by deciding she was nonverbal/I was articulate, she was unsteady on her feet/I was agile, she was dull /I was bright. The illusion of hierarchy divided us. However, we were both hungry to be accepted and included, we both struggled to be seen for who we were, we both endured times of significant vulnerability, and we both believed in love. Our unity contributed to my emerging curiosity about some third way to relate to life that would move me beyond either attempting to conquer or being conquered.

You note Zen Master Shunryu Suzuki's observation: "In the Beginner's mind there are many possibilities; in the expert's mind there are few." How might a person remove himself from the limitation of possibilities that come with the expert's mind? What sustains a beginner's mind as one gains experience?

Sustaining a beginner's mind as one gains experience is a tall order for the average ego, certainly my ego. The ego is not thrilled about the idea that life is a journey. It wants to arrive and arrive feeling damn good about itself.

The beginner's mind is sustained by reminding myself that I must remain vigilant to the seductions calling me away from it. That gentle watchfulness can be very helpful. I also appreciate the rewards of defining myself as a student and taking that definition seriously. It means that I'm willing to remain in a relationship with life, an intimate one.

I notice that gratitude helps keep me grounded in the beginner's mind as it anchors me in appreciation, rather than the self-aggrandizement of how much I know. Returning to holding myself with compassion and kindness is also very helpful to supporting my acceptance of the journey, rather than occupying some alleged station in life.

Lastly, I would say remaining conscious of my devotion to serve can be very useful. I offer many of my workshops at a local yoga center. The owner of the center has asked us to clean the facility before leaving. Each time, I make it a point to clean the bathroom. After being the recipient of loving, respectful eyes all day, cleaning the bathroom becomes a sanctuary to reclaim my beginner's mind.

What commonalities exist between secular mysticism and Buddhism? Do you believe it is beneficial to promote dialogue among various faiths and philosophies?

I think that the major commonality between secular mysticism and Buddhism is the emphasis upon a relationship with life that generates equanimity and kindness. The primary difference is that although the secular mysticism I write about places a great deal of emphasis upon unity with life, it does not exclude unity with a deity or Transcendent Other, while Buddhism would not include some reference to God in its cosmology. The path of the novice mystic is to a great extent an eclectic mysticism. That is, there remains a receptivity and openness to a wide range of faiths and philosophies. I see varying perspectives as muses potentially offering inspiration and arousal to new insight. I strongly encourage conversation amongst varying ideologies with a willingness to suspend competition and right/wrong thinking. A more appropriate approach might be "What can I take from this exchange that might help me live with more courage, more compassion, and more understanding?"

Do you think any potential danger lies in the deification of Sophia? Do you believe Sophia and the Socratic paradox (the insistence upon "knowing nothing") are mutually exclusive?

I would caution about the tendency to deify Sophia. It can easily be a way of distancing the energy and giving ourselves an excuse for not pursuing wisdom. In a number of esoteric circles, Sophia is depicted as both divine and earthly. I'm content with an understanding that she represents something deeply feminine, essentially heartful, and wise. Socrates held the self-examined life in the highest esteem, which is very compatible with Sophia imploring us to be receptive to what our hearts are asking for.

The epistemology of Sophia and Socrates can be labeled phenomenological, in that we are informed through our experience, which includes heartknowing, intuition, imagination, sense data, abstract reasoning, and primal instincts. What is most accessible to our inquiries is who we are: the one who desires to know. Hence, both paradigms honor curiosity as the primary energy of seeking understanding, rather than taking solace in substantiating conclusions. Both ways of knowing are interested in being informed about ignorance, biases, and a reluctance to be further informed. I think of Sophia's question as "What else is here?" This is very Socratic in nature, as opposed to the position "I know what's here." I like the notion that both Sophia and Socrates would see wonder, awe, and curiosity as the energies that create a relationship to that which we desire to know. In this regard, we remain in a state of relatedness, rather than occupying some objective position collecting data. They both value humility as a gracious acceptance of limits, viewing all inquiry as evolving and reflecting some approximation of the truth. Both Sophia and the Socratic invitation suggest we become familiar with he or she who doesn't know. We can learn to welcome what it means to experience the tension of feeling lost, challenged by ambiguity and uncertainty. With an increased sensibility for being able to not know, remaining curious, we deepen our capacity for living the important questions of life, rather than prematurely demanding some answer aimed at ease the tension.

The inability to relax appears to be a widespread issue in our society today. What do you feel is the most intriguing benefit of giving in to "stillness and hereness" and allowing ourselves to live in the moment?

We are challenged as a culture to understand the benefits of stillness. We erroneously define fully alive as constant movement. It would better serve us to define fully alive as the passage from a state of rest to a state of movement and back to rest. We seem confused about the benefits of restoration and renewal. We actually become more productive and efficient when we rest appropriately. An attachment to movement and activity can easily be a way to move away from ourselves by living mostly where we are headed, that event or place in the future. If we were able to let go of our obsession to move and embrace stillness, we would discover our emotional lives waiting for us. We would need to learn how to experience a wide range of emotion. As we did that, our emotional intelligence would likely increase dramatically. When this happens, we get more competent at resolving conflict, we understand ourselves more deeply, we can discover our life's purpose, we can engage in authentic emotional intimacy, we can be clearer about what's in our control and what we need to let go of, we can more fully incubate information and not act impetuously, we can heal, and we can grow a greater capacity to give and receive love.

What effects have you seen in your own life since building your personal philosophy and succumbing to the world's mystery?

The idea of building a personal philosophy as I understand it is mostly a love affair. I have become a lover of Sophia and as such, my life has become devotional. Like any man in love, I can't stop the devotion that runs through my mind and body. I am a devoted student of the unknown and I choose to ground my learning in several areas. The first is how much truth, accompanied by compassion, am I presently living with? This reference to truth refers to my beliefs, my values, my desire, and my feelings. I honor the self as an impenetrable mystery that calls to my curiosity. Secondly, I am devoted to the authentic life, which means a willingness to remain conscious of where I might lead with pretense. Thirdly, I am devoted to living with integrity, where my behavior reflects my values and my heart's desire. I am also willing to notice when I step out of integrity, where I am either living someone else's wishes or have dismissed my own values for some form of immediate gain. Finally, I strive to live with a greater capacity to experience gratitude and generosity. The hope is that this kind of devotion will help clarify the spiritual errand I have been sent on, which means a greater understanding of my purpose. This devotion has helped me to make greater peace with the inherent mystery of life. However, my ego regularly insists upon knowing more than is possible. At those times, I have learned to ask for guidance from allies who are embodied in humans and those who may be from the other side.

What is the role of ego in relation to the Path of the Novice Mystic?

In many personal growth circles, ego is represented as something that needs to be eradicated in order to support spiritual growth. The Path of the Novice Mystic acknowledges the beneficial offerings of ego. These benefits render the novice mystic able to feel, name, and voice desire; able to feel entitlement to pursue desires; able to identify personal values; able to employ effective boundaries; and able to live with integrity, where actions are compatible with personal values and heart's desire. These perks provided by ego can be underdeveloped, in which case there isn't enough *us* to bring to whatever unity we are trying to create. We will need more *us* to truly create a dynamic connection with others, nature, or God. True unity happens because two distinct entities have decided to join. Ego strengths can also be overdeveloped or inflated, in which case we bring too much *us* to our attempts at unity, resulting in a diminished capacity to welcome and receive who or what is attempting to reach all of us. The Path of the Novice Mystic honors a devotion to an ongoing rightsizing of ego in support of deeper experiences of unity.

ENDNOTES

1. Tukaram. *Love Poems from God: Twelve Sacred Voices from the East and West.* Translated by Daniel Ladinsky. New York: Penguin, 2002. Reprinted with permission.

2. Teresa of Avila. *The Essential Mystics: The Soul's Journey into Truth.* Edited by Andrew Harvey. Edison, NJ: Castle Books, 1998.

3. Rumi. "Out Beyond Ideas" and "The Guest House" from *The Essential Rumi.* Translated by Coleman Barks. San Francisco: Harper, 2004. Reprinted with permission.

4. Matthews, Caitlin. *Sophia: Goddess of Wisdom, Bride of God.* Wheaton, IL: Quest Books, 2001.

5. O'Donohue, John. *To Bless the Space Between Us.* New York: Doubleday, 2008.

6. Whyte, David. "What I Must tell Myself" from *The House of Belonging.* Langley, WA: Many Rivers Press, 1997. Reprinted with permission from Many Rivers Press, www.davidwhyte.com.

7. H. H. the Dalai Lama. *How to Expand Love.* Translated by Jeffrey Hopkins. New York: Atria Books, 2006.

8. Plato. *Dialogues.* Translated by Benjamin Jowett. Oxford: Clarendon Press, 1964.

9. Aristotle. *Introduction to Aristotle.* Edited by Richard McKeon. New York: Random House, 1947.

10. Oliver, Mary. "Sleeping in the Forest" from *Twelve Moons.* New York: Hachette, 1992. Copyright 1972, 1973, 1974, 1976, 1977, 1978, 1979 by Mary Oliver. Reprinted by permission of Little, Brown and Company. All rights reserved.

11. Rumi. "Out Beyond Ideas" and "The Guest House" from *The Essential Rumi*. Translated by Coleman Barks. San Francisco: Harper, 2004. Reprinted with permission.

12. Kabir. *Kabir: Ecstatic Poems*. Translated by Robert Bly. Boston: Beacon Press, 2004. Copyright 2004 by Robert Bly. Reprinted with permission of Beacon Press, Boston.

13. O'Donohue, John. *Eternal Echoes*. New York: Harper Perennial, 2000.

14. King, Martin Luther, Jr. "Where Do We Go From Here?" Speech delivered at the eleventh Convention of the Southern Christian Leadership Conference, Atlanta, Georgia, August 16, 1967. Reprinted by arrangement with The Heirs to the estate of Martin Luther King Jr., c/o Writers House as agent for the proprietor New York, NY. Copyright 1967 by Dr. Martin Luther King Jr. Copyright renewed 1995 by Coretta Scott King.

15. O'Donohue, John. *To Bless the Space Between Us*. New York: Doubleday, 2008.

16. Gonzales, Laurence. *Deep Survival*. New York: W.W. Norton, 2003.

17. Dante. *Divine Comedy*. Translated by Allen Mandelbaum. New York: Knopf, 1984.

18. Ibid.

19. Ibid.

20. Ibid.

21. Powell, Robert. *The Sophia Teachings*. New York: Lantern Books, 2001.

22. Ibid.

23. Thoreau, Henry David. *Walden*. Edited by Philip Van Doren Stern. New York: C.N. Potter, 1970.

24. Powell, Robert. *The Sophia Teachings*. New York: Lantern Books, 2001.

25. Kabir. *Kabir: Ecstatic Poems*. Translated by Robert Bly. Boston: Beacon Press, 2004.

26. Heaney, Seamus. "Postscript" from *Opened Ground: Selected Poems 1966–1996*. New York: Farrar, Straus and Giroux, 1996. Copyright 1998 by Seamus Heaney. Reprinted with permission of Farrar, Straus and Giroux.

27. Kornfield, Jack. *A Path with Heart*. New York: Bantam Books, 1993.

28. Plato. *Dialogues*. Translated by Benjamin Jowett. Oxford: Clarendon Press, 1964.

29. Ibid.

30. Oliver, Mary. "Wild Geese" from *Dream Work*. Boston: Grove/Atlantic, 1986. Copyright 1986 by Mary Oliver. Any third party use of this material, outside of this publication, is prohibited. Reprinted here with permission.

31. Keeley, Edmund. C.P. Cavafy's *Collected Poems*. Translated by Edmund Keeley and Philip Sherrard. Princeton, NJ: Princeton University Press, 1992. Reprinted by permission.

32. O'Donohue, John. *To Bless the Space Between Us*. New York: Doubleday, 2008.

33. Eliot, T.S. "The Hollow Man" from *Collected Poems 1909-1962*. New York: Houghton Mifflin Harcourt Publishing Company. Copyright renewed 1964 by Thomas Stearns Eliot. Reprinted by permission of Houghton Mifflin Harcourt Publishing Company. All rights reserved.

34. Moore, Robert L. *Facing the Dragon*. Wilmette, IL: Chiron, 2003.

35. Becker, Ernest. *Escape from Evil*. New York: Free Press, 1985.

36. Hollis, James. *Why Good People Do Bad Things*. New York: Gotham, 2008.

37. Ibid.

38. Moore, Robert L. *Facing the Dragon*. Wilmette, IL: Chiron, 2003.

38. Fromm, Erich. *The Heart of Man*. New York: Harper & Row, 1964.

40. Goldberg, Herb. *Hazards of Being Male*. New York: Signet, 1976. Reprinted with permission.

41. Hare, Robert D. *Without Conscience*. New York: Guilford Press, 1999. Reprinted with permission.

42. Ibid.

43. Ibid.

44. Ibid.

45. Ibid.

46. Ibid.

47. Sanford, John. *Evil: The Shadow Side of Reality*. New York: Crossroad Publishing, 1982.

48. Buber, Martin. *I and Thou*. Translated by Walter Kauffman. New York: Scribner, 1970.

49. Sanford, John. *The Strange Trial of Mr. Hyde*. New York: Harper & Row. 1987.

50. Buber, Martin. *I and Thou*. Translated by Walter Kauffman. New York: Scribner, 1970.

51. O'Donohue, John. *To Bless the Space Between Us*. New York: Doubleday, 2008.

52. Rilke, Rainer Maria. *Letters to a Young Poet*. Translated by Reginald Snell. Mineola, NY: Dover, 2002.

53. Moore, Thomas. *Dark Nights of the Soul*. New York: Gotham Books, 2004.

CPSIA information can be obtained at www.ICGtesting.com
Printed in the USA
BVOW01s2007160913

331333BV00001B/6/P